ID0466970

TRUE
LOVE
WAITS

Other Books by Wendy Kaminer

It's All the Rage
I'm Dysfunctional, You're Dysfunctional
A Fearful Freedom
Women Volunteering

WENDY
KAMINER

TRUE
LOVE
WAITS

ESSAYS
AND CRITICISM

♦♦ *Addison-Wesley Publishing Company*
Reading, Massachusetts   Menlo Park, California   New York
Don Mills, Ontario   Harlow, England   Amsterdam   Bonn
Sydney   Singapore   Tokyo   Madrid   San Juan
Paris   Seoul   Milan   Mexico City   Taipei

Many of the designations used by manufacturers and sellers to distinguish their products are claimed as trademarks. Where those designations appear in this book and Addison-Wesley was aware of a trademark claim, the designations have been printed in initial capital letters (e.g., Wheaties).

Library of Congress Cataloging-in-Publication Data
Kaminer, Wendy.
    True love waits, and other essays and criticism / Wendy Kaminer.
      p. cm.
    Includes index.
    ISBN 0-201-48914-7 (acid-free paper)
    1. Women—United States—Social conditions.   2. Feminism—United States.   3. Feminist theory—United States.   4. Social problems—United States.   5. United States—Social conditions—1980–
I. Title.
HQ1421.K26—1996
305.42′.0973—dc20   95-43807
                                                CIP

Copyright © 1996 by Wendy Kaminer

All rights reserved. No part of this publication may be reproduced, stored in a retrieval system, or transmitted, in any form or by any means, electronic, mechanical, photocopying, recording, or otherwise, without the prior written permission of the publisher. Printed in the United States of America. Published simultaneously in Canada.

Jacket design by David High
Text design by Diane Levy
Set in 11-point Simoncini Garamond by Pagesetters, Inc.

1 2 3 4 5 6 7 8 9-DOH-0099989796
First printing, March 1996

Credits

A portion of the Introduction originally appeared in *The Atlantic*, October 1995, under the title "My Reputation."

"The Privacy Problem" originally appeared in *Mirabella*, April 1994. Reprinted with permission of *Mirabella* magazine, published by Hachette Filipacchi U.S.A., Inc.

"Bimbo Feminism" originally appeared in *New York Newsday*, March 20, 1994 under the title "The Imaginary Politics of Bimbo Feminism."

"No Sex Is Good Sex" originally appeared in *The New York Times Book Review*, April 10, 1994, as a review of *Women, Passion, and Celibacy* by Sally Cline.

"What Is This Thing Called Rape?" originally appeared in *The New York Times Book Review*, September 19, 1993, as a review of *The Morning After* by Katie Roiphe and *Sexual Violence* by Linda A. Fairstein.

"Feminism's Third Wave: What Do Young Women Want?" originally appeared in *The New York Times Book Review*, June 4, 1995.

"Feminism's Identity Crisis" originally appeared in *The Atlantic*, October 1993.

"A Virtuous Woman" originally appeared in *The New York Times Book Review*, September 10, 1995, as a review of *The Education of a Woman* by Gloria Steinem.

"Put the Blame on Mame" originally appeared in *The Atlantic* December 1991, as a review of *Backlash* by Susan Faludi.

"Just Like a Woman" originally appeared in *The Village Voice*, May 6, 1981, as a review of *The Cinderella Complex* by Colette Dowling, *Pioneer Women* by Joanna Stratton, *Women in the Wilderness* by China Galland, and *Tracks* by Robyn Davidson.

"20th Century Foxes" originally appeared in *The Village Voice* May 7, 1986, as a review of *Lives of Modern Women* by Fay Weldon, *Freya Stark* by Caroline Moore, *Jean Rhys* by Carole Angier, and *Bessie Smith* by Elaine Feinstein.

"Feminism and the Devaluation of Rights" originally appeared in *Dissent*, Summer 1991.

"Feminists Against the First Amendment" originally appeared in *The Atlantic*, November 1992.

"Porn Again" originally appeared in *The New York Law School Review*, volume 38, numbers 1–4, 1993, under the title "Toward Safety, Equality, and Freedom." It is a reprint of a talk delivered in 1992.

"Harassed and Abandoned" originally appeared in *California Lawyer*, May 1995.

"Of Face Lifts and Feminism" originally appeared in *The New York Times*, September 6, 1988.

"Crashing the Locker Room" originally appeared in *The Atlantic*, July 1992.

"Divorce" originally appeared in *7 Days*, February 22, 1989.

Laying Down the Law on Sex originally appeared in *The Village Voice* March 30, 1982, as a review of *Prostitutes*, edited by Claude Jaget.

"Second Thoughts on the Second Amendment" originally appeared in *The Atlantic*, March 1995.

"Murder Most Feminine" originally appeared in *The Village Voice* November 26, 1980, as a review of Women Who Kill by Ann Jones.

"Not a Love Story" originally appeared in *The Village Voice* June 29, 1982, as a review of *The Killing of Bonnie Garland* by Willard Gaylin and *The Yale Murder* by Peter Meyer.

"The Avengers" originally appeared in *The Village Voice* January 3, 1984, as a review of *Wild Justice* by Susan Jacoby.

"The Wrong Men" originally appeared in *The Atlantic* December 1992 as a review of *In Spite of Innocence* by Michael Radelet, Hugo Adam Bedau, and Constance E. Putnam.

"Morality—The Newest Deal" originally appeared in *Mirabella*, September 1993. Reprinted with permission of *Mirabella* magazine, published by Hachette Filipacchi U.S.A., Inc.

"When Freedom of Speech Meant Not Saying the Pledge" originally appeared in *Newsday*, June 11, 1990.

"Church & State, Inc." originally appeared in *The Village Voice* September 25, 1984, as a review of *Redemptorama* by Carol Flake.

"Sweet Sin" originally appeared in *7 Days*, November 23, 1988.

"The Borrowing Kind" originally appeared in *Mirabella*, January 1994. Reprinted with permission of *Mirabella* magazine, published by Hachette Filipacchi U.S.A., Inc.

"The Berlin Wall of Foley Square" originally appeared in *Art & Auction*, May 1985, under the title "Tilted Arc."

"The Shrunken Reality of Lives in Therapy" originally appeared in *Newsday*, June 27, 1993.

"Do You Want to Talk About It?" originally appeared in *The Washington Post Book World*, September 27, 1992, as a review of *The Patient Who Cured His Therapist* by Stanley Speigel and Ed Lowe, Jr., and *We've Had a Hundred Years of Psychotherapy* by James Hillman and Michael Ventura.

"I'm O.K., You're Dead" originally appeared in *The New York Times Book Review* October 18, 1992, as a review of *Irresistible Impulse* by Robert Lindsey.

"Tolstoy, Gandhi, and Shirley MacLaine" originally appeared in *The Washington Post Book World*, August 23, 1992, as a Review of *Prophets of a New Age* by Martin Green.

"Just Good Friends" originally appeared in *The Village Voice* November 5, 1985, as a review of *Just Friends* by Lillian Rubin, *Women and Friendship* by Joel D. Block and Diane Greenberg, and *The Best of Friends, the Worst of Enemies* by Eva Margolies.

"It's a Wonderful Life" originally appeared in *The Village Voice* August 6, 1985, as a review of *The Human Animal* by Phil Donahue.

Contents

INTRODUCTION

My friend Abbe, a radical law professor, is worried about my reputation. "Wendy Kaminer? Isn't she a conservative?" one of her colleagues asked her recently. So she was not amused when I told her about the call from the *National Review.* Literary editor David Klinghoffer phoned and asked me to write a book review.

"Why are you calling me?" I asked. "I'm a liberal."

"That's okay," he assured me. "You're sensible."

I asked him how much they paid. "You guys are conservative. You believe in money. How much?"

"$225," he said. "We believe in money, but we have none."

"For $225 I can write for the *Nation,*" I told him, which wasn't quite true. The *Nation* hasn't called. They probably think I'm too conservative. I really am a liberal, an old-fashioned liberal, I kept assuring Klinghoffer, as if I were trying to get Navasky on the line. He kept reassuring me that I was sensible.

"But you don't understand," I explained. "I believe in the welfare state. People think I'm conservative because there are messages about self-reliance in my work, and I value self-reliance; but I don't expect it of children." There was a long pause. He stopped telling me I was sensible.

Once, I was secure in my political identity. Once, my seventh-grade homeroom teacher threw me out of class, after calling me a

Commie, when I refused to stand and recite the Pledge of Allegiance. (I haven't recited it since.) No one called me a conservative then. Once, I was accused of being a feminist. In fact, just last year, the *National Review* cited me as an example of a politically correct feminist. (At least not everyone there considers me sensible.) But some feminists dismiss me as a "backlasher." That's what someone called me in the locker room one day, while one of my friends eavesdropped on a discussion about my politics. ("What is it with Wendy Kaminer? Is she a conservative?" one woman asked, sparking the conversation.)

Although I'm flattered when women in locker rooms talk about my politics instead of their weight, I find my reputation for conservatism disconcerting. I've decided to blame it on the talk shows and declare that it reflects, in part, the increasing polarization of political debate, encouraged by TV. When a producer calls to book you on a show, she usually checks to be sure you will stake out a position that's diametrically opposed to the position staked out by the other guests scheduled to appear. If you express even a little sympathy for what's supposed to be an opposing position, much less a mushy view that attempts to balance concerns on either side, you'll probably forfeit your slot on the show. Analysis, much less judiciousness, is dismissed as equivocation. In any case, it's not good TV. "We're looking for a debate," the producer will say, and her vision of a debate is one person saying "Is too!" and the other responding "Is not!"

In this talk show culture, your "liberalism" or "conservatism" has to be pure, all-encompassing: you can't adopt liberal-like positions on some issues and conservativish positions on others. It puzzles people if you value self-reliance and support the payment of welfare benefits to poor people, as if self-reliance cannot coexist with social service, as if respect for self-reliance is inconsistent with the belief that none of us have the opportunity or capacity to rely on ourselves at every stage of life.

And your social criticism should not be qualified. As Camille Paglia's success has demonstrated, what is most marketable is absolutism and attitude undiluted by thought. I am, for example, known as a critic of "victimism," because of my quarrels with the recovery movement, which suggests that virtually everyone is a victim of abuse, and my critique of a therapeutic brand of feminism that tends to exaggerate women's victimization. This should hardly brand me as an apologist for incest and child battering or an enemy of sexual equality. Still, it confuses people when I acknowledge that some children (we don't know how many) are badly abused by their families. In a highly charged public debate, challenging the notion that abuse is ubiquitous is like denying that abuse exists. It confuses people as well if I say that we still need affirmative action to redress sex and race discrimination. Suggesting that some feminists encourage women to see themselves as victims is considered the equivalent of asserting that women are no longer victimized at all.

Personally, I reserve the right to complain and even whine about whatever injustices are visited upon me—bad haircuts, bad boyfriends, and bad reviews. I have always believed in complaining, and in one view, that makes me a liberal. But I complain only in private, to friends and relations, not to the public at large, and maybe that makes me conservative. My friend Sue says that my reputation as a conservative has nothing to do with my political beliefs; it reflects my attitude problem. "You sound tough and unsentimental," she says. "You're not nice enough to be liberal."

"Be sweet young maid. Let those who will be clever," my mother used to say, worried that my attitude would get me into trouble. She called me a few months ago when the *New York Times Magazine* ran an essay on young conservatives. She is an old liberal. "Did you notice how many of them are Jewish?" she said with wonder. Then she paused. "You're not a conservative, are you?"

■ ■ ■

We arm ourselves with ideologies. "It's scary out there," a college senior said to me last year. "You need to be identified with a group; you need a side and a label." But sometimes the sides are fluid; the labels shift. Rereading the essays in this collection, I'm struck by how little my views have changed from the days when I passed easily as a liberal. At least, after all these years, I am still in relative agreement with myself. If a lot of other people start agreeing with me, I'll know it's time to change my mind.

Still if it might be preferable for people to arm themselves with ideas instead of ideologies, it is probably a sign of progress when a young woman seeks to identify with an ideology instead of a man. When I entered college in 1967, many women aspired to graduate with engagement rings as well as diplomas. When I was a child, most careers, much less ideologies, were the province of a few exceptional women, none of whom lived in my neighborhood.

So, at about age ten, recognizing that I'd never make it as a musical comedy star, lacking any desire to become a teacher or nurse and sensing that I'd never be a housewife, I decided that when I grew up, I'd marry a writer. Twenty years and many bad dates later, it finally occurred to me that I might become a writer instead. I quit my job, aborted my legal career, and began writing book reviews for the *Village Voice*; they focused on sex, violence, and self-reliance, my primary interests ever since. I have included several early *Voice* pieces in this collection, because I like them and because they anticipate much of my later work on feminism, criminal justice, and the American fascination with self-help.

If law gave me one of my primary subjects, the women's movement gave me my career. It created new markets for women writers and imbued our work with a sense of urgency; it encouraged me to be a writer instead of a writer's wife. I was lucky enough to come of age with feminism. I graduated from high school when demands for sexual equality were beginning to intrude on the public consciousness, although I didn't recognize the need for a movement to achieve it. As a teenager, I heard feminists saying, "Women are as smart as men, as good as men, and ought to be treated as well as men," and that had always seemed obvious to me.

Yet, despite the faith and pride I had in my own intelligence, despite the pleasure I took from competing with boys in my classes, I clung to some privileges of femininity. When I was quite young, in grade school, I decided that I was lucky to be a girl because, unlike my brother, I would not be forced to be Bar Mitzvahed; he had to go to Hebrew School on weekday afternoons and Saturday mornings, while I was free. Nor would I ever be drafted, I realized thankfully. I'd always hated summer camp, and soldiers seemed like campers stuck in a perpetual color war, saluting their counselors. (I was even more grateful for the particular injustice of my draft exemption in the 1960s, when the men of my generation faced the prospect of going to war.)

I mention my youthful desire for both equality and the pedestal because it exemplified a historic conflict for feminists that has been the focus for much of my work. Many essays in this collection explore competing notions of sexual justice that follow from competing views of gender roles. I have always believed fiercely in a feminism that demands equal rights for women, not special protections, partly because I have never subscribed to the notion that women constitute a more compassionate, nurturant sex with a different moral voice, any more than I have regarded women as a congenitally weaker sex, needful of protection. I have always suspected that in terms of cognition, character, talent, and temperament, women differ as much from each other as they do from men. My preoccupation has been the historic conflict between protectionist feminism, which emphasizes traditional notions of gender difference (the moral strengths and practical weaknesses associated with motherhood), and equality feminism, which challenges gender stereotypes and roles.

I expected to exhaust this subject in my second book, *A Fearful Freedom: Women's Flight from Equality,* but I keep coming back to it, as many of these essays attest, because it keeps cropping up. Its most recent guise is a debate about "victim feminism," which reflects, in part, the influence of popular therapies on politics. The marriage of feminism with personal development fashions (notably the recovery movement) has spawned a strain of therapeutic feminism that exaggerates women's weaknesses and confuses psychic healing with political action.

Laments about victimism from inside and outside the women's movement have become quite common in recent years, but in the 1980s, when I began writing about feminism's conflicting demands for special protections and equal rights, the belief in women's different voice and need for different treatment under law was strong among feminists. Various forms of protectionism—from the censorship of pornography to special preferences for mothers in custody disputes—had gained support. My own equal rights feminism felt anachronistic. By the early 1990s, however, protectionism was under attack, along with the cult of victimhood. Writers who had little in common but their strong mutual disdain—the young, conciliatory Naomi Wolf and the angry, middle-aged Camille Paglia—critiqued feminism's emphasis on female vulnerability.

Conservatives gleefully joined the attack, lending credence to the charge that it was "backlash" and discouraging liberal feminists from publicly questioning the increasingly dogmatic focus on women's victimization, which was especially marked in debates about sexual violence. The absurdly expansive definitions of sexual harassment and date rape adopted by some feminists reflect equally absurd definitions of addiction and abuse popularized by the recovery movement, and they have a similar effect: if child abuse comprises any form of "inadequate nurturance," as some recovery experts claim, if rape is any sexual encounter that "feels" less than unequivocally consensual to a woman, as some feminists assert, then serious instances of abuse and sexual violence are trivialized while lesser instances (the insensitivity of a parent or boyfriend) are exaggerated.

For conservative critics of feminists, the excesses of the sexuality debates and the rise of "sexual correctness" provided an opportunity to erode support for the policing of sexual violence in general and, not so incidentally, to discredit continuing campaigns for economic equality, particularly when they involved government intervention in the marketplace. Conservative professional women formed self-proclaimed feminist groups such as the Women's Freedom Network that provided women's forums for attacks on affirmative action and antidiscrimination laws. A conference by the Women's Freedom Network that I attended in 1994 included a panel advocating comprehensive deregulation—abolition of virtually all occupational health and safety laws and any restrictions on worker's "freedom to contract," (such as the minimum wage), as well as antidiscrimination laws. The hook for this presentation was an attack on the silly side of sexual harassment regulations.

Missing from both extremes of these debates was a little reality testing. Rules banning dirty jokes from the workplace are inapt metaphors for rules prohibiting discrimination in hiring or firing or policing working conditions in factories, just as pornography is an inapt metaphor for rape. The sexuality debates, in particular, like the therapeutic culture in general, confuse metaphor with reality because they confuse feeling with fact. If you feel "violated" by a *Playboy* pinup or a rude remark, you've been violated, therapeutic feminists say; but, in the real world, most would prefer being assaulted by a magazine to being assaulted by a man, just as they'd prefer an assailant armed only with a magazine to an assailant armed as well with a gun.

Whether the right to own a gun enjoys similar constitutional protection as the right to read or write a magazine is a troublesome question that many civil libertarians on the left have steadfastly ignored. Or, not liking guns, they regard the Second Amendment with the same disdain with which people who don't like pornography regard the First. So it seems fitting that this essay collection segues from feminism to criminal justice with a discussion about the constitutional right to own a gun. My own view is that guns are considerably more dangerous than speech and less essential to a free society, which means that gun controls are much easier to justify than speech controls. But advocates of gun ownership argue that guns protect people from crime (and the government), and, in fact, evidence about the use of guns in self-defense is inconclusive. In any case, if there is a liberty interest in owning guns, then, to a civil libertarian, empirical evidence about the effect of guns is not necessarily controlling.

Whether they focus on feminism, religion and morality in public life, or criminal justice, many of these essays are concerned with civil liberties and civil rights. Together, with pieces on plagiarism and pop psychology, they seem like pleas for independent thought and individual autonomy. Reviewing this collection, I recall that I became a writer not to wield influence over other people's opinions but to have an outlet for my own. I have a compulsion to hold forth. I used to say that if I weren't a writer I'd be a crazy lady on a soapbox; then I learned that when my father was a teenager he was a soapbox speaker on Second Avenue, so maybe it's hereditary. "Were you a Communist?" I asked him. "No," he said, "an anarchist."

--- • • • ---

TRUE LOVE WAITS
(*October 1995*)

Fifteen years ago, when safe sex meant not going home with an axe murderer, Princess Di was the only woman I could name who had saved herself for marriage. But if in 1980 Shy Di was The Last Virgin—a pretty remnant of tradition—in 1994, she might seem avant-garde. American princess Brooke Shields confides to millions that she holds virginity sacred. Athlete A. C. Green finds prominence off the court as a founder of "Athletes for Abstinence." An estimated twenty-five thousand teenagers converge on Washington to promote chastity; they plant some two hundred thousand "pledge cards," from teens nationwide who made at least a momentary promise to remain "sexually pure" until marriage. Add the occasional TV virgin—Donna on *90210* or Jane Halliday on *L.A. Law*—and you have what passes for a trend, if not a movement, at least in the popular press. "Sex Can Wait," the cover story of *USA Weekend* proclaims. "Chastity until marriage? Celebrities are endorsing it, thousands of teens are pledging it."

Meanwhile, millions of teens are doing it. "Ten million teenagers will engage in about 126 million acts of sexual intercourse this year," according to Douglas Besharov of the American Enterprise Institute. Well, maybe not exactly 10 million teens and 126 million acts; sexual activity is difficult to document, as Besharov notes. People can always be trusted to lie about their

10

sex lives, exaggerating their sexual experiences or minimizing them, depending on the mores to which they're expected to conform. But there are objective indicators of increased teen sex, like babies, and the most reliable statistics we have generally confirm what preachers lament and parents fear: the number of teens having sex has increased in the past decades while the age of first sexual encounter has decreased. Media hype about virginity tells us more about cultural fears and ideals than realities. Concern about chastity exerts about as much control over sexual behavior as the obsession with dieting exerts over eating habits. Typical American teens are no more virginal than their parents are thin.

Overeating, however, has long been a national pastime. Unabashed pre-marital sex is a more recent phenomenon, spawned by the sexual revolution (which is generally cited by social conservatives as the beginning of the end for Western civilization). As the mother of a friend once said about the sexual freedom we enjoyed in the 1970s, "In my day, we had affairs after we married; now you have affairs before you marry."

AIDS, of course, has since had a chastening effect on pre-marital and extramarital sex. "Serial monogamy" has replaced "casual sex" in the vernacular of the middle class (just as "quality time" has replaced "quantity time" in discussions of child care). College students today are not more pure than their counterparts twenty-five years ago, but they do seem more monogamous. "In the 1960s and '70s, you had many sexual partners," one twenty-five-year-old explains to me. "Today, people have several partners."

This may seem a semantic difference to conservatives who preach no sexual partners before marriage, but the change in attitudes toward promiscuity on college campuses does seem striking. My own thoroughly unscientific investigation suggests that it is respectable and not at all uncommon for young women to sleep with their boyfriends, but women who sleep around risk being labeled "whorish" by other women. Women who are spotted in last night's dress the morning after, headed toward their dorm, are said to be "doing the Walk of Shame." (You can kid a man about doing the Walk of Shame but not a woman.) Women were cockier twenty-five years ago. When I was in college, in the late 1960s and early 1970s, virginity was becoming more a badge of shame than promiscuity; the pill was becoming a status symbol.

The sexual revolution was primarily a revolution in women's sexual behavior. It was the decline of the double standard. At the time, it surely felt like liberation, a release from the hypocrisies that made men proud of their sexual experiences and women ashamed (not that sex should be a source of pride or shame). Looking back, many of us still feel relatively lucky. "I would have been a much unhappier person had I grown up with the taboos of the 1950s," one of my friends observes. "I would have married the first man I slept with and been miserable."

Is this sanguine view of the sexual revolution typical? In recent years, popular wisdom has focused on the harm of sleeping around. In magazine articles, women talk about being damaged by sexual freedom. Although, outside of the antipornography movement, I can't recall ever hearing this complaint from a woman in real life, feminists have divided over whether the sexual revolution was good or bad for women.

The debate about the costs and benefits of sexual permissiveness is familiar. One hundred years ago, many feminists opposed contraception because they feared it would increase women's vulnerability to marital rape, by taking away their best excuse for saying no. Some also opposed the liberalization of divorce laws, because they feared it would encourage men to abandon their wives. Today, if "Do Me feminists" celebrate sexual freedom, in the belief that women are strong, Don't Me feminists dismiss it as one more turn of the screw. In a sexist society, women are free only to be exploited, they say, pointing to an allegedly high incidence of date rape and the presumed evils of pornography. Even staunch pro-choice feminists sometimes complain that abortion rights provided another disincentive for men to make commitments.

Despite or because of the increased sexual activity of teens, which increases the pressure on young women to say yes, Don't Me feminism has an impressive following on college campuses, among women who identify as feminists, that is; others turn away from feminism precisely because they associate it with a martial view of sexual relations. At their most extreme, Don't Me feminists advocate celibacy. Or they condone relationships only with those men who admit their collective, historic guilt for the oppression of women while they struggle to rid themselves of masculinity, as we know it. (Even celibacy might be preferable to the tedium of a pious, self-flagellating male.)

Given this revival of feminist sexual conservatism, bolstered by fear of AIDS, it's not surprising that chastity would be heralded as a reemerging cultural ideal. The most vociferous organized support for chastity comes from the antifeminist religious right, but it's fueled partly by the same anxiety about sex that underlies the more regressive forms of feminism.

"Casual sex is fraught with risk," emotional and spiritual as well as physical, Dave Scherrer stresses. Scherrer is an organizer with True Love Waits, the teen chastity campaign, sponsored by the Baptist Church, that brought twenty-five thousand teens to Washington last summer. Founded in 1993, True Love Waits asks teenagers to sign a "covenant card," promising to remain sexually pure until marriage. True Love Waits is being marketed by the Baptists as a nondenominational campaign, and it offers instructional materials to church youth groups nationwide, along with True Love Waits "activewear"—tee shirts and baseball caps—and Christian bubble-gum music.

This is what's new about True Love Waits—its marketing strategy. Exhortations about sexual purity have issued from conservative pulpits before, but not with baseball caps and tape cassettes. What's most striking, however, and most effective about the True Love Waits campaign is its celebratory (not celibatory) tone. It focuses on the joys of chastity—the preservation of a "gift you can only give once"—not the sins of casual sex. And it offers redemption, not rejection, to teens who have fallen; through True Love Waits, they can enter into a covenant with God and emerge purified—born-again virgins.

Teenagers who have taken the pledge are a minority, not part of the cultural mainstream (they tend to be devoutly religious and culturally conservative), but, as one youth group leader stresses, "they are not freaks." They engage in normal teenage activities—athletics and hanging out—and "they have hormones." They must also have fears about sexually transmitted diseases, anxieties about their sexual appeal, and hopes of finding true love that are shared by many of their sexually active peers.

Because of AIDS, "it's getting realistic to wait until marriage," one sixteen-year-old girl tells me. She also wants to remain a virgin and marry one "because of the whole comparison thing. I wouldn't want my husband to compare me to someone else he had been with. I think that would kill me." But, most of all, I suspect, her patience reflects the conviction that "God has put someone out there for me." The phrase "true love waits," after all, is not just a directive to abstain from sex until you're truly in love (and legally married); it's a promise that you will find true love—which waits for you. True Love Waits organizers preach chastity for unmarried adults as well as teens, but teens aren't asked to pledge that they will remain pure forever; they're asked to pledge purity until marriage: for each of them, the prospect of marriage is assumed.

My own perspective on this is skewed, I admit. At forty-four, I'm still engaged in premarital sex. But I wonder about the romantic idealism embedded in the True Love Waits campaign and the culture at large. Ideals will turn into illusions for kids who don't marry or marry badly or indifferently, or marry well for a time, only to discover that what begins as true love can end in betrayal.

The irony for advocates of traditional families is that a romantic ideal of marriage can encourage divorce. People who expect personal fulfillment in marriage are less likely to settle for security, stability, or status. But the increased incidence of divorce can, in turn, introduce some realism into the world of romance. "I'm in love with my husband," a recently married, recent college graduate affirms. "But conceivably the marriage could end. Most of my friends expect to get married more than once. Just like you expect to have more than one job in your life, you expect to have more than one relationship."

Without minimizing the cost of divorce, particularly for children, the realization that not all marriages will last, or remain a source of contentment, seems like progress to me. Romance, much more than sexual freedom, has been bad for women. It glamorizes dependence and stigmatizes autonomy. For generations, it prettified traditional gender roles and stereotypes; it still makes passivity and celibacy in women sexy. True Love Waits promotes romance, as it must, to promote virginity: romance must displace desire. You can sell gratification delayed to teens, but few will buy gratification denied. Few will pledge to remain celibate until they marry or die, whichever comes first.

"What are the benefits of abstinence?" I asked a group of five women friends who came of age in the 1960s. They were momentarily stumped. Everyone readily recited the evils that abstinence avoided—disease, unwanted pregnancies, and considerable heartache—but we had trouble identifying the goods that it offered, even to young women in their late teens. Self-discipline was rejected; celibacy seemed more like self-denial. Finally someone pointed out that chastity might help some young women achieve autonomy. It allows them to focus on satisfying themselves instead of pleasing their boyfriends. It puts school before sex. But chastity is a path to autonomy only when it is divorced from romance.

The sexual revolution didn't eliminate romance but did temper it a little, with experience, and the opportunity for autonomy without abstinence. At least, that's how it looks in retrospect. Did we take advantage of our opportunities? Were we even aware of them? It's difficult to recall the women we were in our twenties. "I can't tell you if I had affairs because I enjoyed them or because it was expected of me," a friend remarks. "I can't imagine what I felt back then. Today, sleeping with a man you barely know seems such an odd thing to do. I can't tell you why I went to bed with people or why I began and ended relationships." The past is not easily reconstructed. "We're such unreliable witnesses to our own histories."

My friends and I seem detached from the libertinism of our past, and somewhat bemused but not regretful. The sexual revolution was, after all, inextricably tied to revolutions in gender roles, and our conversation about sexual freedom quickly evolves into a conversation about the discrimination that preceded it—want ads divided into male and female job columns, exclusionary quotas for women in college and graduate schools. "Can you believe it?" someone says, recalling the ban on women in Harvard's undergraduate library. It seems much more bizarre than sleeping with strangers.

THE PRIVACY PROBLEM

(April 1994)

"There no longer exists an unpolitical sphere of life." It sounds like a line from a feminist sampler, but it was uttered by a German court in 1937. The Nazis declared that the personal was political long before any contemporary feminist had her consciousness raised, before many contemporary feminists were even born.

With their all-inclusive definition of political life, the Nazis sought complete control over private thoughts in addition to private relations, as totalitarian regimes do. They defined sexual assaults broadly to include thought crimes and metaphorical assaults, such as uninvited glances—eerily prefiguring some feminist protests against pornography and harassment.

Consider these cases reported by Ingo Müller in his book *Hitler's Justice*: In 1939, a Jewish man was sentenced to prison for one month for looking at an Aryan girl. His look constituted an assault, the court ruled. It "had a clearly erotic basis and could only have had the purpose of effecting an approach to the girl who interested him. This approach failed to occur only because the witness refused to cooperate and summoned the police to her aid." In another case, a Jewish man was sentenced to two years in prison for allegedly being "excited" by a massage, despite the masseuse's insistence that the defendant did not appear to have been aroused. Based on a "confession" to the Gestapo, which he later recanted, the man was convicted of having "attained sexual gratification," thereby dishonoring the Aryan race. The court held that the defendant had obtained a massage for "lascivious purposes and to abuse women as objects of his sexual lust, regardless of whether or not they were aware of it."

Like the slogan there is no "unpolitical sphere of life," neither of these cases would be terribly out of place, rhetorically or ideologically, in some hard-line feminist tract on sexual misconduct. The Nazi view of Jewish male sexuality, like the white supremacist view of black male sexuality, has an unsettling resemblance to the demonization of generic male sexuality that infects the antipornography movement. The more extreme feminist protests against harassment, as well as virtually all demands to censor pornography, assume, as did the Nazis, that the state should punish private, "lascivious" thoughts and glances. Women are encouraged to confuse actual and metaphorical assaults: we're said to be violated or assaulted by a leer, just as we're said to be abused or subordinated by a man's reading or viewing of pornography. If merely enjoying pornography, in a room all by yourself, is a crime or a tort, it can only be a thought crime. Catharine MacKinnon says that men who use pornography are engaging in actual discrimination, which is a little like saying that Jimmy Carter engaged in actual adultery when he harbored lust in his heart.

I point all this out at the considerable risk of inadvertently implying that Rush Limbaugh may have reason to call us feminazis. Apart from its democratic history, feminism is too complicated and diverse a movement to be characterized by invective (or encomium). Nor is this quick review of the Nazi campaign to politicize the personal offered as a reproach to feminists who fought for more equitable regulation of the private sphere. It's not as if a democratic state has no interest in family life or

procreative behavior and no history of regulating them—
through tax laws, for example, domestic relations laws, inheritance laws, and social security benefits. For much of our history,
these laws were grossly discriminatory and sometimes dangerous
for women. In the 1970s, feminists declared that the personal
was political partly so that men would stop beating their wives,
not so that kids would inform on their parents.

Privacy has been a mitigated good for women, given its role in
shielding marital rape and other forms of family violence. Privacy
had pitfalls for women even when it was invoked in their favor. In
1973, in *Roe* v. *Wade,* the Supreme Court grounded abortion
rights in the right to privacy, which made it easier for the government to deny Medicaid funding for abortions. Privacy rights
(rights to be let alone) arguably impose no obligation on government to provide abortions for women who cannot afford them.
As many feminists have pointed out, the Court could have based
abortion rights in equality rights: since abortion prohibitions
impose unique restrictions on women and pose unique obstacles
to their economic advancement, they are fundamental bars to full
equality. Had the Supreme Court recognized this in 1973, the
government would have had a clearer responsibility to ensure
equal access to abortion services.

But if privacy rights do not imply rights to social services, they
do include fundamental civil liberties. The Nazis' utter oblitera-
tion of the private sphere is a reminder that in a free society, the
personal is not simply political—which should be obvious. Do
we want the government tapping our phones or reading our
letters and diaries? Do we want the states enforcing archaic laws
against adultery, oral sex, or contraception? In 1986 the Supreme
Court devalued the privacy rights of homosexuals when it upheld the sodomy conviction of a gay man in Georgia who was
apprehended by police in his own home while engaged in consensual sex with another adult. This was a highly controversial

decision; had it involved heterosexuals, it would have been universally condemned.

Many people agree that consensual relations between adults should be private, but they disagree about what constitutes consent and how it should be monitored. Do we want the state or any other official body, like a college administration, deciding what men and women should say to each other in private? Is it possible or desirable to regulate private relations so that no one is ever hurt, deceived, manipulated, or merely misunderstood? Some attempts to dictate dating and mating rituals or to police private conversations between men and women reflect the childish belief that there is a political solution, and a public policy, for every interpersonal problem.

That is the kind of thinking that leads people into court. Last year, Northwestern University law professor Jane Larson created a small stir with a law review article proposing a new civil action for sexual fraud—"an act of intentional, harmful misrepresentation made for the purpose of gaining another's consent to sexual relations." This might make sense if applied to cases involving knowing transmission of disease, when the harmfulness of the misrepresentation is clear and sometimes deadly. But some of these cases are already being successfully pursued without Professor Larson's proposed cause of action, which is intended to provide a remedy for intangible, emotional harm as well. Questions about emotional damage in workplace sexual harassment cases have been plaguing the courts for several years, and the effort to control "abusive" sexual behavior (particularly when only speech is involved) has been quite controversial. How do we formulate a fair, relatively objective standard for abusiveness, while maintaining respect for free speech? In employment cases, the effort to monitor harassment is worth the trouble: the public interest in eradicating sexism from the workplace is clear, unlike the interest in eradicating sexism from the bedroom. Attempts at regulating sexism in private, nonviolent relations could, at best, be only marginally successful—and would involve substantial sacrifices of sexual privacy. If heterosexual relations in a sexist society are inherently abusive, as some feminists say, the prospects for regulating sexism in the bedroom take your breath away. We'd have an orgy of litigation.

Private lives have long been played out in court, especially in divorce cases, but at least the litigants had the grace to be embarrassed by the dramas; today, they're supposed to feel empowered. And if their trials aren't televised by Court TV, they can take their indiscretions to Geraldo. Feminism's denigration of privacy has been greatly exacerbated by talk shows and personal-development experts who warn that privacy is "toxic." Indiscriminate sharing of intimacies is considered therapeutic.

There is also a kind of incipient totalitarianism in the insistence that public revelation is the route to private redemption. It's reminiscent of political prisoners recanting their beliefs and denouncing false consciousness. Privacy is one of the first casualties of totalitarian states, which aim to control thinking, sexual and reproductive behavior, and religion—the passions in which we seek freedom from politics. Imagine a world with no personal sphere and you imagine a world with no refuge.

BIMBO FEMINISM

(March 1994)

If it ultimately fails as a liberation movement, feminism will at least have achieved considerable literary success. Since *The Feminine Mystique,* by Betty Friedan, became a best-seller in the early 1960s, the feminist movement seems to have consisted partly of a proliferation of feminist books. In the late 1960s and early 1970s, contemporary feminism's renaissance, best-selling authors such as Robin Morgan, Germaine Greer, Kate Millett, and Susan Brownmiller, along with Friedan and journalist Gloria Steinem, were widely regarded as movement leaders. Of course, many of these women were activists as well, but they were known primarily for their writing, which was essential in the popular promotion of feminist ideals. Feminism has given numerous women writers their careers and, in return, they gave feminism its public voice.

Now, a new generation of feminist writers is emerging, women who grew up not just with feminism but with feminist mothers. They also grew up with the notion that the personal is political, which means for some that a mere rendering of personal experience—a memoir—is a form of political commentary. Combine this with a reaction against the puritanism and revilement of men evident in some extreme feminist rhetoric, notably in the antipornography movement, and you get the newest strain of feminism popular among some young women writers—bimbo feminism.

"I see proposals every month from young feminists who want to write about their sex lives and their mothers," one veteran feminist book editor remarks. "They confuse discussion of political and social equality with discussions about their wars with the opposite sex and intergenerational conflicts with Mom." Many of these young women translate anger at their mothers into anger at feminism, the editor surmises, partly because they equate the feminism of their mothers with the sexual authoritarianism of prominent feminists such as Andrea Dworkin and Catharine MacKinnon. Dworkin and MacKinnon say that heterosexual activity may be inherently abusive, implying that women should avoid it. (You only think you're experiencing sexual pleasure with men; they know you're experiencing abuse.) Meanwhile, mothers say what they have always said to their adolescent and twenty-something daughters—"Don't sleep with him." In this context, complaining about your mother or pondering your boyfriend looks like a political act.

I offer this critique of bimbo feminism with some trepidation, knowing that it does not describe young feminists in general. That bimbo feminism may be a publishing trend does not make it a social movement. I know too that I'll be accused of generational snobbery, but, in fact, I don't believe that my generation of feminists (I'm forty-four) was smarter or more special than the generation of twenty- and thirty-year-olds today. They were simply members of my generation, which was disproportionately large and came of age with the civil rights movement and antiwar protests, when political activity focused on politics and not personal development. Counterculture activists, notably Abbie Hoffman, drew on psychologist Abraham Maslow's work on self-actualization, but many, like Hoffman, channeled their creative energies into political protests, which were generally supposed to take priority over personal problems. The call to political action was a stronger moral imperative than simply getting in touch with your feelings; at least, political activism was, for a time, the preferred route to personal fulfillment.

This is not to deny that there may be personal agendas behind political positions—there would not have been much of an anti-war movement in the 1960s if college men had not been subject to the draft. Still, there's a difference between politics that are personally motivated and personal preoccupations that are labeled political even when they involve no engagement in public life. Fighting with your mother about sexual freedom, and writing about fighting with your mother, are not, in and of themselves, political acts. At most, fighting with your mother may lead to political acts, such as lobbying for legislation to provide minors with access to birth control.

The distinctions between private and public behavior—between conducting personal relationships and changing the social and political context of relationships—is fairly simple. It's obviously absurd to call someone an activist because she argues with her boyfriend. But, absurd as this may seem, the young feminist writers my editor friend describes are not alone in mistaking their personal stories for political analyses. They're following fashions in high and low culture that date back at least ten years.

In the late 1980s, the recovery movement celebrated our natural tendency to care more about ourselves than society at large, exaggerating our own importance. Recovery experts told us that the problems of middle-class people who shop too much and have difficult relationships with their parents were as devastating and even as deadly as the problems of homeless drug addicts. (All bad habits were said to be addictions; all suffering was said to be equal.) Recovering from your particular addiction and feeling good about yourself became primary moral imperatives.

At the same time, intellectual and academic trends—deconstructionism and multicultural movements—mirrored popular ideals about recovery. While recovering codependents offered testimony about their personal addictions on TV talk shows, academics engaged in discourse about the personal experiences and desires underlying political, legal, and literary theories. Theory itself was reduced to a personal narrative. (Of course, young women educated in the post-modern 1980s are likely to present their own narratives as theory.) Personal narratives or experiences also became the basis for group identity. Favoring separatism over assimilation, advocates of multiculturalism suggested that the boundaries between people with different backgrounds and experiences were nearly impermeable. The promise of trust, empathy, and shared values and interests between different racial and ethnic groups seemed merely illusory. It has by now become a cliché that there are no objective public realities or values; there are only the subjective private perspectives of different individuals and interest groups, divided by race, sex, ethnicity, and class.

This insistence on the primacy of feelings and beliefs over political ideas is often cloaked in polysyllabic, academic jargon, but it is essentially anti-intellectual. (That is one of the ironies of current intellectual fashions.) Sometimes, at their most extreme, deconstructionists and advocates of multiculturalism sound a lot like mass-market recovery experts who exhort us to think with our hearts and not with our heads. Sometimes, focusing on what are presumed to be the hidden personal agendas of people who offer dissenting views, they sound like schoolyard bullies, attempting to resolve disputes with personal attacks. Labels like "racist," "sexist," and "classist" are indispensable to their arguments.

Am I getting personal? Deconstructionists who have read this far will by now be wondering what searing personal experience I'm cloaking with this critique. And, I have been provoked, in small part, by something personal; but it wasn't quite searing and it wasn't exactly an experience, just something I heard secondhand: A law school writing seminar was assigned my book, *I'm Dysfunctional, You're Dysfunctional,* a critical look at the personal-development tradition. One of the students told me how the book was deconstructed by some members of his class. They assumed that I was motivated by a bad experience with a support group, although I stated at the beginning of the book that I'd never been involved in support groups or any self-help movements and had never been a consumer of self-help books. This statement was dismissed as a lie, along with my own explanation of my interest in the subject of self-help. I claimed to be writing an intellectual critique, which in today's intellectual climate is highly suspect.

It's worth noting, however, that the students who assumed I wrote out of unhappy personal experiences generally disagreed with my perspective on the recovery movement. In keeping with the personalization of political arguments, they disputed my views by attempting to discredit me. Students also questioned my relationship with my father, whom I described briefly and affectionately, chronicling his abusive childhood and using him as an example of someone who withstood early traumas, retaining a sense of humor and compassion. This portrait of my father was presumed to be a lie: I was thought to be hiding from my readers, and perhaps from myself, the abuse they figured my father had inflicted on me. Of course, the students who accused me of lying about my father tended to disagree with the underlying point that child abuse does not always beget child abuse and that some people have strengths that allow them to cope successfully with trauma.

It should be obvious that readers who believe only those authors with whom they agree are in no danger of opening their minds, much less changing them. What was most striking to me about this report on students' reactions to my book was the ease with which they assumed their conclusions. With absolute faith in the notion that no abused child can ever become a nonabusive parent (without enrolling in a program), they dismissed all facts to the contrary as lies.

Faith is an odd phenomenon in a climate marked by disdain for unchanging, objective realities. On the one hand, there are only shifting, subjective perceptions. But on the other hand, it seems, there are objective, immutable truths—that child abuse is ubiquitous and hereditary in every case, that pornography is rape, that oppressed people are virtuous. It is a central and often overlooked paradox of a culture regularly accused of moral relativism that "truths" like these have the force of revelation. Challenging them is like challenging a devout Christian's belief that Jesus was the son of God or a Hasidim's belief that he wasn't.

My student informant, a former scientist, has little patience for revealed truths. Scientists are supposed to test their theories against the facts, discarding the theories, not the facts, when they conflict. Law lent itself to subjectivism because legal doctrines are invented (except for people who believe in a transcendent set of natural laws). Science is supposed to be discovered.

Feminism, for me, is both invented and discovered. It rests on at least one general, revealed truth: that whether or not it is natural, the subordination of women is wrong. Even so, we argue about what constitutes subordination and how it should be remedied, which means that feminism is mostly a process of invention, not revelation. It's built on political debate and the messy business of forging political consensus, not merely voicing personal truths.

Bimbo feminism may be a productive developmental stage for young women who need to address personal conflicts before they take on political ones. The trouble is that bimboism is not simply the province of the young; indeed, they learned it from their elders—forty-year-old teachers and theorists. It's time for middle-aged feminists to consider the implications of their cherished belief in the unity of the personal and political spheres. In general, the personal is only prelude to the political. Personal truths need to be mediated by political processes. That is a fundamental tenet of democracy. The gods may speak to Catharine MacKinnon about such matters as the evils of pornography; they do not speak to me.

---· · · ---

NO SEX IS GOOD SEX

(*April 1994*)

Femininity long denied women the pleasures of appetite. In the 1800s and through much of our century, corsets and girdles penalized the desire for food, at least in public. Cultural mores demonized even the private desire for sex. In the 1920s, changing ideals of marriage and sexual health expanded women's prerogative to enjoy marital sex. But until the sexual revolution, outside the confines of marriage, women were supposed to remain chaste as well as shapely.

Then female promiscuity became as respectable as dieting. In fact, increased sexual activity for women came partly at the cost of decreased eating. What is often described as an epidemic of anorexia may well be women's recompense for sexual freedom, not the backlash to new economic opportunity it is commonly supposed to be. Since the sexual revolution, in equal measure, women have been taught to hate food and love sex.

Given the prevalence of sexual violence and disease as well as eating disorders, it's not surprising that feminism has become, in part, a campaign for women to eat more and have sex less. In *Women, Passion and Celibacy,* Sally Cline recommends "passionate celibacy." The prescription is for lesbians as well as heterosexual women, although Cline, a British feminist, does present intercourse with men as particularly onerous: she paints men as doltish, if not dangerous, as well as bad in bed, and she asserts

29

(with more reason) that the aggressive marketing of heterosexuality is hard to resist. In Cline's view, the male-dominated consumer culture has responded to the challenge of feminism with "mandatory heterosexual consumption."

Cline has a knack for inartful phrasing and the self-help writer's penchant for capitalization. She calls the sexual revolution the "Genital Appropriation" era. (I have no idea what that means.) Surveying the sexual landscape, she sees an androcentric world that prescribes "mandatory penis empowering" and "symbolic penis enhancement," both of which are integral to something called the "Genital Myth," which is propagated by the "Genital Geniuses of the medical profession," along with "male genital mythologists like Norman Mailer," who join Martin and Kingsley Amis in being "literary sperm salesmen." (And she suggests that *men* are sophomoric.) Ms. Cline lacks the wit to leaven her outrage and the polemical skills to make it persuasive. Her book is cluttered with sentences that might have been written by a feminist computer: "Women who opt for celibacy should have their positive choice in the direction of personal independence and political empowerment validated and approved."

■   ■   ■

Writing like this makes it hard to concede that Cline has a point. Sexual freedom should comprise the freedom to be celibate without shame, as well as the freedom to be sexually or, as Cline would say, "genitally" active. (She defines celibacy as sexual behavior, stressing that it does not entail a loss of sexuality.) Sexual activity ought not to be the measure of every important relationship, although it is surely not news to many women that friendships are often more enduring and sustaining than affairs or even marriages. For women who were consigned to financial and social dependence on men and conditioned to define themselves by their mates, celibacy may be one route to autonomy.

Cline interviews many women who gained confidence and independence through celibacy, without sacrificing physical affection. She posits "connected autonomy" as the primary goal of celibacy, which in her view allows women to enjoy relationships without getting lost in them. Sexual activity leads to possessiveness, she suggests; celibacy satisfies a need for both love and separation.

■ ■ ■

For Cline, however, celibacy is not simply one honorable and useful choice for some women; it is the best and maybe the only feminist choice for all. If popular culture idealizes sex and pathologizes celibacy, she idealizes celibacy and pathologizes sex. Women who don't opt for celibacy, it seems, can only hope to be "genitally enslaved." Cline endorses what has become a familiar critique of heterosexual activity as generally oppressive to women: it "rarely" offers equal pleasure and passion; focused on satisfying "masculine needs and desires," it requires the "passivity and masochism" of women. A striking number of the women she interviews flesh out this critique: they have histories of bad sex or abuse; they're afraid of violence or troubled by appearance anxiety.

Given her bleak view of male-female relations, Cline has little sympathy for men who are not totally supportive of wives and lovers who choose celibacy. For her, sex is only an instrument of power for men, never a way of expressing affection. In her view, men have nothing to lose but their dominance.

■ ■ ■

How does Sally Cline know what all men and women experience in bed? Why must she dictate female celibacy with the same fervor with which antifeminists dictate female submissiveness? Why has so much feminist theorizing about sexuality become so presumptuous and authoritarian? Fundamentalist feminists seem to share the unthinking belief that the personal is political—absolutely. If all relations are suffused with power plays, then a personal predilection, like celibacy, becomes a political imperative. And simplistically equating the personal and political spheres not only allows you to tell other people how to conduct their lives but also transforms your problems and preferences into important public issues. So Sally Cline can girlishly list her favorite "passions" in the belief that she's engaging in political debate.

Sex is, after all, a social construct, she asserts (hoping to help us reconstruct it), in keeping with the fashionable academic notion that there are no natural, essential realities or truths; there are only political dogmas. Of course, her assertion is partly true. Sex, like eating, is partly a social construct, as a review of the different sexual mores and dietary habits of different cultures would reveal. Is it really necessary to point out that sex, like eating, also has some basis in biology?

Like many advocates of a new feminist sexual correctness, Cline tries to make her case by overstating it. If human relations are partly political, they must be purely political. If sexual abuse is prevalent, it must be ubiquitous. If some men are intent on acquiring power over women, no men are capable of love.

Feminists have long been labeled "man haters," usually with little reason. Some protest the label, some are indifferent to it, some wear it as a badge of honor. Men need not take offense. It's nothing personal.

WHAT IS THIS THING CALLED RAPE?

(September 1993)

In 1965 a doctor at Brown University hastened the decline of Western civilization by distributing birth control pills to women students twenty-one years of age and older. With "college girls everywhere" using the pill, "mating" might become "casual and random—as among animals," *U.S. News & World Report* warned the following year, bemoaning the loss of "the last vestige of self-restraint"—women's fear of unwanted pregnancies. The sexual revolution was, after all, a revolution in sexual mores for women, and twenty-five years ago, public concern about the new promiscuity reflected concern about the aggressiveness, even shamelessness, of the then new ideal woman.

Today, concern about promiscuity has been replaced with concern about date rape. Stories about sex on campus tend to focus on women's passivity and vulnerability rather than their aggressiveness. It's not that college women, in general, have embraced a traditional feminine ethic of sexual purity, as some skeptics about date rape suggest. *Cosmopolitan,* the magazine makeover spawned in 1965 by the sexual revolution, designed partly as a woman's answer to *Playboy,* is a campus best-seller today. But feminism on campus does sometimes appear a bit Victorian; for the minority of women who might pledge their

33

allegiance to *Ms.* magazine instead of *Cosmo,* feminism seems less a celebration of women's liberation than a lament about their inevitable oppression by men.

This partly reflects the left-wing equation of oppression and virtue. Protesting their sexual victimization enables privileged, heterosexual white women to claim a share of the moral high ground ceded to the victims of racism, classism, and homophobia. But, perhaps one of the primary differences between third-wave feminism and the nascent feminism of twenty-five years ago is the difference between women who came of age with the pill and women who came of age with AIDS.

Katie Roiphe's brave first book, *The Morning After: Sex, Fear, and Feminism on Campus,* will be both heralded and condemned for its angry attack on "rape-crisis feminism." But feminists on all sides of the date rape debate can find evidence in Ms. Roiphe's anger of the psychic damage wrought by AIDS on her twenty-something generation. Ms. Roiphe, a graduate student at Princeton, directs more impatience than compassion toward her peers who turn their fear into ideology, but she seems equally impatient with herself.

■   ■   ■

With a palpable desire for sexual freedom and pleasure as her subtext, Roiphe offers a persuasive critique of what might be called the effemination of feminism—the increasing emphasis on woman's essential weakness and man's essential bestiality that underlies many of the current debates about rape, harassment, and pornography. She reports on campus speak-outs, sexual behavior workshops, and feminist orthodoxies in the classroom, and perceptively analyzes "antiporn star" Catharine MacKinnon's appeal to undergraduates. As Roiphe points out, MacKinnon's rhetoric is an arresting combination of polysyllabic jargon and four-letter words. She talks dirty: "Imagine you are tied down to a table. Imagine you are having hot wax poured onto your nipples." (Listening to her is like watching a foreign "art" film; you get to feel smart and titillated at the same time.) MacKinnon is also an evangelist, and Ms. Roiphe captures the unthinking religious devotion she inspires.

The sheer mindlessness that infects campus debates on sexuality is striking. Ms. Roiphe underscores the fashionable emptiness of the terms "date rape" and "harassment." Like the word "codependency," they are sometimes used to signify practically everything and are beginning to signify nothing at all. The suffering of women who are subject to sexual abuse will be taken less seriously, as Roiphe notes, if the term "harassment" is used for whatever makes a person feel uncomfortable and "date rape" is used to describe any regrettable or equivocal sexual encounter.

Roiphe will be vilified for trivializing the problem of sexual violence, but her point is that indiscriminately equating sexual confusion with sexual coercion is trivializing: the experience of being assaulted or threatened with assault should not be reduced to the experience of being manipulated by your boyfriend. Who is Katie Roiphe to decide that the injury suffered by one woman, who is betrayed by someone she knows, is less serious than the injury suffered by another, who is raped by someone she knows? When you deny the possibility of distinguishing between emotional and physical abuse, or between a leer by a coworker and an attempt at sexual blackmail by your boss, you leave the realm of law for therapy.

There are, of course, hard cases in between. In date rape and harassment or other discrimination disputes, it is particularly difficult to separate questions of fact from perspective. Similar difficulties plague self-defense cases; think of the subway shooter Bernhard Goetz. How do we formulate objective standards of liability for behavior that involves so much subjective apprehension or harm? Roiphe doesn't have the answer (which might easily fill a law review), but at least she has the nerve to raise the question.

The Morning After is a nervy rather than a judicious book (injudiciousness is part of its charm), and Roiphe will be adopted by antifeminists who will use her portrait of feminism at its silliest to characterize feminism in its entirety. Roiphe has not done justice to the many feminist teachers and scholars who share her concerns. (Some of them are historians who have seen it all before; feminism has always been divided by conflicting visions of sexuality.) She thoughtlessly uses the term "rape-crisis feminists" to describe the most extreme feminist protesters, which implicates in campus foolishness women who work in rape-crisis centers and battered women's shelters, confronting daily what Roiphe would probably agree are acts of unquestionable violence. And she is rather unfair to Susan Brownmiller, suggesting that her 1975 book, *Against Our Will; Men, Women and Rape,* was partly responsible for today's date rape hype. At twenty-five, Roiphe is too young to remember, but she's smart enough to know that when *Against Our Will* was published, marital rape was generally legal, acquaintance rape was generally unrecognized, and women's accusations of rape were commonly presumed to be unreliable. In fact, what has chilled debate about sexual violence among feminists is the memory of the days when, instead of being hyped, rape was routinely ignored, except when white women with impeccable reputations were brutally assaulted by strangers.

Linda Fairstein, director of the Sex Crimes Prosecution Unit in the Manhattan District Attorney's Office, has been prosecuting rape cases since the mid-1970s, when the bad old days were beginning to end. Rape laws began to be reformed about twenty years ago, thanks mostly to feminism and partly to the victims' rights movement. Reform was slow and piecemeal, varying from state to state, but the trend reflected the first glimmers of consciousness of sex bias in the courts. Over time, laws no longer required the corroboration of an alleged rape victim's testimony, women were no longer required to have resisted their attackers in order to prove rape, and, unless they were shown to be relevant, the sexual histories of alleged rape victims were no longer a subject for cross-examination.

In *Sexual Violence: Our War Against Rape,* Fairstein explains these changes and the current state of rape law. Using simple language, she walks readers through rape prosecutions, from complaints to convictions. We don't hear about acquittals or about incompetent lawyers and judges (only the occasional juror seems a bit dim). Fairstein is cautiously optimistic about the criminal justice system: rape is being taken seriously, the treatment of rape victims has greatly improved, and women are finding some justice. She comforts readers with this message and tries to restore their faith, while, for better or worse, she holds their attention with stories of rape.

This is an episodic book—part memoir (Fairstein briefly chronicles her career), part real-life criminal procedural, part true-crime story. Fairstein's skills are legal, not literary, and the seams show. Still, if she is an awkward writer, she is also an earnest one with a good deal of useful information to impart and a valuable perspective on such issues as acquaintance rape, prostitution and rape, sexual fraud, and false reporting. Rape victims are lucky to have her as an advocate and, in a way, defense attorneys should be pleased to have her as an opponent, for she seems as fair minded and honest as she is committed to winning her cases.

Fairstein indulges in none of the rape-hype rhetoric that so irritates Roiphe, and the rapes she describes, with a few exceptions involving sexual cons, would be considered "real rapes" by the most moderate feminists. Fairstein focuses on clearly actionable rapes, and she does not use rape as a metaphor for the institutionalized oppression of women.

Instead, in the tradition of liberal feminism, Linda Fairstein presents rape as aberrant, violent behavior. Radical feminism presents it as normal sexual behavior in a male-dominated world. Tenacious faith in the commonness of benign, consensual heterosexual relations is what distinguishes liberal feminists from their radical sisters. Loss of that faith is what Katie Roiphe laments.

FEMINISM'S THIRD WAVE: WHAT DO YOUNG WOMEN WANT?

(June 1995)

Like the sexual revolution, the feminist movement was said to be over some ten or fifteen years ago, but people keep copulating and feminists keep writing away. Publishing activity, like pre-marital sex, begins early these days. *Listen Up: Voices from the Next Feminist Generation* is a recently published collection of essays by women in their twenties, one of whom, twenty-one-year-old Jennifer DiMarco, reports that she is the author of fourteen novels. Katie Roiphe was a twenty-four-year-old graduate student when she made headlines with her controversial book about date rape. Rebecca Walker, twenty-five, is a contributor to *Ms.* magazine and a leading spokeswoman for third-wave feminism. Veronica Chambers, a twenty-four-year-old editor at the *New York Times Magazine,* is working on a family memoir. Naomi Wolf and Susan Faludi, both in their mid-thirties, are now the elder stateswomen of this wave.

As the best-selling feminist authors of their generation, Faludi and Wolf are both targets and touchstones for emerging writers like Rene Denfeld, author of *The New Victorians,* and the journalists Karen Lehrman and Cathy Young, both of whom are writing books about feminism. Like their older sisters, they are a contentious lot, these young feminists. Whether or not they retain some attachment to the notion that women are essentially nicer than men, their behavior belies pious stereotypes of women as more cooperative than competitive, more interested in relationships than in autonomy and individual achievement.

Vying for shelf space, airtime, and name recognition, as so many writers do, auditioning for the starring role in public debates and inspired by genuine ideological disputes (not merely fighting over fame), they pay a lot of of attention to one another. Denfeld, Lehrman, and Young charge Faludi and Wolf with "victimism," sloppy scholarship and muddled thinking, and are charged in turn with "backlash." In a recent essay in *Ms.,* Faludi dismisses Roiphe, Young, Lehrman, and Denfeld as media-made "pseudo-feminists" or "pod feminists" planted by the right.

Feminism has always been a collection of feminisms, as the bitter debate about pornography has shown: advocates of censorship and aficionados of pornography, as well as free-speech devotees, can all identify themselves as feminists. Self-proclaimed feminists include women who want to extend the welfare state and women who want to dismantle it, women who advocate strengthening sexual harassment laws and women who want to abolish them.

Recently, conservative professional women who tend to oppose government intervention in the marketplace have banded together to form their own groups, like the Women's Freedom Network, which appeals largely to young, professional white women (who make up about two-thirds of its members). These are the women *Ms.* derides as "faux feminists," and the concept of free-market feminism does seem oxymoronic, considering the government's historic crucial role in dismantling employment discrimination: but who holds the copyright on feminism? Historically, faith in women's superior emotional sensitivities and vulnerabilities clashed with the insistence that women are neither a weaker nor gentler sex bereft of supposedly masculine skills—like analytic thinking. Armed with opposing concepts of sexual difference and justice, supporters of protective labor laws once fought advocates of the Equal Rights Amendment.

Conflicts among young feminists today reflect this familiar divide: the drive for individual equality collides with demands for group protection. Generally there is relatively little support among young women on either side for the Victorian belief that women need protection because they are naturally weaker than men; the debate focuses on how much women have been unnaturally weakened by a history of discrimination and how much discrimination they continue to suffer.

This is posited as a debate about "backlash." (I'm dating myself by using the term "discrimination" and classifying myself as a liberal rather than a radical feminist by eschewing the word "oppression.") Backlash comprises a range of evils—from sexual violence to welfare reform and attacks on affirmative action. In the view popularly attributed to Susan Faludi, backlash represents a conspiracy against women, led by the male-dominated media, as well as by the fashion industry and the medical profession (plastic surgery, like baby-doll dresses, is considered a form of backlash).

Faludi is a proponent of equality for women, not protections; she rejects traditional notions of feminine weakness. But the suggestion that backlash is a male-dominated conspiracy has made her vulnerable to the charge that she exaggerates women's victimization. Reviewing *Backlash* for the *New Republic,* Karen Lehrman chastised Faludi for her "ready embrace of an external enemy," which minimizes women's responsibilities for their own failures.

The charge of "victimism" is routinely leveled at civil rights movements in a society that thinks of itself as meritocratic and is loath to blame public evils for private problems. Is it fairly leveled against feminism? The only accurate answer is: some-times. In *The New Victorians,* Rene Denfeld dismisses Faludi's notion of backlash as "paralyzing paranoia." This is hyperbole with a tenuous relation to reality, given the number of women who felt energized by Faludi's book and the revival of interest in feminist issues that its success inspired. (Rene Denfeld might never have had her book contract if Susan Faludi hadn't helped make the women's movement marketable again.)

Still, it's fair to say that Faludi overstated women's passivity and ignored their complicity in antifeminist fashions. Except for a minority of television anchorwomen and others whose liveli-hoods depend on their looking good, most women choose their face-lifts, just as some choose to regard themselves as naturally better parents than men. Although male resistance to sexual equality is a real and costly phenomenon for women, backlash also comes from within, as women retreat from the challenges of equality, taking cover in femininity or in chauvinistic notions of their moral superiority. But that is a complicated, less than inspir-ing phenomenon.

Hyperbole, for and against claims about women's victimiza-tion, is more marketable and politically effective than an analysis suggesting that some claims about backlash are sound and others exaggerated—which the talk show culture would deem equivo-cation. (Consider the attention garnered by Camille Paglia's strident antifeminist performance art and the difficulty of coun-tering it with thoughtful conversation.) Naomi Wolf's breath-lessly melodramatic portrait of backlash in *The Beauty Myth* gave her national prominence as the second feminist voice of her generation. Inviting the comparison of anorexic women to con-centration camp inmates—as if a cultural preference for thinness in women were akin to the Third Reich—Wolf posited not just that standards of beauty are demoralizing and oppressive to virtually every woman, but that they constitute an independent entity, a totalitarian state called the Beauty Myth, which seems possessed of its own malevolent life force, like some disembodied being on *Star Trek.* (It is a counter force to the women's movement that is "poisoning our freedom" and "operating to checkmate the inheritance of feminism in every level in the lives of western women.")

It's not surprising that Wolf's apocalyptic description of the "beauty backlash" generated derision as well as applause. (Either you share a preacher's passion or you don't.) *The Beauty Myth* appeared shortly before an onslaught of attacks on feminist victimology (it is often offered as an example of such excesses), and in her second book, *Fire with Fire,* Wolf offered a critique of "victim feminism," exhorting women to embrace "power feminism" in its stead. Naomi Wolf has emerged as the leading weathervane of her generation.

Rene Denfeld, twenty-eight, continues the attack on victimism in *The New Victorians,* a heartfelt but consistently unoriginal book that offers itself as the young feminist manifesto. Denfeld's central theme—that feminism in the 1980s mirrored the dominant feminism of the 1880s—has been thoroughly explored by historians and journalists critical of the antipornography movement as well as of the notion that women share particular (superior) moral sensibilities. Denfeld's agenda for the 1990s lists all the old concerns: day care, reproductive choice, political parity, and the effective prosecution of sex offenders.

■　■　■

Still, Rene Denfeld's attack on Victorian feminism may resonate with her peers (she received a glowing review in the *Harvard*

Crimson), and it should not be blithely dismissed as backlash, as many dismissed Katie Roiphe's critique of feminist orthodoxies about date rape in *The Morning After.* You may disagree with them, or even consider them naïve about the roadblocks and risks still facing women, but you can hear in both Denfeld and Roiphe a genuine feminist sensibility—a belief in equality, a desire for sexual, psychological, and economic independence. Instead of vilifying them, middle-aged feminists might ask why young women like this feel so misrepresented by feminism.

They argue that feminism's attack on patriarchy is over-wrought, that it demonizes men and exaggerates their resistance to equality and that its critique of the pornographic culture degenerates into prudery. The familiarity of these charges makes them easy to scorn: feminists have always been lampooned as sexually frustrated man haters (or impersonators) by defenders of the status quo. But the recent prominence of the antipornography movement and injudicious critiques of heterosexuality have made the caricatures seem true. Young women for whom sexual freedom is a more immediate concern than jobs are apt to focus on sexuality debates much more than on demands for economic and political equity; to them, feminism must sometimes seem like an embittered, puritanical mother.

The irony is that some of the most vehement rank-and-file crusaders for censorship and sexual correctness are younger women, who may fear sexual freedom as much as they crave it. It's no coincidence that much of the debate about sexual correctness is centered on campus. Antipornography activists Catharine MacKinnon and Andrea Dworkin have a particularly enthusiastic following among the young. Their most vehement opponents, the women who have led the fight against censorship, tend to be middle aged.

A preoccupation with women's victimization is not simply

imposed by older feminists on the young. Some young women raised in a therapeutic culture will turn to feminism in search of explanations for the identity crises and feelings of victimization that often begin in adolescence. They choose between competing ideologies. Like voters in a democracy, young women sometimes get the feminism they seek.

The collaboration between generations is seen in women's studies programs, which introduce many young women to feminism. Women's studies has recently been the subject of devastating critiques, not just by conservatives who feel victimized by campus radicals but by feminists themselves: in *Professing Feminism,* Daphne Patai, who teaches women's studies, and Noretta Koertge, a historian, offer a sorrowful insiders' indictment of the smug, insular, and often silly orthodoxies of academic feminism. In a 1993 article on women's studies courses for *Mother Jones* magazine, Karen Lehrman decried their tendency to elevate ideology over scholarship (precisely the sin of the traditional curriculum, which ignored or belittled women), their therapeutic approach to teaching (classrooms are supposed to be "safe" places in which women can talk about their feelings), and their intolerance of dissent.

As Ms. Lehrman noted, however, her generalizations do not apply to all women's studies programs, which vary greatly; if women's studies has enshrined some silly orthodoxies, it has also produced a rich lode of scholarship. And some students endorse the orthodoxies that critics condemn. "The problem in women's studies is not just a supply-side problem; it's a demand-side problem as well," Susan Reverby, a historian at Wellesley College, remarks. Sometimes, she says, students insist on talking about their personal experiences in class and seek therapy instead of instruction from their teachers. "What do nineteen- and twenty-year-olds think about? They think about themselves."

The attraction of a therapeutic feminism that focuses on identity and self-expression and acknowledges no distinction between the personal and political is evident in *Listen Up* (Seal
Press), an anthology edited by Barbara Findlen, the thirty-year-
old executive editor of *Ms.* Findlen's concise introduction captures the riches and challenges of growing up with a movement
on the ascent. "I became part of a massive, growing, vibrant
feminist movement at the age of eleven," she recalls. It gave her a
sense of entitlement (to play baseball instead of hopscotch) and
also "the burden of high expectations." The women's movement
hasn't eliminated but has substantially limited discrimination,
leaving young women with higher standards of achievement and
fewer excuses for failure. Still, they encounter sexism, and, Findlen writes, "it can take away your breath, your hope, your faith in
yourself, your faith in the world."

Whether you focus on barriers to equality that have been
dismantled or barriers to equality that remain determines
whether you blame internalized victimism or external backlash
for women's troubles. The most vociferous critics charge that in
recent years feminism has manufactured excuses for women,
exaggerating the extent of discrimination, sexual harassment, or
the risk of sexual violence. The contributors to this volume
would generally disagree.

■ ■ ■

A self-consciously diverse group, they write about eating disorders, discrimination against fat people and the disabled, rape,
incest, and homophobia, as well as sexism and racism in its
various forms. They are preoccupied with oppression. Are they
oppressed? Do they collaborate in the oppression of others? "I
have to take into account the fact that I'm an articulate, white,
middle-class college kid, and that provides me with a hell of a lot
of privilege and opportunity for dealing with my oppression, that

may not be available to other oppressed people," Nomy Lamm writes in an essay about being fat.

In the world of therapeutic feminism, oppression is not clearly defined or bounded, but that's part of its appeal. Like codependency, oppression is an affliction that anyone can claim. Even white males can be "oppressed" by masculinity. Fat people who are the subject of ridicule can declare themselves oppressed, like victims of ethnic cleansing—just as people who are misunderstood by their parents can claim to be abused.

The inchoate belief that feeling bad is the equivalent of being oppressed may be especially appealing to the young, whose solipsism can be excused as developmental. But social and political commentary requires detachment from the self as well as engagement in its dramas. Writers, especially critics, are not like athletes; very few of us peak in our twenties. Almost all the young contributors to *Listen Up* focus on themselves with the unchecked passion of amateur memoirists who believe that their lives are intrinsically interesting to strangers. A few, like Ellen Neuborne, who offers a spirited essay about discrimination on the job, use their personal experiences skillfully to illuminate political issues. But most seem to equate political commentary with the telling of a personal story. They write about feminism by writing about growing up, describing conflicts with parents or early sexual encounters, or discussing the evolution of their own identities.

The children of identity politics, they routinely deconstruct themselves. "As an educated, married, monogamous, feminist, Christian, African-American mother, I suffer from an acute case of multiplicity," Sonja D. Curry-Johnson explains. Sometimes the explanations are sad: "I am not just a woman or just an African-American," Cheryl Green writes. "I am also a person with a visible disability, and I have also been shaped by my awareness that my beliefs and experiences conflict with those of white, nondisabled women, nondisabled African-Americans and many women and men with disabilities. I identify partially with all these groups, yet at times I feel contempt and exclusion from each of them."

■   ■   ■

Sometimes the explanations are inadvertently satiric: "I came out as a woman, an Asian-American and a bisexual within a relatively short span of time," Jee Yeun Lee writes in an essay about diversity sliced thin. At a retreat for lesbian Asian and Pacific Island women, she reports, rifts developed among "East Asians, South Asians, Southeast Asians and Pacific Islanders; women of mixed race and heritage; women who identified as lesbians and those who identified as bisexuals; women who were immigrants, refugees, illegal aliens or second generation or more." The list goes on. Finally, one woman concludes, "Our identity as queer A.P.I. women must be a coalitional identity."

Feminists who are so acutely aware of the differences among women struggle to confirm their common bonds. Efforts to form a racially integrated movement are relatively new and not entirely successful. But whether you focus on racial, ethnic, economic, and religious differences or on differences in talents, temperaments, and desires, the problem is the same—how to forge a movement of disparate individuals, or tribes? From opposite ends of the spectrum, identity politics and radical individualism pose a similar challenge.

Karen Lehrman, perhaps the sharpest of the young individualist critics, assails the notion of "gender consciousness" and even a continued focus on discrimination. She asserts that considering the ubiquity of equal opportunity laws, sex discrimination in the workplace should be considered a private matter between women and their employers. Trade unionists, as well as older feminists who experienced discrimination and fought hard to prohibit it, will dismiss Ms. Lehrman as a naif with a lot to learn about persistent, systematic barriers to equality and the futility of confronting your employer individually, especially if you're stuck in a low-level job. Highly skilled professionals (particularly writers who work for themselves, alone) may prosper without much solidarity, but what about minimum-wage service workers?

If an excessively collectivist feminism obliterates the personal sphere by defining private problems as public responsibilities, an excessively individualist feminism obliterates the political. It's easy to understand the appeal of a pure individualism to young women professionals imbued with confidence, an ethic of self-reliance, and the head start of a good education. But it's hard to imagine a women's movement without at least a little "gender consciousness" and some commitment to collective action.

Feminism remains a balancing trick. Negotiating the drive toward individual autonomy and the demand for collective identity, young women must walk the same tightrope as their elders. Individualists define feminism as the acknowledgment that women are human beings, just like men, stressing that sex is not an accurate predictor of character, personality, or intelligence. That's compelling, but incomplete. As a practical matter, feminism also entails the recognition that whatever differences exist among them, women constitute a political class with common interests and goals, reflecting a common history of discrimination, including sexual violence, which is virtually oblivious of personal, racial, or economic differences. Conceiving of continuing discrimination as a private problem, feminism would be less a political movement than an exercise in personal development.

The political is personal to a radical individualist. The personal is political, a therapeutic feminist would stress, or, as a collectivist believer in women's ways of knowing might point out, a wealthy woman may read the same self-help books as her maid. In the end, feminists who exalt women's victimization and feminists who ignore it may have more in common than they know.

FEMINISM'S IDENTITY CRISIS

(*October 1993*)

My favorite political moment of the 1960s was a Black Panther rally in a quadrangle of Smith College on a luxuriant spring day. Ramboesque in berets and ammunition belts, several young black males exhorted hundreds of young white females to contribute money to Bobby Seale's defense fund. I stood at the back of the crowd watching yarn ties on blonde ponytails bobbing up and down while the daughters of CEOs nodded in agreement with the Panthers' attack on the ruling class.

It was all so girlish—or boyish, depending on your point of view. Whatever revolution was supposed to be fomenting posed no apparent threat to gender roles. Still, women who had no political analysis of chauvanism rampant in the anti-war movement or the typical fraternity, planned automatically to attend graduate or professional school and pursue careers that would have been practically unthinkable for them ten years earlier. Feminism may have been relegated to the back of the political consciousness of many middle-class college women in 1969, but it was altering their lives as much as draft avoidance was altering the lives of their male counterparts.

Today, three decades of feminism and one Year of the Woman later, a majority of American women agree that feminism has altered their lives for the better. In general, polls conducted over the past three years indicate strong majority support for feminist ideals. But the same polls suggest that a majority of women hesitate to associate themselves with the movement. As Karlyn Keene, a resident fellow at the American Enterprise Institute, has observed, more than three-quarters of American women support efforts to "strengthen and change women's status in society," yet only a minority, a third at most, identify themselves as feminists.

Many feminists take comfort in these polls, inferring substantial public support for economic and political equality, and dismissing women's wariness of the feminist label as a mere image problem (attributed to unfair media portrayals of feminists as a strident minority of frustrated women). But the polls may also adumbrate unarticulated ambivalence about feminist ideals, particularly with respect to private life. If widespread support for some measure of equality reflects the way women see, or wish to see, society, their unwillingness to identify with feminism reflects the way they see themselves, or wish to be seen by others.

To the extent that it challenges discrimination and the political exclusion of women, feminism is relatively easy for many women to embrace. It appeals to fundamental notions of fairness; it suggests that social structures must change but that individuals, particularly women, may remain the same. For many women, feminism is simply a matter of mommy-tracking, making sure that institutions accommodate women's familial roles, which are presumed to be essentially immutable. But to the extent that feminism questions those roles and underlying assumptions about sexuality, it requires profound individual change as well, posing an unsettling challenge that well-adjusted people instinctively avoid. Why question norms of sex and character to which you've more or less successfully adapted?

Of course, the social and individual changes demanded by feminism are not exactly divisible. Of course, the expansion of women's professional roles and political power affects women's personality development. Still, many people manage to separate who they are in the workplace from who they are in bed, which is why feminism generates so much cognitive dissonance. As it addresses and internalizes this dissonance and women's anxiety about the label "feminism," as it embarks on a "third wave," the feminist movement today may suffer less from a mere image problem than from a major identity crisis.

It's difficult, of course, to generalize about how millions of American women imagine feminism and what role it plays in their lives. All you can say with certitude is that different women define and relate to feminism differently. The rest—much of this essay—is speculation, informed by conversations with editors of women's magazines (among the most reliable speculators about what middle class women want), polling data, and ten years of experience studying feminist issues.

Resistance to the Label

Robin Morgan, the editor in chief of *Ms.,* and Ellen Levine, the editor in chief of *Redbook,* two veterans of women's magazines and feminism, offer different views of feminism's appeal, each of which seems true, in the context of their different constituencies. Morgan sees a resurgent feminist movement and points to the formation of new feminist groups on campus and intensified grassroots activity by women addressing a range of issues, from domestic violence to economic revitalization. Ellen Levine, however, believes that for the middle-class family women who read *Redbook* (the average reader is a thirty-nine-year-old wage-earning mother), feminism is "a non-issue." She says, "They don't think about it; they don't talk about it." They may not even be familiar with terms of art like "glass ceiling," which feminists believe have passed into the vernacular. And they seem not to be particularly interested in politics. The surest way not to sell

Redbook is to put a woman politician on the cover: the January 1993 issue of *Good Housekeeping,* with Hillary Clinton on the cover, did poorly at the newsstands, according to Levine.

Editors at more upscale magazines—*Mirabella, Harper's Bazaar,* and *Glamour*—are more upbeat about their readers' interest in feminism, or at least their identification with feminist perspectives. Gay Bryant, *Mirabella*'s editor in chief, says, "We assume our readers are feminists with a small 'f.' We think of them as strong, independent, smart women; we think of them as pro-woman, although not all of them would define themselves as feminists politically." Betsy Carter, the executive editor of *Harper's Bazaar,* suggests that feminism has been assimilated into the culture of the magazine: "*Feminism* is a word that has been so absorbed in our consciousness that I don't isolate it. Asking me if I believe in feminism is like asking me if I believe in integration." Carter says, however, that women tend to be interested in the same stories that interest men: "Except for subjects like flyfishing, it's hard to label something a man's story or a woman's story. In fact," she adds, "it seems almost obsolete to talk about women's magazines." Carter, a former editor at *Esquire,* recalls that *Esquire*'s readership was 40 percent female, which indicated to her that "women weren't getting what they needed from the women's magazines."

Ruth Whitney, the editor in chief of *Glamour,* might disagree. She points out that *Glamour* runs monthly editorials with a decidedly "feminist" voice that infuses the magazine. *Glamour* readers may or may not call themselves feminists, she says, but "I would call *Glamour* a mainstream feminist magazine, in its editorials, features, fashions, and consumerism." *Glamour* is also a pro-choice magazine; Whitney stresses that it has long published pro-choice articles—more than any other mainstream women's magazine. And it is a magazine for which women seem to constitute the norm: "We use the pronoun 'she' when referring to a doctor, lawyer, whomever, and that does not go unnoticed by our readers."

Some women will dispute one underlying implication of Betsy Carter's remarks—that feminism involves assimilation, the merger of male and female spheres of interest. Some will dispute any claims to feminism by any magazine that features fashion. But whether *Ms.* readers would call *Harper's Bazaar, Mirabella,* and *Glamour* feminist magazines, or magazines with feminist perspectives, their readers apparently do, if Betsy Carter, Gay Bryant, and Ruth Whitney know their audiences.

Perhaps the confident feminist self-image of these upscale magazines, as distinct from the cautious exploration of women's issues in the middle-class *Redbook,* confirms a canard about feminism—that it is the province of upper-income urban professional women. But *Ms.* is neither upscale nor fashionable, and it's much too earnest to be sophisticated. Feminism—or, at least, support for feminist ideals—is not simply a matter of class, or even race.

Susan McHenry, a senior editor at *Working Woman* and the former executive editor of *Emerge,* a new magazine for middle-class African Americans, senses in African American women readers "universal embrace of women's rights and the notion that the women's movement has been helpful." Embrace of the women's movement, however, is equivocal. "If you start talking about the women's movement, you hear a lot about what we believe and what white women believe."

For many black women, devoting time and energy to feminist causes or feminist groups may simply not be a priority. Black women "feel both racism and sexism," McHenry believes, but they consider the fight for racial justice their primary responsibility and assume that white women will pay primary attention to gender issues. Leslie Adamson, the executive secretary to the president of Radcliffe College, offers a different explanation. She doesn't, in fact, "feel" sexism and racism equally: "Sex discrimination makes me indignant. Racial discrimination makes me enraged." Adamson is sympathetic to feminism and says that she has always "had a feminist mind." Still, she does not feel particularly oppressed as a woman. "I can remember only two instances of sex discrimination in my life," she says. "Once when I was in the sixth grade and wanted to take shop and they made me take home economics; once when I visited my husband's relatives in Trinidad and they wouldn't let me talk about politics. Racism has always affected me on a regular basis." Cynthia Bell, the communications director for Greater Southeast Healthcare System, in Washington, D.C., offers a similar observation: "It wasn't until I graduated from college that I encountered sexual discrimination. I remember racial discrimination from the time I remember being myself."

Black women who share feminist ideals but associate feminism with white women sometimes prefer to talk about "womanism," a term endorsed by such diverse characters as Alice Walker (who is credited with coining it) and William Safire. Susan McHenry avoids using the term "women's movement" and talks instead about "women moving." She identifies with women "who are getting things done, regardless of what they call themselves." But unease with the term "feminism" has been a persistent concern in the feminist movement, whether the unease is attributed to racial divisions or residual resistance to feminist ideals. It is, in fact, a complicated historical phenomenon that reflects feminism's successes as well as its failures.

"The Less Tainted Half"

That feminism has the power to expand women's aspirations and improve their lives without enlisting them as card-carrying feminists is a tribute to its strength as a social movement. Feminism is not dependent on ideological purity (indeed, it has always been a mixture of conflicting ideologies) or any formal organizational structure. In the nineteenth century feminism drew on countless unaffiliated voluntary associations of women devoted to social reform or self-improvement. Late-twentieth-century feminism has similarly drawn on consciousness-raising groups, professional associations, grass-roots activism and the growing middle-class female labor force, shaped partly by economic forces and a revolution in birth control. Throughout its 150-year history, feminism has insinuated itself into the culture as women have sought to improve their status and increase their participation in the world outside the home. If women are moving in a generally feminist direction—toward greater rights and a fairer apportionment of social responsibilities—does it matter what they call themselves?

In the nineteenth century many, maybe most, women who took part in the feminist movement saw themselves as paragons of femininity. The great historic irony of feminism is that the supposed feminine virtues that justified keeping women at home—sexual purity, compassion, and a talent for nurturance—eventually justified their release from the home as well. Women were "the less tainted half of the race," Frances Willard, the president of the National Woman's Christian Temperance Union, declared, and thus were the moral guardians of society.

But in the long run, identifying feminism with femininity offered women limited liberation. The feminine weaknesses that were presumed to accompany feminine virtues justified the two-tier labor force that denied women executive positions and political office along with arduous, high-paying manual-labor jobs (although women were never considered too weak to scrub floors). By using femininity as their passport to the public sphere, women came to be typecast in traditional feminine roles that they are still playing and arguing about today. Are women naturally better suited to parenting than men? Are men naturally better suited to waging war? Are women naturally more cooperative and compassionate, more emotive and less analytic, than men?

A great many American women (and men) still seem to answer these questions in the affirmative, as evidenced by public resistance to drafting women and the private reluctance of women to assign, and men to assume, equal responsibility for child care. Feminism, however, is popularly deemed to represent an opposing belief that men and women are equally capable of raising children and waging war. Thus feminism represents, in the popular view, a rejection of femininity.

Feminists have long fought for day-care and family-leave programs, but they still tend to be blamed for the work-family conundrum. Thirty-nine percent of women recently surveyed by *Redbook* said that feminism had made it "harder" for women to balance work and family life. Thirty-two percent said that feminism made "no difference" to women's balancing act. This may reflect a failure of feminists to make child care an absolutely clear priority. It may also reflect the association of feminism with upper-income women like Zoë Baird (President Clinton's first nominee for Attorney General), who can solve their child-care problems with relative ease. But, as Zoë Baird discovered, Americans are still ambivalent about women's roles within and outside the home.

Feminism and the careerism it entails are commonly regarded as a zero-sum game not just for women and men but for women and children as well, Ellen Levine believes: wage-earning mothers still tend to feel guilty about not being with their children and to worry that "the more women get ahead professionally, the more children will fall back." Their guilt does not seem to be assuaged by any number of studies showing that the children of wage-earning mothers fare as well as the children of full-time homemakers, Levine adds. It seems to dissipate only as children grow up and prosper.

Feminists who dismiss these worries as backlash risk trivializing the inevitable stresses confronting wage-earning mothers (even those with decent day care). Feminists who respond to these worries by suggesting that husbands should be more like wives and mothers are likely to be considered blind or hostile to presumptively natural sex differences that are still believed to underlie traditional gender roles.

To the extent that it advocates a revolution in gender roles, feminism also comes as a reproach to women who lived out the tradition, especially those who lived it out unhappily. Robin Morgan says, "A woman who's been unhappily married for forty years and complains constantly to her friends, saying 'I've got to get out of this,' might stand up on a talk show and say feminism is destroying the family."

The Wages of Equality

Ambivalence about equality sometimes seems to plague the feminist movement almost as much today as it did ten years ago, when it defeated the Equal Rights Amendment. Worth noting is that in the legal arena feminism has met with less success than the civil rights movement. The power of the civil rights movement in the 1960s was the power to demonstrate the gap between American ideals of racial equality and the American reality for African Americans. We've never had the same professed belief in sexual equality: federal equal employment law has always treated racial discrimination more severely than sex discrimination, and so has the Supreme Court. The Court has not extended to women the same constitutional protection it has extended to racial minorities, because a majority of justices have never rejected the notion that some degree of sex discrimination is only natural.

The widespread belief in equality demonstrated by polls is a belief in equality up to a point—the point where women are drafted and men change diapers. After thirty years of the contemporary women's movement, equal rights feminism is still considered essentially abnormal. Ellen Levine notes that middle-class family women sometimes associate feminism with lesbianism, which has yet to gain middle-class respectability. Homophobia is not entirely respectable either, however, so it may not be expressed directly in polls or conversations; but it has always been a subtext of popular resistance to feminism. Feminists have alternately been accused of hating men and of wanting to be just like them.

There's some evidence that the fear of feminism as a threat to female sexuality may be lessening: 77 percent of women recently surveyed by *Redbook* answered "yes" to the question "Can a woman be both feminine and a feminist?" But they were answering a question in the abstract. When women talk about why they don't identify with feminists, they often talk about not wanting to lose their femininity. To the extent that an underlying belief in feminine virtues limits women to feminine roles, as it did a hundred years ago, this rejection of the feminist label is a rejection of full equality. In the long run, it matters what women call themselves.

Or does it? Ironically, many self-proclaimed feminists today express some of the same ambivalence about changing gender roles as the "I'm not a feminist, but . . ." women (". . . but I believe in equal opportunity or family leave or reproductive choice"). The popular image of feminism as a more or less unified quest for androgynous equality, promoted by the feminists' nemesis Camille Paglia, is at least ten years out of date.

The Comforts of Gilliganism

Central to the dominant strain of feminism today is the belief, articulated by the psychologist Carol Gilligan, that women share a different voice and different moral sensibilities. Gilligan's work—notably *In a Different Voice* (1982)—has been effectively attacked by other feminist scholars, but criticisms of it have not been widely disseminated, and it has passed with ease into the vernacular. In a modern-day version of Victorian True Woman-hood, feminists and also some antifeminists pay tribute to women's superior nurturing and relational skills and their general "ethic of caring." Sometimes feminists add parenthetically that differences between men and women may well be attributable to culture, not nature. But the qualification is moot. Believers in gender difference tend not to focus on changing the cultural environment to free men and women from stereotypes, as equal rights feminists did twenty years ago; instead they celebrate the feminine virtues.

It was probably inevitable that the female solidarity at the base of the feminist movement would foster female chauvinism. All men are jerks, I might agree on occasion, over a bottle of wine. But that's an attitude, not an analysis, and only a small minority of separatist feminists turn it into an ideology. Gilliganism addresses the anxiety provoked by that attitude—the anxiety about compromising their sexuality that many feminists share with nonfeminists.

Much as they dislike admitting it, feminists generally harbor or have harbored categorical anger toward men. Some would say that such anger is simply an initial stage in the development of a feminist consciousness, but it is also an organizing tool and a fact of life for many women who believe they live in a sexist world. And whether or not it is laced with anger, feminism demands fundamental changes in relations between the sexes and the willingness of individual feminists to feel like unnatural women and be treated as such. For heterosexuals, feminism can come at a cost. Carol Gilligan's work valorizing women's separate emotional sphere helped make it possible for feminists to be angry at men and challenge their hegemony without feeling unwomanly. Nancy Rosenblum, a professor of political science at Brown

University, says that Gilliganism resolved the conflict for women between feminism and femininity by "de-eroticizing it." Different-voice ideology locates female sexuality in maternity, as did Victorian visions of the angel in the house. In its simplest form, the idealization of motherhood reduces popular feminism to the notion that women are nicer than men.

Women are also widely presumed to be less warlike than men. "Women bring love; that's our role," one woman explained at a feminist rally against the Gulf War that I attended; it seemed less like a rally than a revival meeting. Women shared their need "to connect" and "do relational work." They recalled Jane Addams, the women's peace movement between the two world wars, and Ban the Bomb marches of thirty years ago. They suggested that pacifism was as natural to women as childbirth, and were barely disconcerted by the presence of women soldiers in the Gulf. Military women were likely to be considered self-hating or male identified or the hapless victims of a racist, classist economy, not self-determined women with minds and voices all their own. The war was generally regarded as an allegory of male supremacy: the patriarch Bush was the moral equivalent of the patriarch Saddam Hussein. If only men would listen to women, peace, like a chador, would enfold us.

In part, the trouble with True Womanhood is its tendency to substitute sentimentality for thought. Constance Buchanan, an associate dean of the Harvard Divinity School, observes that feminists who believe women will exercise authority differently often haven't done the hard work of figuring out how they will exercise authority at all. "Many feminists have an almost magical vision of institutional change," Buchanan says. "They've focused on gaining access but haven't considered the scale and complexity of modern institutions, which will not necessarily change simply by virtue of their presence."

Feminists who claim that women will "make a difference" do,

in fact, often argue their case simply by pointing to the occasional female manager who works by consensus, paying little attention to hierarchy and much attention to her employees' feelings—assuming that such women more accurately represent their sex than women who favor unilateral decision making and tend not to nurture employees. In other words, different-voice feminists often assume their conclusions: the many women whose characters and behavior contradict traditional models of gender difference (Margaret Thatcher is the most frequently cited example) are invariably dismissed as male identified.

From Marilyn to Hillary

Confronted with the challenge of rationalizing and accommodating profound differences among women, in both character and ideology, feminism has never been a tranquil movement, or an agreeably divided one. It has always been plagued by bitter civil wars over conflicting ideas about sexuality and gender that lead to conflicting visions of law and social policy. If men and women are naturally and consistently different in terms of character, temperament, and moral sensibility, then the law should treat them differently, as it has through most of our history, with labor legislation that protects women, for example, or with laws preferring women in custody disputes: special protection for women, not equal rights, becomes a feminist goal. (Many feminists basically agree with Marilyn Quayle's assertion that women don't want to be liberated from their essential natures.) But if men and women do not conform to masculine and feminine character models, if sex is not a reliable predictor of behavior, then justice requires a sex-neutral approach to law that accommodates different people's different characters and experiences (the approach championed by Ruth Bader Ginsburg twenty years ago).

In academia this has been dubbed the "sameness-difference" debate, although no one on either side is suggesting that men and women are the same. Advocates of laws protecting women suggest that men and women tend to differ from each other in predictable ways, in accord with gender stereotypes. Equal rights advocates suggest that men and women differ unpredictably and that women differ from one another unpredictably as well.

It's fair to say that both sides in this debate are operating in the absence of conclusive scientific evidence confirming or denying the existence of biologically based, characterological sex differences. But this is a debate less about science than about law. Even if we could compromise, and agree that sex and gender roles reflect a mixture of natural and cultural programming, we'd still have to figure out not only what is feasible for men and women but also what is just. If there are natural inequities between the sexes, it is hardly the business of law to codify them.

In the 1980s this debate about sex and law became a cottage industry for feminist academics, especially postmodernists who could take both sides in the debate, in celebration of paradox and multiculturalism. On one side, essentialism—a belief in natural, immutable sex differences—is anathema to postmodernists, for whom sexuality itself, along with gender, is a "social construct." Sensitivity to race- and class-based differences among women also militates against a belief in a monolithic feminine culture: from a postmodern perspective, there is no such category as "woman." Taken to its logical conclusion, this emphasis on the fragmentation of the body politic makes postmodern feminism an oxymoron: feminism and virtually all our laws against sex discrimination reflect the presumption that women do in fact constitute a political category. On the other side, to the extent that postmodernism includes multiculturalism, it endorses tribalism, or identity politics, which for some feminists entails a strong belief in "women's ways." Thus the theoretical rejection of essentialism is matched by an attitudinal embrace of it.

Outside academia, debates about sex and justice are sometimes equally confused and confusing, given the political and ideological challenges of affirmative action programs and the conflicting demands on women with both career aspirations and commitments to family life. Feminists often have to weigh the short-term benefits of protecting wage-earning mothers (by mommy tracking, for example) against the long-term costs of a dual labor market. Sometimes ideological clarity is lost in complicated strategy debates. Sometimes ideological conflicts are put aside when feminists share a transcendent social goal, such as suffrage or reproductive choice. And sometimes one ideological strain of feminism dominates another. In the 1970s equal rights feminism was ascendant. The 1980s saw a revival of protectionism.

Equal rights feminism couldn't last. It was profoundly disruptive for women as well as men. By questioning long-cherished notions about sex, it posed unsettling questions about selfhood. It challenged men and women to shape their own identities without resort to stereotypes. It posed particular existential challenges to women who were accustomed to knowing themselves through the web of familial relations. As Elizabeth Cady Stanton observed more than a hundred years ago, equal rights feminism challenges women to acknowledge that they are isolated individuals as well. Stressing that like "every human soul" woman "must make the voyage of life alone," Stanton, the mother of seven and a political organizer who spent most of her life in a crowd, exhorted women to recognize the "solitude of self."

This emphasis on individual autonomy didn't just scare many women; it struck them as selfish—as it might be if it were unaccompanied by an ongoing commitment to family and community. Twenty years ago feminists made the mistake of denigrating homemaking and volunteer work. It's hard to imagine how else they might have made their case for paid work, at the time.

Still, the attack on volunteering was simplistic and ill informed. Feminists might have paid attention to the historical experiences of middle-class African American women combining paid work, volunteering, and family life. They might have paid attention to the critical role played by the volunteer tradition in the nineteenth-century women's movement. Women's sense of their maternal responsibilities at home and in the wider world was at the core of their shared social conscience, which feminists ignored at their peril. Feminism will not succeed with American women, as Constance Buchanan notes, until it offers them a vision that reconciles the assertion of equal rights with the assumption of social responsibilities.

That's the vision Hillary Clinton is striving to embody, as a family woman and a feminist, an advocate of civil rights and a preacher of a caring and sharing politics of meaning. I wish her luck: the difficulty she encountered during the 1992 presidential campaign persuading people that she has a maternal side reflects the strong popular presumption that a commitment to equality is incompatible with a willingness to nurture.

We should know better. In fact, millions of American women working outside the home are exercising rights and assuming responsibilities—for better or worse, that's one of the legacies of feminism. Women who sought equal rights in the 1970s have not abandoned their families, like Meryl Streep in *Kramer vs. Kramer*, as antifeminists predicted they would. Instead they have overworked themselves, acting as breadwinners and primary caretakers, too. Given the absence of social and institutional support—family leave and day care—it's not surprising that women would turn for sustenance to traditional notions of sex difference. The belief that they were naturally better suited to child care than men would relieve them of considerable anger toward their husbands. As Victorian women invoked maternal virtue to justify their participation in the public sphere, so contemporary American women have used it to console themselves for the undue burdens they continue to bear in the private one.

Notions of immutable sex differences explained a range of social inequities—the plight of displaced homemakers, the persistence of sexual violence, the problems of women working double shifts within and outside the home. The general failure of hard-won legal rights to ensure social justice (which plagued civil rights activists as well as feminists) might have been considered a failure of government—to enforce civil rights laws and make them matter or to provide social services. It might have been considered a failure of community—our collective failure to care for one another. Instead it was roundly condemned as a failure of feminism, because it provided convenient proof of what many men and women have always believed—that biology is destiny after all. Equal rights feminism fell out of favor, even among feminists, because it made people terribly uncomfortable and because legal rights were not accompanied by a fair division of familial and communal responsibilities.

Feminism Succumbs to Femininity

The feminist drive for equal rights was supposed to have been revitalized last year, and it's true that women were politically activated and made significant political gains. It's clear that women are moving, but in what direction? What does the women's movement comprise?

Vying for power today are poststructural feminists (dominant in academia in recent years), political feminists (officeholders and lobbyists), different-voice feminists, separatist feminists (a small minority), pacifist feminists, careerist feminists, liberal feminists (who tend also to be political feminists), antiporn feminists, ecofeminists, and womanists. These are not, of course, mutually exclusive categories, and this is hardly an exhaustive list. New Age feminists and goddess worshipers widen the array of alternative truths. And the newest category of feminism, personal-development feminism, championed by Gloria Steinem, puts a popular feminist spin on deadeningly familiar messages about recovering from addiction and abuse, liberating your inner child, and restoring your self-esteem.

The marriage of feminism and the phenomenally popular recovery movement is arguably the most disturbing (and potentially influential) development in the feminist movement today. It's based partly on a shared concern about child abuse, nominally a left-wing analog to right-wing anxiety about the family. There's an emerging alliance of antipornography and antiviolence feminists with therapists who diagnose and treat child abuse, including "ritual abuse" and "Satanism" (often said to be linked to pornography). Feminism is at risk of being implicated in the unsavory business of hypnotizing suspected victims of abuse to help them "retrieve" their buried childhood memories. Gloria Steinem has blithely praised the important work of therapists in this field without even a nod to the potential for, well, abuse when unhappy, suggestible people who are angry at their parents are exposed to suggestive hypnotic techniques designed to uncover their histories of victimization.

But the involvement of some feminists in the memory-retrieval industry is only one manifestation of a broader ideological threat posed to feminism by the recovery movement. Recovery, with its absurdly broad definitions of addiction and abuse, encourages people to feel fragile and helpless. Parental insensitivity is classed as child abuse, along with parental violence, because all suffering is said to be equal (meaning entirely subjective); but that's appropriate only if all people are so terribly weak that a cross word inevitably has the destructive force of a blow. Put very simply, women need a feminist movement that makes them feel strong.

Enlisting people in a struggle for liberation without exaggerating the ways in which they're oppressed is a challenge for any civil rights movement. It's a particularly daunting one for feminists, who are still arguing among themselves about whether women are oppressed more by nature or by culture. For some feminists, strengthening women is a matter of alerting them to their natural vulnerabilities.

There has always been a strain of feminism that presents women as frail and naturally victimized. As it was a hundred years ago, feminist victimism is today most clearly expressed in sexuality debates—about pornography, prostitution, rape, and sexual harassment. Today sexual violence is a unifying focal point for women who do and women who do not call themselves feminists: 84 percent of women surveyed by *Redbook* considered "fighting violence against women" to be "very important." (Eighty-two percent rated workplace equality and 54 percent rated abortion rights as very important.) Given this pervasive, overriding concern about violence and our persistent failure to address it effectively, victimism is likely to become an important organizing tool for feminism in the 1990s.

Feminist discussions of sexual offenses often share with the recovery movement the notion that, again, there are no objective measures of suffering: all suffering is said to be equal, in the apparent belief that all women are weak. Wage-earning women testify to being "disabled" by sexist remarks in the workplace. College women testify to the trauma of being fondled by their dates. The term "date rape," like the term "addiction," no longer has much literal, objective meaning. It tends to be used figuratively, as a metaphor signifying that all heterosexual encounters are inherently abusive of women. The belief that, in a male-dominated culture that has "normalized" rape, "yes" can never really mean "yes" has been popularized by the antipornography feminists Andrea Dworkin and Catharine MacKinnon. (Dworkin devoted an entire book to the contention that intercourse is essentially a euphemism for rape.) But only five years ago Dworkin and MacKinnon were leaders of a feminist fringe. Today, owing partly to the excesses of multiculturalism and the exaltation of victimization, they're leaders in the feminist mainstream.

Why is feminism helping to make women feel so vulnerable? Why do some young women on Ivy League campuses, among the most privileged people on the globe, feel oppressed? Why does feminist victimology seem so much more pervasive among middle- and upper-class whites than among lower-income women, and girls, of color? Questions like these need to be aired by feminists. But in some feminist circles it is heresy to suggest that there are degrees of suffering and oppression, which need to be kept in perspective. It is heresy to suggest that being raped by your date may not be as traumatic or terrifying as being raped by a stranger who breaks into your bedroom in the middle of the night. It is heresy to suggest that a woman who has to listen to her colleagues tell stupid sexist jokes has a lesser grievance than a woman who is physically accosted by her supervisor. It is heresy, in general, to question the testimony of self-proclaimed victims of date rape or harassment, as it is heresy in a twelve-step group to question claims of abuse. All claims of suffering are sacred and presumed to be absolutely true. It is a primary article of faith among many feminists that women don't lie about rape, ever; they lack the dishonesty gene. Some may call this feminism, but it looks more like femininity to me.

Blind faith in women's pervasive victimization also looks a little like religion. "Contemporary feminism is a new kind of religion," Camille Paglia complains, overstating her case with panache. But if her metaphor begs to be qualified, it offers a nugget of truth. Feminists choose among competing denominations with varying degrees of passion, and belief; what is gospel to one feminist is a working hypothesis to another. Still, like every other ideology and "ism"—from feudalism to capitalism to communism to Freudianism—feminism is for some a revelation. Insights into the dynamics of sexual violence are turned into a metaphysic. Like people in recovery who see addiction lurking in all our desires, innumerable feminists see men's oppression of women in all our personal and social relations. Sometimes the pristine earnestness of this theology is unrelenting. Feminism lacks a sense of black humor: I know a few Jewish jokes about the Holocaust but no feminist jokes about rape.

This is only an observation, made with some trepidation, not an invitation to laugh about genocide or sex crimes. And I'm not suggesting that the emerging orthodoxy about victimization infects all feminist sexuality debates. Of course, many feminists harbor heretical thoughts about lesser forms of sexual misconduct. But few want to be vilified for trivializing sexual violence and collaborating in the abuse of women.

The Enemy Within

The example of Camille Paglia is instructive. She is generally considered by feminists to be practically pro-rape, because she has offered this advice to young women: don't get drunk at fraternity parties, don't accompany boys to their rooms, realize that sexual freedom entails sexual risks, and take some responsibility for your behavior. As Paglia says, this might once have been called common sense (it's what some of our mothers told us); today it's called blaming the victim.

Paglia is right: it ought to be possible to condemn date rape without glorifying the notion that women are helpless to avoid it. But not everyone can risk dissent. A prominent feminist journalist who expressed misgivings to me about the iconization of Anita Hill chooses not to be identified. Yet Anita Hill is a questionable candidate for feminist sainthood, because she was, after all, working for Clarence Thomas voluntarily, apparently assisting him in what feminists and other civil rights activists have condemned as the deliberate nonenforcement of federal equal employment laws. Was she too hapless to know better? Feminists are not supposed to ask.

It is, however, not simply undue caution or peer pressure that squelches dissent among feminists. Many are genuinely ambivalent about choosing sides in sexuality debates. It is facile, in the context of the AIDS epidemic, to dismiss concern about date rape as "hysteria." And it takes hubris (not an unmitigated fault) to suggest that some claims of victimization are exaggerated, when many are true. The victimization of women as a class by discriminatory laws and customs, and a collective failure to take sexual violence seriously, are historical reality. Even today women are being assaulted and killed by their husbands and boyfriends with terrifying regularity. When some feminists overdramatize minor acts of sexual misconduct or dogmatically insist that we must always believe the woman, it is sometimes hard to blame them, given the historical presumption that women lie about rape routinely, that wife abuse is a marital squabble, that date rape and marital rape are not real rape, and that sexual harassment is cute.

Feminists occasionally need critics like Paglia who are not afraid to be injudicious. Paglia's critiques of feminism are, however, flawed by her limited knowledge of feminist theory. She doesn't even realize what she has in common with feminists she disdains—notably Carol Gilligan and Catharine MacKinnon. Both Paglia and MacKinnon suggest that sexual relations are inextricably bound up with power relations; both promote a vision of male sexuality as naturally violent and cruel. But while Paglia celebrates sexual danger, MacKinnon wants to legislate even the thought of it away. Both Paglia and Gilligan offer idealized notions of femininity. But Gilligan celebrates gender stereotypes while Paglia celebrates sex archetypes. Paglia also offers a refreshingly tough, erotic vision of female sexuality to counteract the pious maternalism of *In a Different Voice*.

To the extent that there's a debate between Paglia and the feminist movement, it's not a particularly thoughtful one, partly because it's occurring at second hand, in the media. There are thoughtful feminist debates being conducted in academia, but they're not widely heard. Paglia is highly critical of feminist academics who don't publish in the mainstream; but people have a right to choose their venues, and besides, access to the mainstream press is not easily won. Still, their relative isolation is a problem for feminist scholars who want to influence public policy. To reach a general audience they have to depend on journalists to draw on and sometimes appropriate their work.

In the end feminism, like other social movements, is dependent on the vagaries of the marketplace. It's not that women perceive feminism just the way *Time* and *Newsweek* present it to them. They have direct access only to the kind and quantity of feminist speech deemed marketable. Today the concept of a feminist movement is considered to have commercial viability once again. The challenge now is to make public debates about feminist issues as informed as they are intense.

It's not surprising that we haven't achieved equality; we haven't even defined it. Nearly thirty years after the onset of the modern feminist movement, we still have no consensus on what nature dictates to men and women and demands of law. Does equality mean extending special employment rights to pregnant women, or limiting the Sixth Amendment rights of men standing trial for rape, or suspending the First Amendment rights of men who read pornography? Nearly thirty years after the passage of landmark federal civil rights laws, we still have no consensus on the relationship of individual rights to social justice. But, feminists might wonder, why did rights fall out of favor with progressives just as women were in danger of acquiring them?

The most effective backlash against feminism almost always comes from within, as women either despair of achieving equality or retreat from its demands. The confident political resurgence of women today will have to withstand a resurgent belief in women's vulnerabilities. Listening to the sexuality debates, I worry that women feel so wounded. Looking at feminism, I wonder at the public face of femininity.

A VIRTUOUS WOMAN

(September 1995)

Gracious, compassionate, fervently devoted to advancing the status of her sex, sometimes at the expense of her self, Gloria Steinem emerges from this reverential biography as an accidental celebrity. It's hard to imagine such a feminine woman, always apt to consider the needs of others before her own, actively seeking power, fame, and the lead role in contemporary American feminism. In fact, as Steinem concedes, she came late to the women's movement, at age thirty-five, in 1969, after attending an abortion speak-out. (The "light began to dawn," she wrote, "I began to read every piece of feminist writing I could lay my hands on, and talk to every active feminist I could find.") Once converted, she attracted the attention of the press more than she sought it out, her authorized biographer Carolyn Heilbrun suggests, because she was "nonthreatening," pretty, and glamorous.

If this is true, it does not diminish Steinem's commitment or contributions to feminism, as Heilbrun stresses. Having been "anointed" by the media, she ably performed the duties of her office, earning her place in the pantheon. She overcame a fear of public speaking to become an itinerant preacher, bringing her message about sexual and racial equality home to women nationwide. (By the late 1980s, Heilbrun writes, "there had, after all, only been one week when she was not in an airplane.") She became active in national politics as well and helped build some enduring institutions—the National Women's Political Caucus, *Ms.,* and the Ms. Foundation, which funds organizing at the grass roots. In the end, Heilbrun suggests, Steinem became the leader the media made her out to be, which is to say that she did not seek leadership so much as consent to it, once it was conferred on her.

Heilbrun, professor of English at Columbia University and author most recently of *Hamlet's Mother,* is alert to the tendency of accomplished women, and their biographers, to deny their quest for power and control. In the traditional view, work discovers and pursues the woman of exceptional achievement, as if it were a "conventional romantic lover," Heilbrun remarked in *Writing a Woman's Life.* So it is puzzling to find her portraying Steinem in the traditional feminine mode—as a woman to whom fame came serendipitously, an exceedingly nice woman with intelligence, integrity, and an abiding concern for social welfare but no discernible personal ambition. Apart from a cursory reference to an undergraduate essay she wrote on fame, in which she declared her desire to see her name in the papers, there is little acknowledgment in *The Education of a Woman* that Steinem may have plotted or at least desired her ascent, partly for her own sake, not merely for the good of womankind. Nor is she seen enjoying her celebrity so much as tolerating it, for the sake of helping others.

What drove Gloria Steinem to become America's preeminent feminist? She has described herself as "codependent with the world," referring to her impulse to rescue people, a legacy of the lonely, relatively impoverished childhood years spent caring for her emotionally unstable mother. Steinem's most popular writings are partly autobiographical, and her readers will be familiar with this explanation of her character and with much of her life story—her childhood, her conversion to feminism, her political experiences, the burnout she suffered in her fifties after two decades of public life marked by little introspection, her subsequent immersion in therapy and embrace of recovery movement teachings about self-esteem and the child within. Heilbrun fills in some details—about Steinem's college experiences, her postgraduate career as a freelance journalist in New York, her experiences at *Ms.,* her trashing by radical feminists in the 1970s, in addition to her love affairs and disinclination to marry—but she fails to illuminate Steinem's "elusive" personality. Instead she tends to take her subject at face value, mirroring the self-image that Steinem presents in her work.

A living icon, whom many feminists loathe to criticize (partly for political reasons, partly because her graciousness makes criticism feel churlish), a public woman who discovered the inner life at fifty, Steinem presents a formidable challenge to a sympathetic biographer. Heilbrun describes her as Godlike, "essential and ubiquitous," and constrained by admiration or etiquette, she is consistently apologetic about whatever might be perceived by feminists as Steinem's shortcomings or political faux pas. Discussing the glamorous life she led in the 1960s as a magazine writer who modeled herself after Holly Golightly, Heilbrun assures us that Steinem was an "internal radical," devoted to causes she could not publicize. The "ease" with which she moved in Mort Zuckerman's Easthampton social circle during their brief relationship in the 1980s is attributed to "profound fatique" and the desire to raise money for her causes. Goddess forbid she simply enjoyed partygoing. Feminists, I guess, aren't supposed to have fun.

Nor are they supposed to have much money; the equation of poverty with virtue often prevails among feminists. (American attitudes toward wealth are generally contradictory: populist mistrust of the rich conflicts with the ethic of upward mobility.) Heilbrun painstakingly explains Steinem's sympathy for wealthy women in paternalistic families, which, she observes, "has always puzzled feminists." Steinem herself, accused of being rich, has carefully explained that much of her income has been diverted to worthy causes. She has also had to apologize for being thin: the child of a food addict, she has an eating disorder, she's explained; she is in recovery.

Known as the pretty, miniskirted feminist with a string of well-placed lovers, Steinem has always had to defend herself against the charge that she owes her success to her looks and her relationships with men. Heilbrun does have the temerity to address one central irony of Steinem's life—that her beauty was "essential" to her success, partly because it enhanced her "ability to persuade and to captivate" as well as her value as a feminist symbol. She was proof that feminists were not simply frustrated women who hated men or were unable to attract them.

Heilbrun is quick to add, however, that while good looks "play(ed) their part" in Steinem's career, "they would not be more significant than her ideas." It would be more accurate to say that her looks would not be more significant than her activism, which was, in turn, facilitated by her looks. (As Heilbrun suggests, beauty helped provide Steinem with a platform and a receptive audience.) It is no criticism of Steinem to say that, although she is a talented journalist, she has not made her mark with ideas (indeed, she disdains intellectualism); she has made her mark as an activist. But while Heilbrun gently criticizes the naïveté of *Revolution from Within,* Steinem's simplistic, derivative book about self-esteem, while she sympathizes with feminist intellectuals who have little patience for her belated discovery of the examined life, she is positively euphemistic when describing Steinem's penchant for unoriginal thinking as a "talent for tolerating restatement."

Nor does Heilbrun offer analysis, much less criticism, of Steinem's "ideas," such as her controversial notions about censoring pornography and her support for proposals by Catharine Mac-

Kinnon and Andrea Dworkin to make pornography, vaguely defined, a violation of women's civil rights. In her brief, one-paragraph defense of Steinem's views, Heilbrun facilely attributes feminist opposition to the MacKinnon/Dworkin position to a lack of information: "Anti-pornography groups are not advocating 'censorship,'" she remarks earnestly, as if imposing civil sanctions on the production and distribution of speech were not an effective way of suppressing it.

If an exceptional capacity for empathy is one of Steinem's strengths, it may also contribute to her intellectual weakness, as her support for censoring pornography suggests. Her rescue fantasies, her sympathy for the oppressed, seem to make her unduly sensitive to claims of victimization and insufficiently skeptical of their sensibleness or veracity. In recent years, Steinem has become a strong advocate of therapeutic feminism, which borrows heavily from the recovery movement and tends to exaggerate women's weakness: we are terrorized by pornography, traumatized by rude remarks as well as behavior; we are oppressed, not merely hurt or irritated, and never amused by cultural standards of beauty and youth. Steinem's writing about the pain endured by women who lie about their age may make you nostalgic for Jack Benny.

But therapeutic feminism, with its excessive concern for the traumas attendant on womanhood, has been ascendant in recent years. What is interesting about Steinem is that her own evolution mirrors the evolution of popular feminism. In the 1970s, she was an advocate of equal rights, who challenged traditional notions of gender difference and natural feminine weakness. In the 1980s she began supporting at least some protection for women in the form of censorship. In the 1990s she stands for feminism as a form of personal development as well as political liberation.

"What if an entire generation of women refused to learn how to type?" Steinem asked my graduating class at Smith College in her controversial commencement speech in 1971. I jabbed my mother in the ribs; a child of the depression, she had insisted that I spend the summer after my junior year taking a typing course at a local secretarial school. Steinem gave a powerful, injudicious speech that day, advocating abortion rights; attacking the politics of marriage, motherhood, and religion; and challenging Smith, a traditional woman's college, to transform itself into a radicalizing feminist institution.

Addressing the class of 1995, last spring, she was more sanguine, acknowledging feminism's progress over the past thirty years, as well as the challenges remaining. And, just like a self-help writer, she suggested that the path to liberation was ultimately subjective, exhorting her listeners to trust their own experiences, above all: "trusting our own experience . . . may be the single most revolutionary thing we can do."

Commencement speakers traffic in hyperbole, but it's true that many women do turn to feminism after a personal epiphany, born of hard experience. And if Steinem embraced feminism partly because of her own experience obtaining an abortion, perhaps she has simply come full circle. So it's not fair to suggest that she has abandoned the political sphere in a quest for personal "empowerment." However naïvely, she has sought instead to underscore a connection between personal and political liberation. Whether this confuses categories or clarifies them, the notion that therapy is political and politics therapeutic comes naturally to feminism.

Whether or not she will help lead women to liberation, at least Steinem has never been tentative or retiring in espousing either equality or enlightenment. If she became a symbol for the women's movement by accident, she remained one by design. If she has a feminine impulse toward self-sacrifice, it has been tempered by a talent for self-promotion and a feminist desire for achievement. The woman who strode through the past twenty-five years of public life strides, along with the feminist movement, beyond the ken of this tentative, feminine book.

PUT THE BLAME ON MAME

(*December 1991*)

She's a cashmere-sweater and camel's-hair-coat girl: no artificial fiber would dare to touch her perfect skin. She's an Ivory Soap girl, with barely styled brown hair falling thickly past her shoulders. Softly pretty and blankly self-assured, she's a tranquilizer: two clean and docile young boys flank her, stuck to her sides like magnets on a refrigerator. One has both arms wrapped fervently around her waist. The other leans into the pleats of her good wool skirt.

She's the New Traditionalist, star of a recent *Good Housekeeping* ad campaign and harbinger of what's supposed to be a trend. In the 1990s women will rediscover domesticity, according to *Good Housekeeping.* "Searching for something to believe in," the postfeminist woman will find "her husband, her children, her home," and last of all "herself." Kicking off the new "social movement" of full-time homemaking, Alan Waxenberg, the publisher of *Good Housekeeping,* offered this historical critique of late-twentieth-century American culture: the 1960s was the decade of "protest," the 1970s was the decade of "feminism," the 1980s was the decade of "yuppieism," and the 1990s will be the decade of the "new traditionalist."

It should be easy to dismiss antifeminist fantasies (and puerile pronouncements on culture) like this, but often they are taken quite seriously. Reactionary visions of femininity have displaced "factual reporting" on women's lives, Susan Faludi stresses in her comprehensive survey of a powerful ten-year backlash against feminism. Faludi, a reporter for the *Wall Street Journal,* briskly exposes the conventional wisdom about women's dissatisfaction with equality and life outside the home as a collection of prejudices and myths.

The first myth, from which all others flowed, began circulating in the early 1980s (I originally heard it from the audience on *Donahue*). It goes something like this: the feminist movement is over, because equality has been achieved. To believe this you have to ignore a lot of facts—about sexual violence and harassment, the wage gap, occupational segregation, the denial of reproductive choice to poor women, the disproportionate numbers of women in poverty, the disproportionate numbers of men in Congress and the judiciary.

The problems these statistics represent have, of course, received some attention in the media—occasional articles about the "glass ceiling," the feminization of poverty, and the unequal treatment of women candidates, a few TV movies about rape victims and battered wives. But feminists who have continued to protest pervasive sex discrimination are likely to be dismissed as complainers. And they're said to be "out of touch" with the average American woman, which brings us to myth number 2: Women today suffer from too much equality, not too little. The high-profile problems for women in the 1980s (middle-class problems all) were infertility, the stress of working outside the home, and the emptiness of professional life. The blame for virtually all these problems was put on feminism, which devolved from a promise to a threat.

Faludi, unabashed about her own feminism and commitment to equal rights, shows how these myths were perpetuated and exploited by the press, the fashion and film industries, the anti-abortion movement, cosmetic surgeons, right-wing ideologues-turned-authors (George Gilder and Allan Bloom), popular psychologists, the men's-movement guru Robert Bly, and a few revisionist feminists (Carol Gilligan, Lenore Weitzman, Sylvia Ann Hewlett). *Backlash* is more descriptive than analytic; Faludi doesn't argue the justice of equality so much as assume it, which will alienate readers (I suspect there are many) who believe that equality is unnatural and bad for women. But Faludi is a good journalist; her assertions about antifeminist propaganda are substantiated. If you believe, as I do, that equality is good for women, and that traditional gender roles are mandated unfairly by culture, not nature, you'll find this book a valuable resource— an encyclopedic review of contemporary antifeminism—and reading it you may feel less alone.

■   ■   ■

Beginning with a critique of the overpublicized 1986 Harvard-Yale study about the diminishing chances that single, educated, heterosexual women over thirty would find mates, Faludi debunks much popular wisdom about the ravages of feminism: the Harvard-Yale marriage findings were preliminary, readily discredited by other statisticians, and deleted from the final marriage study that was formally published three and a half years later. The preliminary findings, encouraging women to marry young, were front-page news; word of their retraction was buried and brief.

In the 1980s, Faludi asserts, "statistics on women stopped functioning as social barometers." Instead of describing women's behavior, they effectively prescribed it. The Reagan administration pressured the Census Bureau into demonstrating "the rising threat of infertility, the physical and psychic risks lurking in abortion, the dark side of single parenthood, the ill effects of day care." Bad news about feminism was heavily promoted by the press and rarely scrutinized, as Faludi demonstrates. The press portrayed the "postfeminist" professional woman as stressed out and frustrated sexually and maternally. It helped create an "infertility epidemic" (there was little hard evidence of one), launching an infertility industry. It seized on questionable news about the dire effects of divorce reform on homemakers, perversely blaming feminists for the inevitable consequences of discrimination. The problems of displaced homemakers are hardly indictments of feminism; they're indictments of the traditional division of labor at home and in the workplace (and of the dearth of day care), which denies women equal earning power and necessitated a feminist movement.

The scapegoating of feminism—the spread of the notion that women suffered from equality, not discrimination—was a product of what Faludi calls trend journalism. (It was trend journalism that allowed *Good Housekeeping*'s publisher to anoint the 1990s as the decade of the "new traditionalist" with a completely straight face.) News accounts of women's lives in the 1980s were marked by "the absence of real women," Faludi asserts.

The press delivered the backlash to the public through a series of "trend stories," articles that claimed to divine sweeping shifts in female social behavior while providing little in the way of evidence to support their generalizations. Underlying Faludi's sometimes familiar critique of antifeminism is a powerful critique of the press.

Faludi is not exactly a conspiracy theorist who believes that the press was part of some antifeminist cabal; it was "just grossly susceptible to the prevailing political currents." She also ascribes the shoddy reporting on feminism to laziness—journalists' "propensity to repeat one another"—and to a concentration of ownership that encouraged the repetition of news items. The persuasiveness of thoughtless, unsubstantiated attacks on feminism was a tribute to the force of repetition, as Faludi observes.

Saying that feminism was bad for women made it so, as long as you said it often. ("If we say it's a quota bill, it's a quota bill," a Republican operative told the *New York Times* recently, explaining President Bush's strategy on the civil rights bill.)

Journalists helped create the new truths about feminism; Hollywood dramatized them. The independent, often unmarried heroines of the 1970s gave way to the frustrated career women of the 1980s who got their comeuppance in the antifeminist *Fatal Attraction*. Faludi doesn't predict fashions in femininity for the 1990s, but if *Thelma and Louise* and *Terminator 2* are indications of a trend, celluloid women may regain their independence with a vengeance. She does provide an entertaining and instructive report on the backlash of the 1980s in the movies and on TV, focusing on the misogynist sentiments of *Fatal Attraction*'s director, Adrian Lyne, its leading man, Michael Douglas, and other rich white guys who feel wounded by feminism. Douglas is "tired of feminists, sick of them. . . . Guys are going through a terrible crisis right now because of women's unreasonable demands," he laments. Marshall Herskovitz, a cocreator of *thirtysomething*, agrees: "I think this is a terrible time to be a man, maybe the worst time in history," he whines. "Manhood has simply been devalued in recent years and doesn't carry much weight anymore."

Womanhood, however, carries no weight at all. It floats down fashion runways in tight, tiny skirts and baby-doll dresses. Faludi chronicles the emergence in the late 1980s of Christian Lacroix and other designers who promoted High Femininity—clinging, revealing fripperies and street-wear lingerie. Fashion designers claimed philosophically that they were doing women a favor: the "tailored look" damaged women "psychologically," Cher's favored designer, Bob Mackie, opined. "It hurt their femininity."

Women consumers did not agree, Faludi believes. She reports that the fashion industry lost money on High Femininity. It was a failure in the ready-to-wear market; it didn't suit women's lives at home or in the workplace. Informal evidence—what you see on the street and in stores—indicates that designers may finally have been more successful in marketing miniskirts than Faludi suggests. (In any case, she wears them.) But their apparent willingness to suffer some financial losses in a High Femininity campaign is unsettling, revealing, as it does, an antifeminist ideology that's stronger than greed.

Not that antifeminism isn't often profitable, as cosmetic surgeons can attest. Not that feminism isn't seen as a financial threat by men who fear losing their monopoly on higher-paying jobs. (Women's advances in employment in the 1970s helped trigger the backlash, as Faludi observes. Blue-collar workers whose earning power was being depleted by a failing economy were especially resentful of feminism.) But Faludi's report on the backlash implies that it is fueled not just by economics but by prejudice arising from a fierce emotional attachment to traditional gender roles and notions about natural gender differences. (Michael Douglas and Marshall Herskovitz can hardly be worried that women will take over their jobs.) The enormous popularity of Carol Gilligan's anecdotal, unsubstantiated paean to women's "different voice" was evidence of a strong belief among women, too, in natural gender differences: men and women differ not just biologically but in terms of character, temperament, and moral perspective in one popular feminist view. The antiabortion movement exploits this belief in the primacy of women's maternal role and their nurturing, compassionate, "relational" proclivities. Reproductive choice is a covert economic threat to men (it expands education and employment options for women), but it also poses an identity crisis for women who define themselves as mothers first.

Faludi acknowledges the emotional appeal of antifeminism, but she believes that it's limited among women. Relying on surveys that indicate women's strong support for an egalitarian feminist agenda, she suggests that backlash was foisted on us by antifeminist men (and their right-wing women's auxiliary). Women have been silenced and isolated by backlash, she says, not persuaded by it.

I'm hopeful she's right, but I'm not optimistic. Despite some evidence of a small gender gap, women help elect antifeminist politicians. Women consume trend journalism, advice by self-appointed experts on "successful" femininity, and tributes to women's special (and superior) ways of knowing, relating, and resolving moral dilemmas. Women believed Clarence Thomas over Anita Hill by about a two-to-one margin, according to the *New York Times,* which reported no significant gender gap in support for the Thomas nomination. Feminism was easily sabotaged by the federal government and gatekeepers of the culture because it lacked the wholehearted support of its constituency. Feminists themselves are deeply divided over the fairness and feasibility of equality, and over strategies for achieving it. Feminists, too, are insecure about aging, gaining weight, and failing the tests of femininity.

Demographic changes and the need to integrate women fully into the civilian workplace and the military may eventually force equality on a recalcitrant public. Reaction to the probable retrenchment on reproductive choice may revitalize the feminist movement. Young women like Susan Faludi may continue the drive for equality with uncompromising confidence and verve. Meanwhile, according to a reliable source, some leading New York feminists are getting face-lifts.

---------------- ∎ ∎ ∎ ----------------

JUST LIKE A WOMAN
(*May 1981*)

Thirty years ago, Simone de Beauvoir wrote: "For a long time I have hesitated to write a book on women. The subject is irritating, especially to women, and it is not new . . . but, the voluminous nonsense uttered during the last century seems to have done little to illuminate the problem." So de Beauvoir wrote *The Second Sex,* one of the most intelligent and comprehensive modern analyses of the "woman problem." Today's feminists have proven her wrong on only one point: women are fascinated by the subject of women. The creation of a new school of feminist literature and criticism may be the greatest single accomplishment of today's movement. Women have excelled at consciousness raising and conversation; it's almost as if we would talk our way to liberation.

"The curse upon woman," de Beauvoir wrote, "is that she is not permitted to do anything, so she persists in the vain pursuit of her true being through narcissism, love and religion." Action is not feminine, and she noted that the "independent" professional woman (of 1952) was trapped in a paralyzing conflict between the hope (bred into her) that a man would one day save her life and the drive for independence and self-realization.

Thirty years and more voluminous nonsense later, Colette Dowling has discovered this conflict for what she apparently thinks is the first time. *The Cinderella Complex: Women's Hidden*

Fear of Independence is a sophomoric, depressingly unoriginal book about the simple truth that middle class women are conflicted about taking care of themselves. Read just one chapter of *The Second Sex* ("The Independent Woman") and Matina Horner's 1968 study on women's "fear of success," and you can write *The Cinderella Complex*. Reading it is like going back to your first consciousness raising.

The book is part confessional—an account of Dowling's own unremarkable brush with the dependency syndrome—and part pop psychology—every cliché about feminine behavior is couched in jargon and buttressed by the usual research ("Studies show . . .") and quotes from "authorities in the field." The conflict between femininity and personal or professional competence becomes "gender panic"; dependency is a "lack of separation individuation"; the tendency to seek fulfillment in personal relationships is an "excessive affiliative" drive. With much ado, Dowling and her experts report the women's magazine news from the last decade: women who are taught to lean on men have a hard time assuming responsibility; they are prone to "performance anxiety" and hold themselves back professionally because of sexual confusion about success and independence. These startling conclusions are italicized for the lazy reader. They are supported by the usual case studies of educated middle- and upper-class women suspended between protective fathers, submissive mothers, career ideals, and traditional marriages.

This is popular feminism at its worst: a narrow, narcissistic analysis that turns the concerns and fixations of one class of women into existential problems for womankind. Dowling barely acknowledges that the women she has studied have all had what many would consider the luxury of choosing between paid work and economic dependency. She only notes, in a passing stumble over the obvious, "It is beginning to become apparent that this conflict over working is strongly related to class." It has, of course, long been apparent to men and women who work for money because they must.

This is not to suggest that middle-class women don't suffer, but the failure to recognize the effect of class on women's attitudes toward themselves and their work trivializes questions about sexuality and independence. How seriously can you take a woman whose conflict stems from her shock at finding that being supported is easier than supporting yourself?

It is distressing that many of the women profiled here, notably the author herself, would have called themselves feminists ten years ago. Has the women's movement been so shallow as this? What did feminism mean to these women—the right to take courses and an occasional job while someone else paid the rent? Did they expect that work was fun and always fulfilling? And did they think that they would rid themselves of a lifetime of social and sexual conditioning by earning pin money and making their husbands do the dishes?

Now, after ten years and much breastbeating over her own dependency lapse, Dowling has some sense of what it means to be responsible and independent. But for all her born-again feminism, she is still shaking her head over the fact that it has not been easy. She hasn't grasped that feminine fears of independence reflect what are among the first facts of life for men and women: it is frightening to be alone, hard to define your own life and to exorcise the myths about sex and gender by which you have been raised. Femininity is not the only problem, the root of every sorrow or wrong ever suffered by a woman.

Dowling ultimately legitimizes Cinderella's complex by overstating the problem of femininity. Her underlying message to women is that all their problems are special and purely a function of sex. Sexual oppression, either in the form of law or social conditioning, becomes an excuse for every fault, and every failure is a noble one in the struggle against a sexist culture.

This is hardly the kind of feminism that encourages independence and personal responsibility. It's easy to see *The Cinderella Complex* leading to nothing but more soul searching and consciousness raising. Colette Dowling, like a talk show therapist, reassures women that it is not possible to act until the "inner self" is "clear and unconflicted"; they have to "work through conflict" by paying "scrupulous attention" to themselves. Yes, the process of defining the "inner self" (growing up) requires some thought, but you don't need to be completely cured to take a few small steps off the couch. Haven't women been staring into the mirror long enough?

What's needed is a voyage out. *Pioneer Women: Voices from the Kansas Frontier* is a collection of memoirs from women who settled Kansas during the last half of the nineteenth century. Their voices are remarkably unself-conscious; their subjects, the details and work of daily life: farming (often for the first time), feeding and clothing a family, providing medical care, fighting prairie fires, or simply making soap. Their stories live up to our myths about the pioneers. These were strong, resourceful women who learned to care for themselves and their families through droughts, blizzards, locusts, and Indian wars.

These are, of course, the records of survivors—the women who did not turn back or give out along the way. But many of them were unprepared for the hardships of the frontier. Living conditions at first were unexpectedly primitive. The homes of the early settlers were underground hillside dugouts or freestanding sod cabins, fifteen foot square. We get only glimpses of the initial despair of women from comfortable homes in the East on their first view of the "bleak and lonely" Kansas prairie. There is little mention of fears, self-doubt, or personal unhappiness. These women are always shaking their heads and getting on with it.

Their own pioneering spirits surface not only in a stoic strength in the face of danger and physical deprivation but in the simple ethos that you are what you do. It's not surprising that as the frontier developed pioneer women became politically active. After homes and farms were established, they started schools, churches, and libraries, they became temperance workers and suffragists. The self-portraits that emerge in their reminiscences are of women who defined themselves through their work and their communities.

Joanna Stratton has compiled these memoirs with respect and in a coherent chronology. She does indulge in a few of her own renderings of frontier life, which some may find intrusive, but her narration provides a historical thread that shapes the book. The job of organizing and editing these materials must have been formidable; they are part of a collection of eight hundred pioneer stories solicited by Stratton's great-grandmother. If we want to hear from the voices left out of the book, it is only because the ones included are compelling.

Women in the Wilderness is an account of contemporary pioneering—a more deliberate, feminist quest for what a Kansas pioneer unabashedly called the "wisdom of the wilderness" and for a "female heroic." China Galland has skillfully combined a record of her own wilderness experiences with stories of other women explorers, past and present, into an intelligent, ebullient rendering of the process of trailblazing that makes you want to leave home.

At first, her tone is too self-consciously holy. Galland calls her book a "rudder"—the map of "a length of coastline I have travelled as a woman." She introduces it with a bit of Eastern wisdom and a quote from Eliot that highlights a recurring theme: "And the end of all our exploring / Will be to arrive where we started / And know the place for the first time. . . ." This sounds at first like the familiar pretensions of self-discovery but there are substance and sense in this book.

It is grounded in straightforward accounts of Galland's own

wilderness treks, beginning with her logs of the first all-women's rafting trip down the Grand Canyon and her subsequent voyage to Baja, Mexico—ocean kayaking in the Sea of Cortez. (This is an engrossing travel and adventure book, photographed in black and white.) The record of wilderness experiences is complemented by a discussion of Eastern and Western mythologies, the literature of (male) heroic quests, contemporary feminism, environmental science, and a range of quotes—from Eliot to Adrienne Rich to Ben Franklin.

Galland just manages to carry this off (like the English teacher she once was) because her own voice is strong and commonsensical and her focus is clear: how to overcome passivity, dependence, and fear, how to act to save yourself. Her approach is practical and nondoctrinaire. Galland is a founder of Women in the Wilderness, an organization that runs expeditions and training programs for women, from trekking Nepal to day hikes in neighborhood parks. She looks to the wilderness to teach women to care for themselves, to be alone, and to develop a feminist style of leadership—one that informs without dictating decisions so that every woman is ultimately responsible for herself and her companions.

The models of female leadership and heroism are drawn from stories of political activists and women explorers—an Argentine human rights activist, the first women to climb Annapurna, and Alexandre David-Neel, a Frenchwoman who, in 1911, in her mid-thirties, ran away from a traditional marriage to explore Tibet, Nepal, India, and China. She became a scholar of Tibetan Buddhism, spent three years by herself, living in a cave, studying under a Tibetan hermit, hiked unmapped country through China to the forbidden capital of Tibet, and never gave up the financial support of her husband, who handled her business affairs from afar for forty years.

Of course, notwithstanding the supportive husband, this is

caring for yourself on the grand scale. Fortunately, Galland is modest and practical in pursuit of her ideal. (It is reassuring to hear that as the single mother of three, she does not spend all her time hanging off cliffs.) *Women in the Wilderness* is a wonderfully balanced book—dreamy, idealistic, and practical. It's both a how-to book for "working through" conflict and a book of imaginings, of fantasies and myths of explorations.

Tracks is Robyn Davidson's story of her trek across seventeen hundred miles of Australian desert; she was accompanied only by her dog, three camels, and, for two weeks, an aborigine named Eddy whom she befriended along the way. It took her six months to cross the desert and two years to prepare and train for the trip, living in the Outback.

Davidson, a native Australian, was twenty-seven when she began her trek. She knew nothing about camels or about surviving by herself in the wilderness. She set out to cross the desert because she was "vaguely bored" with her life, disaffected, disgusted with her "self-indulgent negativity." She speaks with self-conscious disdain of the "malaise of my generation, my sex, my class." This was not an informed, deliberate journey. It's as if Cinderella got up, smashed her mirror, and jumped out the window blindfolded.

She landed in Alice Springs, a redneck town on the edge of the desert (for a woman alone, this seems a more dangerous place than any wilderness). Preparation for the trip meant serving as a sort of stable girl on a camel ranch run by a violent, abusive man, working only for room, board, and the promise of three camels. The first half of *Tracks* describes the time in Alice Springs, learning about camels and living alone in a hostile environment. It is a hard, frustrating, and angry period. The trip seems forgotten or simply impossible. She is withdrawn, defensive, confused. She stays, it seems, out of the blind desperation that drove her there.

The desert does not cure her; it is not what she envisioned. Instead of enjoying a solitary trek across a wilderness, she encounters obnoxious tourists, depressing settlements of oppressed aborigines, and a *National Geographic* photographer who is chronicling her trip. She is angry at the government for destroying the aborigines, angry at herself and *National Geographic* for going commercial, angry at the tourists for being crass and stupid and crossing her path. After five months in the desert, she finds "so much of the trip wrong, empty, and small."

There are moments, of course, when the trip is exactly right, and she seems to be bravely following her instincts. It is a great release to set out by herself for the first time. She is at her best in the desert—calm, strong, and purposeful. And she gains some understanding of her need for solitude, her compulsiveness, and of more deliberate ways of dealing with fears, "using your fears as a stepping stone."

Tracks is an odd sort of wilderness book. Its heroine is not very likable; she's insular, hostile, with an adolescent's anger at the world. She does not fit the classic romantic image of an explorer, man or woman. Her journey nearly completed, she is still a runaway who doesn't know what she's doing in the desert. "There had been no point at which I could say 'Yes, this is what I did it for' or 'Yes, this is what I wanted for myself.' "

Davidson says the trip was a gentle catharsis that helped her to "see" herself, but she is at her most expressive when describing her disappointments and her sense of failure. She can't quite articulate what she has learned from the trek. Her sentences build to conclusions that are never drawn: "What I'm trying to say is when you walk on, sleep on, stand on, defecate on, wallow in, get covered in, and eat the dirt around you, and when there is no one to remind you what society's rules are, and nothing to keep you linked to that society, you had better be prepared for some startling changes."

Perhaps because Davidson can't describe the change, it seems to us that it never happened. (I want her to come out of the desert cleansed and calm, and she is still angry.) At least she is not suffering paralysis of the will. She has survived the leap off the cliff. It is a start. Only in myths and fairy tales would one trip through the desert make her whole.

20TH CENTURY FOXES

(*May 1986*)

Whether they are inspirational or cautionary, biographies are great escapes: when you tire of contemplating your own life, it is a relief to imagine someone else's. These brief, impressionistic portraits, intended primarily for young women in search of role models, are diverting introductions to the lives and works of four "significant twentieth-century women." The first entries in a series on modern women, they are billed as "creative" rather than "rote" life histories (as if biographies were, by nature, mundane recitations of dates and happenings). Take "creative" to mean idiosyncratic. The modern women series was born when contemporary writers—journalists, novelists, and poets— were invited to portray their favorite female achievers, to "reconstruct," in their own styles, "a person and a milieu." Still to come are biographies of Edith Piaf, Sylvia Plath, Simone Weil, and Margaret Mead. Books are being published in order of completion; the primary connection between the first four is that they were finished first. But read together they also illuminate the ways gifted women survive adversity, resist or give in to femininity. The emergence of this as a common theme is hardly serendipitous: what woman hasn't succeeded in spite of her sex?

Rebecca West managed not to be sandbagged by motherhood, to the dismay of her son, who took his revenge in a book published after her death. West may or may not have been a "bad" mother, but she was a good writer—which, in Fay Weldon's view, redeems her. We don't expect "niceness" of male writers, she notes; we shouldn't demand it of females. Still, Weldon creates a likable as well as redoubtable Rebecca West in this entertaining account of West's youthful affair with H. G. Wells and the birth of their son.

Hardly a biography, Weldon's portrait is a personal meditation on a fictionalized character—"the young Rebecca" (she was twenty-one when her son was born). Weldon addresses her directly, in a series of "letters from the future," describing her situation and emotional state, praising her creative, intellectual powers, and "making up" scenes between Rebecca, H. G. Wells, her mother, and sister. Instead of summarizing the facts of this long and fruitful life, Weldon hopes with a little fiction to capture the spirit that shaped it. Some may find her approach presumptuous, even coy; West might have understood it. Only artists, she once suggested, can be "sure about people they don't know."

Weldon's young Rebecca, a "rising intellectual star," is passionately devoted to her art and politics, ambitious, brave, and vulnerable—miscast in the conventional role of mistress to an older married man and mentor. She believes, naïvely, that her affair with Wells is different, that he is different; she still hopes that he will leave his wife, not yet knowing, as Weldon knows, that he doesn't take their affair as seriously as she does and doesn't want to be bothered for too long with a mistress and her out-of-wedlock child. She hasn't learned, Weldon writes, that "men like women to appear and disappear, to exist and not exist, at their convenience, and are most put out when it doesn't happen."

West might have suspected as much; she was prepared in childhood for independence. Her father, whom she adored, was hopelessly irresponsible and eventually left the family in genteel poverty. She idealizes him in her autobiographical novel, *The Fountain Overflows,* as a principled, crusading journalist who squandered the family's money in bad investments and was at his best when caring for strangers. ("I had a glorious father. I had no father at all," Rose Aubrey, the novel's young narrator remarks.) Rose's mother is a loving, creative, charming, and childlike woman who "did seem to look to her daughters for protection," and Rose imagines herself "a big, tall man . . . filling the need" for a male in the house. (Mamma is unimpressed: "Why are you giving an imitation of Henry the VIII, or is it Napoleon?" she asks.)

Still, for all the troubles it describes, *The Fountain Overflows* is a hopeful book; Rose always felt sure that "in the end we would be *all right.*" She has chosen not to give in to fear or anger at her parents; instead she pretends to be "all right," as if she can make herself "all right" by pretending. Survival is an act of will or, as Weldon suggests, a matter of "dissimulation." Young Rebecca learned the "art of not admitting defeat," which would pull her through the unhappy affair with Wells and propel her professionally: "You know that you must love the dawning day or else it will be the death of you."

Freya Stark, a contemporary of West's, learned a similar lesson early on. Stark, who became famous for her travels through the East in the 1930s and her travel books, had a solitary, itinerant childhood, shadowed by her parents' unhappy marriage and her much-beloved father's eventual departure for Canada. Stark and her younger sister grew up mostly in Italy with their mother, whom it became Freya's job to manage. "Some lives, like my mother's," she wrote, "are terribly expensive in the lives of other people."

For much of her life, Stark was plagued by ill health and

loneliness: she was a spinster who wanted badly to be married, who finally wed at fifty-four only to divorce a few years later. Through it all, she was self-reliant, brave, and very British. A strong, "no-nonsense" sort of woman (alive today at ninety-three), she set goals for herself and met them, believing that "the secret of life does lie in our own hands," and after making a name for herself as a traveler, she became an established member of British diplomatic circles in the 1940s. Stark never lost what she described as the "capacity for complete diffusion in delight." A born traveler who spoke three languages by the time she was five years old, she never ceased to see the world as a wondrous, "beckoning" place.

Stark wrote extensively about her own life in four volumes of autobiography, and her biographer, Caroline Moorehead, has relatively little to add. Moorehead deftly summarizes Stark's story but doesn't quite bring her character to life. Stark is, however, a difficult subject. There is much to admire about her— the unflagging strength to carry on—and much to dislike. She is imperialistic, "greatly fond of Empire." Thirty years after India gained independence, Moorehead notes, she could still suggest that Britain's civilian rulers may not have been sufficiently "pater-nal" toward the Indians and that "deification of the Viceroy and his wife" might have benefited "the British rule." She is anti-Semitic: "I don't think anyone but a Jew can really like the Jews," she wrote. And she is ill disposed toward other women, "unques-tionably preferred men," and complained of the "arrogance of the unfeminine woman."

Yet reading Stark's autobiography, you can't help liking her a little, as she relaxes her guard and tries to uncover at least some truth about herself. The first volume, *Traveller's Prelude,* resur-rects the troubled girl—plain, sexually insecure, and pained by the separation from her father and premature death of her

sister—who underlies the soldierly woman she becomes. Moorehead describes this side of Freya Stark without, somehow, evok-
ing much sympathy for her. In Stark's own words, the story is
much more poignant.

Anxiety about her appearance and failure to fulfill a traditional female role for which she was thoroughly unsuited are
recurring themes. If she disliked "unfeminine" women, she
could be quite caustic about feminine ones and the male adula-
tion they inspired. "A very delicate woman called Mrs. Riley
came to stay," Stark recalls. "She was always lying about on
sofas in lacy tea-gowns, and her husband adored her. I rather
think many husbands prefer wives whom they can leave safely
on a sofa. . . ."

Although she eventually accepted and learned to enjoy her
status as a single woman, she always wanted to be pretty and
yearned to be loved: "To be just middle-aged with no particular
charm or beauty and no position is a dreary business," she
wrote in *Beyond Euphrates,* a chronicle of her first years in the
East. "I feel as if I had been going uphill all the time to nowhere
in particular, and feel . . . most dreadfully lonely, envying all
these women with their nice clean husbands . . . and their nice
flaxen children . . . I feel as if I had no people of my own . . . no
one any longer makes love to me except when they are drunk."

Despite moments of weakness, Stark spent a lifetime never
giving up; she buried her troubles so that they would not defeat
her. Fay Weldon describes Rebecca West as a "self . . . layered
in youth in the interest of survival." What makes a writer,
Weldon suggests, is the impulse to "probe" each layer, "touch-
ing sore places as a tongue insists on searching out a loose
tooth." Stark, too, found relief in this. Concluding the very
"private history" of *Traveller's Prelude,* she wrote, "I try to
forget and indeed have long succeeded in not thinking of the

unhappy things among all these memories—but now . . . I realize that it was rather a burden to have them entirely all to myself." But she had never been afraid of exploring strange and secret places, and you believe Freya Stark when she says that for her traveling was never "running away." She went "not to escape but to seek."

While Stark set out on the open road and West invaded England's intellectual elite, Jean Rhys crouched in furnished rooms—never a seeker (life would have nothing good to offer her) and hardly one for a stiff upper lip. The world never beckoned Rhys; it stalked her.

This paranoid, passive, and unhappy woman was, however, a gifted writer, and Carole Angier does her justice in an astute and eloquent biography that blends a critique of Rhys's work with an account of her life; one informs the other. In general, you expect a fiction writer to write fiction and try not to confuse her with her character. With Jean Rhys, it's hard not to. If her novels aren't strictly autobiographical, they are entirely solipsistic. Rhys had no capacity for empathy; others were barely human to her. "I see them as trees walking," she wrote.

Rhys was always an outsider, an unloved child who emigrated from the West Indies to Edwardian England in the care of an aunt. Introverted, awkward, essentially alone, she couldn't fit in or get used to the cold. After a few unhappy years in school, she changed her name, became a chorus girl, had an ill-fated affair with a respectable Englishman, broke down, overwhelmed with despair when he left her, and started in desperation to write a diary. She also began a version of *Voyage in the Dark,* an account of this first unhappy love, which would be revised and published years later. From the beginning, Rhys wrote to relieve her suffering. What distinguished her from millions of other anguished diarists was the mysterious talent that transformed suffering into art.

But Rhys had always made an art of suffering. Her life story reads like one of her novels—except that, unlike her heroines, Jean was a survivor, a perennial victim who always found someone to save her. After recovering, more or less, from her first affair, she married (in 1919), moved to Paris, had a child, and was relatively happy for a brief period, until her husband was jailed for swindling. She entered into a disastrous ménage à trois with Ford Madox Ford (her literary patron) and his common-law wife, and was devastated, once again, by this affair, in which everyone behaved rather cruelly. But she drew from it her first novel, *Quartet,* which launched her career.

She returned to England in the 1920s and married her literary agent, a decent man, according to Angier, who put up with her drinking, despair, temper tantrums, and occasional violence and nursed her through her best work—*After Leaving Mr Mackenzie, Good Morning, Midnight, Voyage in the Dark,* and the first drafts of *Wide Sargasso Sea.* They stayed together nearly twenty years, until his death. Then, broke and alone, Jean was rescued, once again, by a man intent on taking care of her: like her first husband, he ended up in jail for swindling. Angier speculates that her aggressive helplessness and incessant demands for support may have contributed to the downfall of both men.

Rhys was, perhaps, like Freya Stark's mother, a woman whose life was "terribly expensive" to others; like Anna in *Voyage in the Dark,* she was "a stone that [you] try to roll uphill that always rolls down again." Rhys developed a "habit of anguish," Angier writes; her "tragic and pessimistic" worldview was inexorably self-fulfilling. Not believing in happy endings, she was incapable of forging one. Embittered about not having love, she was incapable of giving it. This was the "unbearable" knowledge that writing finally gained her: Rhys's isolation "wouldn't end because she wouldn't let it end . . . people wouldn't love and trust her, because she wouldn't love and trust them."

Locating Jean the tormented, self-destructive woman is relatively easy; Jean the artist is elusive, probably because, as Angier observes, she wrote only about being an unhappy woman, not about being a writer. But reviewing the novels against the backdrop of her life, Angier reveals the growing self-knowledge (and artistic control) that Rhys's best work reflects. Her heroines in *Good Morning, Midnight*, and *After Leaving Mr Mackenzie* are not just victims but collaborators in their own destruction; she assigns to them the responsibility for suffering that she could never assume herself.

Rhys earned her belated recognition as a "modern" woman writer, Angier notes, but she was never a "modern woman." Dependent, self-pitying, irresponsible, hardly a feminist role model, she was everything you never want to be. Not weak (Rhys lived to be eighty-eight), not helplessly but willfully unhappy, she was, at her best, resigned. She always yielded to loneliness and despair and found no solace in pretending not to. For her, there was no make-believing life was "all right"; "You can pretend for a long time," she wrote in *Wide Sargasso Sea,* "but one day it all falls away and you are alone"—not just accepting defeat but embracing it.

What a pleasure to turn to Bessie Smith. Underlying her bluest laments there seemed a stubborn, sensual strength, combining sorrow with resilience. Poet and novelist Elaine Feinstein hears pride and a "sense of freedom" in her voice—rejection of the feminine "habit of submission." "Her voice has given me courage," she writes. ". . . We still take fire when we listen to her."

Feinstein recognizes, however, that she's better off knowing Smith from a distance, paying tribute to her combative spirit without romanticizing it. Tough times—growing up poor and black in turn-of-the-century Tennessee—made Smith a tough woman. Life was a battle, so was love, and if she was generous in victory (Smith always took care of her family and friends), she was rarely gracious in defeat.

Her career spanned most of her life; at age nine she was singing in the streets for nickels. At eighteen she was on the road with Ma Rainey and a few years later had her own troupe and her own hit records (for which she did not receive royalties) on Columbia's "race records" label. Smith's career thrived in the 1920s, on her own terms. She never tried to conform to white standards of beauty or behavior, Feinstein writes. An unfashionably big, dark-skinned woman, she didn't expect acceptance from the white community and didn't care to seek it. She was also unfashionably defiant for a successful black performer of the period, and took some pleasure in provoking "polite society" with her crudeness.

Bessie Smith was no lady. ("A lady," Jean Rhys wrote. "Some words have a long, thin neck that you'd like to strangle.") She drank a lot, slept around, and got into fights. Her affairs were the stuff of soap operas—tempestuous. She married twice, the first time to the love of her life; they were happy for a few years, occasionally beat each other, and split up in 1929, as Smith's career was beginning to decline with the onset of the depression. Her second marriage seems to have been more tranquil and helped her through hard times in the early 1930s. In the end, Feinstein writes, her life was taking a "turn for the better."

The end came prematurely, in a car crash in 1937; Smith was forty-three. Feinstein discounts the popular theory that Smith died because she was turned away from a nearby white hospital but suggests that there was probably some unwarranted (although not necessarily "decisive" delay) in treating her. She speculates that a doctor on the scene may have been more concerned with tending to an injured white couple. It's unfortunate that, as Feinstein notes, Smith's death brought her more attention in the white press than her music ever did. "I'm always like a tiger," Bessie sang. She shared with Rebecca West and Freya Stark a will to endure, an unfeminine penchant for victory. Bessie Smith was a modern woman—not the type to take pleasure in martyrdom.

ON FEMINISM AND THE DEVALUATION OF RIGHTS

(Summer 1991)

Justice William Brennan's retirement from the Supreme Court was "exciting news" for Beverly LaHaye, president of Concerned Women for America, an organization boasting a God-given mandate to protect American families from feminists and other "liberal humanists," like William Brennan. Chief among his sins according to LaHaye were support for legalized abortion, the First Amendment, and sexual equality, all of which are at stake in two cases now before the Court: this term the Supreme Court will decide whether employers may bar all fertile women, pregnant or not, from jobs that may pose risks to fetal health, a decision that will help shape the prospects for economic equality; and it will decide whether the administration may bar federally funded family planning clinics from providing abortion counseling. If it is unclear how Justice Souter will rule in these cases, it is certain that Justice Brennan will be missed.*

Still, if Brennan was a friend to feminism, he was hardly a hero to all feminists; among feminists, his tenacious respect for indi-

---

* In *Auto Workers* v *Johnson Controls, Inc.,* the Court struck down fetal protection policies, holding that they violated federal equal employment law. In *Rust* v *Sullivan,* the Court upheld prohibitions on abortion counseling in federally funded clinics.

vidual rights is falling out of favor. Privacy rights, in which the Court has grounded women's abortion rights, are anathema to some feminists who want to dismantle traditional divisions between the public and private sphere because they effectively condone family violence. (The preferred feminist argument for abortion rights is based on the Fourteenth Amendment guarantee of equal protection.) To some feminists, privacy rights, like First Amendment rights that "shield pornographers," are mere instruments of patriarchy: they're said to reflect a masculine obsession with property and the individual accumulation of power that shapes the masculine approach to government, business, and personal relations.

Women are more concerned with feelings than with rights, Carol Gilligan suggested nearly ten years ago, while Andrea Dworkin was dismissing the First Amendment as a boy toy. Or, as Phyllis Schlafly once declared, men are "analytical minded" and women "more personal." Instead of rights, women have a natural moral claim to male protection, conventional antifeminist wisdom held. Instead of rights, women need and seek connectedness, the new feminist champions of femininity assert: women need laws and policies affirming the primacy of their maternal roles, their natural sexual vulnerability, and the special value of their different voice.

Retreating from equality and questioning the efficacy of rights, feminists in the 1980s began demanding special protections for women—special preferences for mothers in child custody disputes, a return to traditional alimony laws, special benefits for wage-earning mothers, and the censorship of pornography considered harmful to women. (Sometimes protectionism confers putative privileges on women; sometimes it restricts men's rights.) Only women get pregnant (and almost only women get raped), opponents of equality intone; so they demand laws that treat the sexes differently, in respect of their reproductive roles, as if the mere possibility of becoming pregnant makes women uniformly more compassionate, nurturing, cooperative, more sexually submissive, and more interested in family life than men, whose inability to bear children is presumed to make them uniformly more ambitious, analytic, sexually aggressive, and emotionally dull.

Traditional notions of gender difference like these have always been at odds with women's rights, as the first generation of contemporary feminists, demanding equality, made clear. Assumptions of difference justified, even glorified, double standards of sexual behavior (which justified rape), traditional divisions of labor within the home and workplace, and the male monopoly on wealth and political power. Mainstream contemporary feminism began with radical visions of assimilation and gender neutral laws, stressing what men and women shared—the capacity to reason and the right to determine their own destinies—instead of how they differed biologically.

But progress toward equality has been slow. Equal opportunity laws do not always provide equal access, much less equal results, and new rights for women have not been accompanied by much-needed social services—day care, health care, support for battered women, training for women who enter the job market late in life or with severe educational disadvantages. Without support services or a federal commitment to affirmative action and the enforcement of civil rights laws, equality remained elusive throughout the 1980s. Despite dramatic gains infiltrating male strongholds—law, medicine, business, even police work—women were still plagued, as a class by occupational segregation, the wage gap, poverty, sexual violence, and the struggle to combine wage earning and child care.

These persistent inequities can be blamed on politics or nature; people are either collectively unwilling or collectively unable to change. In the 1960s and 1970s, feminists generally blamed politics or culture and gender stereotypes for institutionalized gender inequities, which strengthened the drive for equality. Blaming politics, equality feminism has always reflected a belief in the possibility of change.

In the 1980s feminists began losing that belief; they lost courage or hope and began blaming nature, or, rather, blaming earlier equal rights feminists for challenging nature and the maternal ideal. Instead of strengthening their resolve, the slow pace of change convinced some feminists that biology might be destiny after all.

The second generation of contemporary feminists is leaning back toward separatism, advocating separatist workplace policies such as mommy tracking or educational reforms such as new gynocentric curricula. Feminists today are embracing an old belief in gender difference and a concomitant disdain for equal rights, arguing that rights are inherently masculine (as caring and sharing are feminine) and that in the competitive marketplace of rights, women are naturally handicapped by pregnancy. No longer do the majority of feminists challenge assumptions of gender difference because they're inimical to women's rights. Instead rights are considered inimical to women.

This feminist rejection of rights is partly cowardice. Having lost the ERA and whatever public support they gained in the 1970s, feminists seem afraid to challenge mainstream ideals of femininity and family life. Wellesley students who protested Barbara Bush's appointment as commencement speaker last June initially found relatively little support among their middle-aged feminist mentors, who chastized students for being careerists. The students' simple point—that Barbara Bush was not known as a homemaker or community volunteer, much less a career woman, but was known primarily as an important man's wife— was buried at first in an anxious, irrelevant feminist defense of female nurturance.

Still, the new protectionist feminism is not simply political cowardice or conformity; it also reflects justifiable, if confused, concern about women's welfare and the failure of legal rights to ensure social justice. In recent years, feminists and advocates of minority rights have been confronted with the irony of extending rights to people who are in no position to take advantage of them: Abortion rights are merely academic to poor women when public funding for abortions is denied. Equal employment rights are irrelevant to illiterate teenagers who have not enjoyed access to decent public schools.

Perhaps this proves that rights will not lead us to justice. Perhaps it proves we need more rights still. Social inequities are arguments not just for social services but for the underlying recognition of economic needs as rights, a point made and lost by the welfare rights movement some twenty years ago before a Supreme Court that was considerably more liberal than the one presiding today. With the Court and an entrenched Republican administration now more intent on restricting the rights of women and minority males than expanding them, with the gap between legal equality and social inequality increasing, women looking around for something to blame find feminism.

If the natural order is inequality, then feminist hubris may be faulted for disrupting it and placing women at risk. Divorce law reform, for example, based on a feminist ideal of marriage as a voluntary union of equals, is said to have been bad for women who are not, in fact, the economic equals of their husbands. So equal rights feminists are blamed for the problems of displaced homemakers, which is a little like blaming advocates of fair housing laws for white flight from neighborhoods in which houses are sold to blacks or for the crosses that burn on their lawns.

Displaced homemakers might blame the dual labor market for their plight. They might blame a culture that encourages women to sacrifice their careers to their husbands and values middle-aged men more than middle-aged women. They might blame judges for applying the new laws unfairly to deny women the postdivorce support to which they're legally entitled. Generally, the new divorce laws give judges the discretion to award long-term maintenance or generous property settlements to women (or men) who have been long-term homemakers. Egalitarian notions of justice do not require courts to presume equality that has yet to be achieved.

In fact, the gap between legal equality and social inequality is a central concern for equal rights feminists too. How should laws treat women who are still only potentially equal? Feminists on both sides of the debate about gender difference, protections, and rights can generally agree that justice sometimes requires treating differently situated people differently: A woman who has suffered discrimination early on in her career may have a right to be evaluated by different standards from men when decisions about promotion are made.

Still, the suggestion that legal rights should be shaped partly by historical realities and socially constructed roles and relations (an argument for affirmative action) doesn't end the debate about protections and rights for women. Even feminists who agree that men and women are not essentially, consistently different in character, but also agree that the different circumstances of women's lives and women's history may sometimes require their differential treatment, disagree about precisely what circumstantial differences are relevant to the allocation of rights; they also disagree about how rights should be allocated—to women as a class or in a gender-neutral fashion to individuals who are similarly situated.

When is the fact that only women get pregnant relevant in the workplace and how should employment policies account for pregnancy? Does it require or justify different maximum hour laws for men and women, promulgated in the early 1900s in the interests of motherhood, or maternal leave instead of parental leave policies, or different disability benefits for pregnant and nonpregnant workers?

To suggest, as some equality feminists do, that disability policies should be gender neutral, that women disabled by pregnancy should receive equal but not extra benefits, is not to ignore the uniqueness of pregnancy and its effect on women's lives. It is to recognize that men and women workers disabled for different reasons should receive comparable benefits, just as some men and women in different jobs ought to receive comparable pay. Of course, only women get pregnant. But not all women get pregnant. Not all women are temporarily disabled by pregnancy, and not only women suffer from a range of temporary disabilities. It shouldn't matter for purposes of a disability plan whether a worker is disabled by pregnancy or a bad back. What matters are not the unique causes of disabilities but their common effects— temporary inability to work and increased medical expenses.*

Nor should sex matter in a child custody dispute or to the extension of child-care benefits. What matters is the division of labor within the home. (Not only women can care for children.) Women who take primary responsibility for child care probably should enjoy a presumptive advantage in custody disputes, but so should the small minority of men who stay home. Parental instead of maternal leave policies allow men to participate more fully in family life and women to pursue careers, without denying couples the opportunity to play traditional roles if they choose.

This egalitarian demand for gender-neutral laws does not den-

---

* See Wendy W. Williams, "Equality's Riddle: Pregnancy and the Equal Treatment/Special Treatment Debate," New York University review of Law and Social Change, 325 (1985): 13.

igrate what are commonly considered natural feminine values, as protectionist feminists charge; it does resist the attempt to feminize what ought to be considered human values and human rights. Equality and respect for choice generally require that laws focus on characteristics other than sex when they parcel out rights. Surely history has taught women that much.

Like contemporary feminism, the first women's rights movement began in the mid-1800s protesting the male monopoly on rights, which complemented the female monopoly on feelings. But it too was torn by debates about protections and rights and femininity (in the 1920s, feminist supporters of protective labor laws vigorously opposed the ERA), and the first movement for legal equality lost momentum after women won the vote. Until some twenty-five years ago, laws continued subordinating women by making presumptions about them based on a maternal ideal, instead of treating them as individuals. Women were presumed to be homemakers and men breadwinners, so a range of state and federal laws extended greater rights, responsibilities, and benefits to men: male wage earners received greater social security benefits because it was assumed that men were supporting their families while women worked for fun, or pin money. This was conventional wisdom and generally perfectly legal until the early 1970s when, in a victory for the equal rights movement, the Supreme Court recognized that wage-earner/homemaker laws were discriminatory and ought to be prohibited under the Fourteenth Amendment.

So sex discrimination is a relatively new concept for the Supreme Court and one the justices haven't fully embraced, which is another reason the equal rights movement stalled. The Court has failed to fashion a gender-neutral approach to equality that accommodates pregnancy (in the 1970s it upheld the exclusion of pregnancy-related disabilities from employee disability plans, allowing less than equal treatment of women workers). It has refused to recognize that abortion rights are essential to achieving sexual equality. And it has refused to grant women the same equality rights it grants racial minorities, because a majority of justices have never believed that men and women are equal to the same extent that people of different races are equal.

The Court often has trouble locating discrimination in laws allocating different rights or liabilities to men and women in cases involving sex and children. It has, for example, upheld statutory rape laws applying only to men and limited the parental rights of unwed fathers, assuming that their reproductive roles make women sexually submissive, superior parents. But male sexual aggressiveness and a tendency to exploit women as well as widespread paternal neglect aren't simply biologically compelled; they reflect cultural conditioning too. The Court can't see discrimination in laws limiting fathers' rights or making only men liable for statutory rape because it can't see the difference in these cases between biology and culture.*

Of course, defining that difference and its relevance to law has always been the challenge for feminists. Reasonable people always will disagree about whether or to what extent traditional familial roles or male sexual aggressiveness and violence are natural or the results of socialization, which is why a sameness/difference debate is polarizing the feminist community today. Among scholars, that debate is a sophisticated cottage industry. Periodically a feminist scholar devises a new theory promising to take us beyond sameness or beyond difference and beyond rights to some new, unspecified way of distributing power. But the subtleties of much feminist scholarship are lost in public policy discussions, not to mention the popular forums of talk shows and women's magazines where theories of gender difference are most crudely construed.

---

* See Sylvia A. law, "Rethinking Sex and the Constitution," University of Pennsylvania Law review, 955 (1984): 132.

And sometimes the central question for women is lost in subtleties. Although strategies for achieving equality may involve convoluted compromises—affirmative action or special workplace benefits that provide short-term relief to women until comparable benefits may be extended to men—the ideological question facing women is simple: Is biology destiny, are women defined by motherhood, or not? Should law treat women as variable individuals, equally imbued with rights, or as members of a class defined by its capacity to care, nurture, and breed?

Protectionism has always been essentially pronatalist and anti-choice, revolving as it does around sex and reproduction. It also has a historic connection to racism, incorporating white, middle-class standards of femininity that black women were considered naturally incapable of meeting. Turn-of-the-century labor laws limiting women's hours of work or denying them manual labor jobs reflected a belief in white women's natural physical weakness and their exclusive responsibility to bear and care for children. (Occupations in which black women were clustered—agriculture and domestic service—were not generally covered by protective laws.) The labor laws did make life easier for some women, at the expense of maintaining a dual labor market and reinforcing traditional familial roles. Protective family laws, making only men liable for alimony or giving women preferences in custody disputes, helped preserve the patriarchal family. Protective criminal laws distorted the prosecution of rape cases, protecting only "good" women—chaste, passive, white women—from sexual assaults. Protective laws regulating speech and sexual behavior, championed by nineteenth-century social purists and anti-pornography activists today, inevitably restrict access to sex education and birth control.

Protectionism is a seamless web for women, and that's what makes it so dangerous. It reflects an ideology of gender difference that has shaped labor laws, family laws, criminal laws, and laws limiting First Amendment rights and reproductive behavior that keep women in place. When protectionists demand special benefits for women instead of equal rights, they justify the imposition of special restrictions on them, like maximum hour laws or fetal protection policies, and establish a basis for state control of procreation.

The frequently overlooked connection between protective laws for women and abortion prohibitions dates back to the Supreme Court decision in *Muller* v *Oregon,* the landmark 1911 case that upheld special labor laws for women. Hailed as a great victory by Progressives and feminist reformers, this case provided a constitutional rationale for sex discrimination and restriction of reproductive choice.

In *Muller* the Court upheld an Oregon law limiting women's hours of work, despite the fact that only three years earlier it had struck down a New York law limiting men's hours of work because it interfered with men's freedom of contract. The Court reconciled these two irreconcilable cases on the basis of sex. Because women get pregnant they were said to be weaker than men and less able to endure long workdays. Regulations of women's behavior would be upheld when regulations of men's behavior would not, the Court held, rationalizing sex discrimination.

The Court went on to provide a basis for what are now known as fetal endangerment cases (prosecutions of pregnant women for endangering the fetus): the production of healthy children depends on the existence of healthy mothers, the Court stressed. Protective labor laws were good not only for women but for the future of "the race." (The Court was concerned, of course, with the white race; *Muller* was decided during the eugenics movement.) This suggests that the state has not only the option but the obligation to regulate women's behavior during or even before pregnancy, in the interests of future generations. When it upheld protective labor laws in *Muller,* the Supreme Court upheld state power to regulate women's behavior and restrict their freedom of choice in the interests of children who have yet to be born, or even conceived. It is not a great leap from this to *The Handmaid's Tale*.

It is only a step to fetal protection policies that prohibit women from working at jobs considered hazardous to fetal health, whether or not they are pregnant or plan ever to become pregnant. These policies deny women equal employment rights by treating them categorically as potentially pregnant and deny men occupational safety rights by ignoring threats to male reproductive health, as protective labor laws generally do. The Supreme Court will determine the legality of fetal protection policies under federal employment law this term. Given the Court's emerging sympathy for theories of fetal rights, its upcoming decision on fetal protection in the workplace may teach protectionist feminists to be careful what they wish for.

The popularity of new fetal rights theories, spawned by the antiabortion movement, and the persistent appeal of abortion prohibitions demonstrate pervasive, emotional opposition to granting women's rights and dismantling gender roles, as well as the pitfalls of protectionism. It is probably impossible to overestimate how much men and women, including some feminists, have invested in stereotypes of male and female temperament, morality, and behavior.

Antiabortion activists exploit this when they characterize abortion as selfish. The charge of selfishness resonates. Women who demand their rights have always been called selfish, which is partly why nineteenth-century feminists demanded the vote not for its own sake, as a matter of right, but as a means of achieving womanly reforms. It was as if voting would simply provide women with a better route to public service, as if by fighting for the ballot women were doing their communities a favor.

There are echoes of this today when a woman politician reminds voters that she speaks in a different voice, that a woman in office will be more compassionate, better at delivering social services and cleaning up the environment (women are, after all, natural housekeepers), more cooperative and less confrontational than men—qualities that make her ultimately less self-serving.

The charge of selfishness resonates, and women run from it and from the goal of equal rights. There are echoes of it too in the communitarian critique of feminism, the association of feminism with narcissism and a "selfish" emphasis on the individual over the family. Imagine a woman defining herself as an independent person and not just, not first, as a member of her family. The authors of *Habits of the Heart* worry about this, warning that sexual equality "could lead to a complete loss of the human qualities long associated with 'women's sphere.' "

Which human qualities, feminists might ask: the qualities of self-sacrifice and abnegation? Or they might point out that human qualities can hardly be, ought not to be, confined to women's sphere. Presumably some men, like the ones who helped write *Habits of the Heart,* have human qualities too. Feminists might also ask why the civil rights movement is praised by communitarians as a paradigm of community when, like equality feminism, it was a movement to acquire individual rights. They might remind their communitarian critics that there is such a thing as a feminist community; in fact, without a sense of community among women, there would be no such thing as feminism.

But a statement blaming feminists for eroding human qualities does not invite a reasoned response. It invites a knee jerk about feminist selfishness in demanding equal rights and attacking traditional values. Which values you don't need to ask: the values associated with one-income nuclear families or, at least, a dual labor market and mommy track jobs; the values of women who always choose childbirth over abortion. Abortion, a powerful act of self-assertion, has become our most powerful symbol of feminist selfishness, which protectionist feminists may find difficult to defend. Women who believe that they're naturally better parents than men have an especially hard time conceding that some women prefer not to be parents at all.

Support for reproductive choice cannot be reconciled with traditional ideals of femininity, ideals underlying virtually all protective legislation. Choice blurs gender distinctions, suggesting that women may naturally be autonomous, self-interested creatures too, for whom the drive to parent may not always be primary. It suggests, conversely, that compassion, empathy, and cooperativeness should not be considered unique to women, as primary functions of motherhood.

Feminists who persist in celebrating femininity, demanding protections for women instead of rights, may sabotage the pro-choice movement. Pro-choice advocates are demanding reproductive rights, not protections. The pro-choice movement begins with an egalitarian image of women as thoughtful, self-reliant individuals and a belief in the primacy of individual rights over familial and community relations. Protectionists, like opponents of abortion rights, begin with an image of the family that pre-empts women's rights and what Elizabeth Cady Stanton called their "self-sovreignty." For protectionist feminists and antifeminists alike, the ideal woman—nurturing, attuned to the emotional needs of others—is shaped by a commitment to children and family life, which transcends what's dismissed as men's cold concern for rights. She's a vessel of maternal virtue, shaped by faith in the justice of love, rather than a love of justice.

FEMINISTS AGAINST THE FIRST
AMENDMENT

(*November 1992*)

Despite efforts to redevelop it, New York's Forty-second Street retains its underground appeal, especially for consumers of pornography. What city officials call "sex-related uses"—triple-X video (formerly book) stores, peep shows, and topless bars—have declined in number since their heyday in the 1970s, and much of the block between Seventh and Eighth Avenues is boarded up, a hostage to development. New sex businesses—yuppie topless bars and downscale lap-dancing joints—are prospering elsewhere in Manhattan. But Peepland (MULTI-VIDEO BOOTHS! NUDE DANCING GIRLS!) still reigns in the middle of the block, and Show World, a glitzy sex emporium, still anchors the west end, right around the corner from the *New York Times*.*

In the late 1970s I led groups of suburban women on tours through Show World and other Forty-second Street hot spots, exposing them, in the interests of consciousness raising, to pornography's various genres: Nazi porn, nurse porn, lesbian porn, bondage porn—none of it terribly imaginative. The women

---

*Redevelopment efforts have progressed since this article was published, and recent zoning proposals by the Guiliani Administration would greatly limit the number of sex-related businesses in Manhattan.

didn't exactly hold hands as they ventured down the street with me, but they did stick close together; traveling en masse, they were not so conspicuous as individuals. With only a little less discomfort than resolve, they dutifully viewed the pornography.

This was in the early days of the feminist antiporn movement, when legislative strategies against pornography were mere gleams in Andrea Dworkin's eye, when it seemed possible to raise consciousness about pornography without arousing demands for censorship. The period of innocence did not last long. By 1981 the New Right had mounted a nationwide censorship campaign to purge schools and public libraries of sex education and other secular-humanist forms of "pornography." Sex education was "filth and perversion," Jerry Falwell announced in a fund-raising letter that included, under the label "Adults Only. Sexually Explicit Material," excerpts from a college health text. By the mid-1980s, right-wing advocates of traditional family values had co-opted feminist antiporn protests—or, at least, they had co-opted feminist rhetoric. Feminist attorney and law professor Catharine MacKinnon characterized pornography as the active subordination of women, and Phyllis Schlafly wrote: "Pornography really should be defined as the degradation of women. Nearly all porn involves the use of women in subordinate, degrading poses for the sexual, exploitative, and even sadistic and violent pleasures of men." Just like a feminist, Schlafly worried about how pornography might "affect a man who is already prone to violence against women." President Ronald Reagan deplored the link between pornography and violence against women.

Pornography as Sex Discrimination

Of course, while feminists blamed patriarchy for pornography, moral majoritarians blamed feminism and other humanist rebellions. The alliance between feminists and the far right was not ideological but political. In 1984 antiporn legislation devised by Andrea Dworkin and Catharine MacKinnon, defining pornography as a violation of women's civil rights, was introduced in the Indianapolis city council by an anti-ERA activist, passed with the support of the right, and signed into law by the Republican mayor, William Hudnut.

With the introduction of this bill, a new legislative front opened in the war against pornography, alienating civil-libertarian feminists from their more censorious sisters, while appealing to populist concerns about declining moral values. By calling for the censorship of pornography, some radical feminists found their way into the cultural mainstream—and onto the margins of First Amendment law.

The legislation adopted in Indianapolis offered a novel approach to prohibiting pornography that had all the force of a semantic distinction: pornography was not simply speech, Catharine MacKinnon suggested, but active sex discrimination, and was therefore not protected by the First Amendment. (In her 1989 book *Toward a Feminist Theory of the State,* MacKinnon characterized pornography as "a form of forced sex.") Regarding pornography as action, defining it broadly as any verbal or visual sexually explicit material (violent or not) that subordinates women, presuming that the mere existence of pornography oppresses women, the Indianapolis ordinance gave any woman offended by any arguably pornographic material the right to seek an order prohibiting it, along with damages for the harm it presumably caused. In other words, any woman customer browsing in a bookstore or patrolling one, glancing at a newsstand or a triple-X video store, was a potential plaintiff in a sex discrimination suit. Given all the literature, films, and videos on the mass market that could be said to subordinate women, this ordinance would have created lots of new business for lawyers—but it did not stand. Within a year of its enactment the Dworkin-

MacKinnon law was declared unconstitutional by a federal appeals court, in a decision affirmed by the U.S. Supreme Court.

The feminist antiporn movement retreated from the legislative arena and passed out of public view in the late 1980s, only to reemerge with renewed strength on college campuses. College professors following fashions in poststructuralism asserted that legal principles, like those protecting speech, were mere rhetorical power plays: without any objective, universal merit, prevailing legal ideals were simply those privileged by the mostly white male ruling class. The dominant poststructural dogma of the late 1980s denied the First Amendment the transcendent value that the liberal belief in a marketplace of ideas has always awarded it.

Massachusetts Mischief

This unlikely convergence of First Amendment critiques from multiculturalists, poststructuralists, and advocates of traditional family values, recently combined with high-profile rape and harassment cases and women's abiding concern with sexual violence, buoyed the feminist antiporn movement. This year it reemerged on the national and local scene with renewed legislative clout. The presumption that pornography oppresses women and is a direct cause of sexual violence is the basis for bills introduced in the U.S. Senate and the Massachusetts legislature. Last June the Senate Judiciary Committee passed the Pornography Victims' Compensation Act, which would make producers, distributors, exhibitors, and retailers convicted of disseminating material adjudged obscene liable for damages to victims of crimes who could claim that the material caused their victimization. The Massachusetts legislature held hearings on a much broader antiporn bill, closely modeled on the Indianapolis ordinance. Disarmingly titled "An Act to Protect the Civil Rights of Women and Children," the Massachusetts bill not only would make purveyors of pornography liable for crimes committed by their customers but also would allow any woman, whether or not she has been the victim of a crime, to sue the producers, distributors, exhibitors, or retailers of any sexually explicit visual material that subordinates women. (The exclusion of verbal "pornography" from the antitrafficking provision would protect the likes of Norman Mailer, whom many feminists consider a pornographer, so long as his works are not adapted for the screen.) What this bill envisions is that the First Amendment would protect only that speech considered sexually correct.*

The feminist case against pornography is based on the presumption that the link between pornography and sexual violence is clear, simple, and inexorable. The argument is familiar: censorship campaigns always blame unwanted speech for unwanted behavior: Jerry Falwell once claimed that sex education causes teenage pregnancy, just as feminists claim that pornography causes rape. One objection to this assertion is that it gives rapists and batterers an excuse for their crimes, and perhaps even a "pornography made me do it" defense.

The claim that pornography causes rape greatly oversimplifies the problem of sexual violence. We can hardly say that were it not for pornography, there would be no rape or battering. As feminists opposed to antiporn legislation have pointed out, countries in which commercial pornography is illegal—Saudi Arabia, for example—are hardly safe havens for women.

This is not to deny that there probably is some link between violence in the media and violence in real life, but it is complicated, variable, and difficult to measure. Not all hate speech is an incantation; not all men are held spellbound by misogynist pornography. Poststructural feminists who celebrate subjectivism should be among the first to admit that different people respond to the same images differently. All we can confidently claim is

---

* Neither the Massachusetts bill nor the Federal bill was enacted.

that the way women are imagined is likely to have a cumulative effect on the way they're treated, but that does not mean any single image is the clear and simple cause of any single act.

The Dworkin-MacKinnon bill, however, did more than assume that pornography causes sex discrimination and other crimes against women. It said that pornography *is* violence and discrimination: the active subordination of women (and it assumed that we can all agree on what constitutes subordination). MacKinnon and her followers deny that prohibiting pornography is censorship, because they effectively deny that pornography is speech—and that is simply Orwellian. The line between speech and behavior is sometimes blurred: dancing nude down a public street is one way of expressing yourself that may also be a form of disorderly conduct. But if pornography is sex discrimination, then an editorial criticizing the president is treason.

Most feminists concerned about pornography are probably not intent on suppressing political speech, but the legislation they support, like the Massachusetts antiporn bill, is so broad, and its definition of pornography so subjective, that it would be likely to jeopardize sex educators and artists more than it would hard-core pornographers, who are used to operating outside the law. Feminist legislation makes no exception for "pornography" in which some might find redeeming social value; it could, for example, apply in the case of a woman disfigured by a man who had seen too many paintings by Willem de Kooning. "If a woman is subjected," Catharine MacKinnon writes, "why should it matter that the work has other value?"

With this exclusive focus on prohibiting material that reflects incorrect attitudes toward women, antiporn feminists don't deny the chilling effect of censorship; they embrace it. Any speech that subordinates women—any pornography—is falsely yelling "Fire!" in a crowded theater, they say, falling back on a legal canard. But that's true only if, just as all crowds are deemed potential mobs, all men are deemed potential abusers whose violent impulses are bound to be sparked by pornography. It needs to be said, by feminists, that efforts to censor pornography reflect a profound disdain for men. Catharine MacKinnon has written that "pornography works as a behavioral conditioner, reinforcer and stimulus, not as idea or advocacy. It is more like saying 'kill' to a trained guard dog—and also the training process itself." That's more a theory of sexuality than of speech: pornography is action because all men are dogs on short leashes.

The bleak view of male sexuality condemns heterosexuality for women as an exercise in wish fulfillment (if only men weren't all dogs) or false consciousness (such as male-identified thinking). True feminism, according to MacKinnon, unlike liberal feminism, "sees sexuality as a social sphere of male power of which forced sex is paradigmatic." With varying degrees of clarity, MacKinnon and Dworkin suggest that in a context of pervasive, institutionalized inequality, there can be no consensual sex between men and women: we can never honestly distinguish rape from intercourse.

An Esoteric Debate

A modified version of this message may well have particular appeal to some college women today, who make up an important constituency for the antiporn movement. In their late teens and early twenties, these women are still learning to cope with sexuality, in a violent and unquestionably misogynistic world. Feminism on campus tends to focus on issues of sexuality, not of economic equity. Anxiety about date rape is intense, along with anxiety about harassment and hate speech. Understanding and appreciation of the First Amendment is a lot less evident, and concern about employment discrimination seems somewhat remote. It's not hard to understand why: college women, in general, haven't experienced overt repression of opinions and ideas, or many problems in the workplace, but from childhood they've known what it is to fear rape. In the age of AIDS, the fear can be crippling.

Off campus the antiporn feminist critique of male sexuality and heterosexuality for women has little appeal, but it is not widely known. MacKinnon's theoretical writings are impenetrable to readers who lack familiarity with poststructural jargon and the patience to decode sentences like this: "If objectivity is the epistemological stance of which women's sexual objectification is the social process, its imposition the paradigm of power in the male form, then the state will appear most relentless in imposing the male point of view when it comes closest to achieving its highest formal criterion of distanced aperspectivity." Dworkin is a much more accessible polemicist, but she is also much less visible outside feminist circles. Tailored, with an air of middle-class respectability and the authority of a law professor, MacKinnon looks far less scary to mainstream Americans than her theories about sexuality, which drive the antiporn movement, might sound.

If antipornography crusades on the right reflect grassroots concern about changing sexual mores and the decline of the traditional family, antipornography crusades on the feminist left reflect the concerns and perceptions of an educated elite. In the battle for the moral high ground, antiporn feminists claim to represent the interests of a racially diverse mixture of poor and working-class women who work in the pornography industry—and they probably do represent a few. But many sex-industry workers actively oppose antiporn legislation (some feminists would say they've been brainwashed by patriarchy or actually coerced), and it's not at all clear that women who are abused in the making of pornography would be helped by forcing it deeper underground; working conditions in an illegal business are virtually impossible to police. It's hard to know how many other alleged victims of pornography feel represented by the antiporn movement, and I know of no demographic study of the movement's active members.

Leaders of the feminist antiporn movement, however, do seem more likely to emerge from academia and the professions than from the streets or battered-women's shelters. Debra Robbin, a former director of the New Bedford Women's Center, one of the first shelters in Massachusetts, doesn't believe that "women on the front lines," working with victims of sexual violence, will "put much energy into a fight against pornography." Activists don't have time: "They can barely leave their communities to go to the statehouses to fight for more funding." The poor and working-class women they serve would say, "Yeah, pornography is terrible, but I don't have food on my table." Carolin Ramsey, the executive director of the Massachusetts Coalition of Battered Women Service Groups, says that the pornography debate "doesn't have a lot to do with everyday life for me and the women I'm serving." She explains: "Violence in the home and the streets that directly threatens our lives and our families is more pressing than a movie. Keeping my kids away from drugs is more important than keeping them away from literature."

Ramsey is sympathetic to antiporn feminists ("there's room in the movement for all of us"), and she believes that "violence in the media contributes to violence in real life." Still, she considers the pornography debate "esoteric" and "intellectual" and feels under no particular pressure from her constituents to take a stand against pornography.

If censoring pornography is the central feminist issue for Catharine MacKinnon, it is a peripheral issue for activists like

Robbin and Ramsey. Robbin in particular does not believe that eliminating pornography would appreciably lessen the incidence of sexual abuse. David Adams, a cofounder and the executive director of Emerge, a Boston counseling center for male batterers, believes that only a minority of his clients (perhaps 10 to 20 percent) use hard-core pornography. He estimates that half may have substance-abuse problems, and adds that alcohol is more directly involved in abuse than pornography. Adams agrees with feminists that pornography is degrading to women but does not support legislation regulating it, because "the legislation couldn't work and would only open the door to censorship."

What might work instead? Emerge conducts programs in Boston and Cambridge public schools on violence, aimed at both victims and perpetrators. "There's a lot of violence in teen relationships," Adams observes. Debra Robbin wishes that women in the antiporn movement would "channel their energies into funding battered-women's shelters and rape-crisis centers."

Reforming the criminal justice system is also a priority for many women concerned about sexual violence. Antistalking laws could protect many more women than raids on pornographic video stores are ever likely to; so could the efficient processing of cases against men who abuse women.

Sensationalism as an Organizing Tool

Why do some women channel their energies into a fight against pornography? Antiporn legislation has the appeal of a quick fix, as Robbin notes. And, she adds, "there's notoriety to be gained from protesting pornography." The "harder work"—promoting awareness and understanding of sexual violence, changing the way children are socialized, and helping women victims of violence—is less sensationalist and less visible.

Sensationalism, however, is an organizing tool for antiporn

feminists. If questions about the effects of pornography seem intellectual to some women involved in social service work, the popular campaign against pornography is aggressively anti-intellectual. Although advocates of First Amendment freedoms are stuck with intellectual defenses of the marketplace of ideas, antiporn feminists whip up support for their cause with pornographic slide shows comprising hard-core pictures of women being tortured, raped, and generally degraded. Many feminists are equally critical of the soft-core porn movies available at local video stores and on cable TV, arguing that the violence in pornography is often covert (and they include mainstream advertising images in their slide shows). But hard-core violence is what works on the crowd. Feminist rhetoric often plays on women's worst fears about men: "Pornography tells us that there but for the grace of God go us," Gail Dines, a sociology professor at Wheelock College, exclaimed during her recent slide show at Harvard, as she presented photographs of women being brutalized.

Dines's porn show was SRO, its audience some three hundred undergraduates who winced and gasped at the awful slides and cheered when Dines pointed to a pornographic picture of a woman and said, "When I walk down the street, what they know about me is what they know about her!" She warned her mostly female audience that pornographers have "aggressively targeted college men." She seemed preoccupied with masturbation. Part of the problem of pornography, she suggested, is that men use it to masturbate, and "women weren't put on this world to facilitate masturbation." She advised a student concerned about the presence of *Playboy* in the college library that library collections of pornography aren't particularly worrisome, because men are not likely to masturbate in libraries.

In addition to condemnations of male sexuality, Dines offered questionable horror stories about pornography's atrocities, like this: rape vans are roaming the streets of New York. Women are dragged into the vans and raped on camera; when their attackers sell the rape videos in commercial outlets, the women have no legal recourse.

A story like this is impossible to disprove (how do you prove a negative?), but it should probably not be taken at face value, as many students in Dines's audience seemed to take it. William Daly, the director of New York City's Office of Midtown Enforcement, which is responsible for monitoring the sex industry in New York, has never heard of rape vans; almost anything is possible on Forty-second Street, but he is skeptical that rape vans are a problem. Part of Dines's story, however, is simply untrue: under New York State privacy law, says Nan Hunter, a professor of law at Brooklyn Law School, women could seek damages for the sale of the rape videos, and also an injunction against their distribution.

It would be difficult even to raise questions about the accuracy of the rape van story, however, in the highly emotional atmosphere of a slide show; you'd be accused of "not believing the women." Just as slides of bloody fetuses preempt rational debate about abortion, pornographic slide shows preempt argumentative questions and rational consideration of First Amendment freedoms, the probable effect of efforts to censor pornography, and the actual relationship between pornography and violence.

A Pornographic Culture?

Does pornography cause violence against women, as some feminists claim? Maybe, in some cases, under some circumstances involving explicitly violent material. Readers interested in the social science debate should see both the report of the Attorney General's Commission on Pornography, which found a link between pornography and violence against women, and the feminist writer Marcia Pally's *Sense and Censorship,* published by Americans for Constitutional Freedom and the Freedom to Read

Foundation. In addition to the equivocal social science data, however, we have the testimony of women who claim to have been brutalized by male consumers of pornography. Antiporn feminists generally characterize pornography as "how to" literature on abusing women, which men are apparently helpless to resist. But evidence of this is mainly anecdotal: At a hearing last March on the antiporn bill in the Massachusetts legislature, several women told awful, lurid tales of sexual abuse, said to have been inspired by pornography. Like a TV talk show, the Attorney General's Commission presented testimony from pornography's alleged victims, which may or may not have been true. It's difficult to cross-examine a sobbing self-proclaimed victim; either you take her testimony at face value or you don't.

Still, many people don't need reliable, empirical evidence about a link between pornography and behavior to believe that one exists. When feminists talk about pornography, after all, they mean a wide range of mainstream media images—Calvin Klein ads, Brian De Palma films, and the endless stream of TV shows about serial rapist stranglers and housewives who moonlight as hookers. How could we not be affected by the routine barrage of images linking sex and violence and lingerie? The more broadly pornography is defined, the more compelling are assertions about its inevitable effect on behavior, but the harder it is to control. How do we isolate the effects of any particular piece of pornography if we live in a pornographic culture?

Narrowly drawn antiporn legislation, which legislators are most likely to pass and judges most likely to uphold, would not begin to address the larger cultural problem of misogynist pornography. Feminists themselves usually claim publicly that they're intent on prohibiting only hard-core pornography, although on its face their legislation applies to a much broader range of material. But if you accept the feminist critique of sexism in the media, hard-core porn plays a relatively minor role in shaping attitudes and behavior. If feminists are right about pornography, it is a broad social problem, not a discrete legal one—that is, pornography is not a problem the law can solve, unless perhaps we suspend the First Amendment entirely and give feminists the power to police the mainstream media, the workplace, and the schools.

The likelihood that feminists would not be the ones to police Forty-second Street should antiporn legislation pass is one reason that many feminists oppose the antiporn campaign. If society is as sexist as Andrea Dworkin and Catharine MacKinnon claim, it is not about to adopt a feminist agenda when it sets out to censor pornography. In fact, the history of antiporn campaigns in this country is partly a history of campaigns against reproductive choice and changing roles for men and women. The first federal obscenity legislation, known as the Comstock Law, passed in 1873, prohibited the mailing of not only dirty pictures but also contraceptives and information about abortion. Early in this century birth-control advocate Margaret Sanger and sex educator Mary Ware Dennett were prosecuted for obscenity violations. Recently right-wing campaigns against socially undesirable literature has focused on sex education in public schools. Antiporn activists on the right consider feminism and homosexuality (which they link) to be threats to traditional family life (which, in fact, they are). In Canada a landmark Supreme Court ruling this year that adopted a feminist argument against pornography was first used to prohibit distribution of a small lesbian magazine, which a politically correct feminist would be careful to label erotica.

Gay and lesbian groups, as well as advocates of sex education and the usual array of feminist and nonfeminist civil libertarians, actively oppose antipornography legislation. Some state chapters of the National Organization for Women—New York, California, and Vermont—have taken strong anticensorship stands, but at the national level NOW has not taken a position in the pornography debate. Its president, Patricia Ireland, would like to see pornography become socially unacceptable, "like smoking," but is wary of taking legal action against it, partly because she's wary of "giving people like Jesse Helms the power to decide what we read and see." But for major, national feminist organizations, like NOW and the NOW Legal Defense and Education Fund, the pornography debate is a minefield to be carefully avoided. Pornography is probably the most divisive issue feminists have faced since the first advocates of the ERA, in the 1920s, squared off against advocates of protective labor legislation for women. Feminists for and against antiporn legislation are almost as bitterly divided as pro-choice activists and members of Operation Rescue.

Renewed concern about abortion rights may drain energy from the antiporn movement. Feminists may awaken to the danger that antipornography laws will be used against sex educators and advocates of choice. (The imposition of a gag rule on family planning clinics may have made some feminists more protective of the First Amendment.) Politicians courting women voters may find that antiporn legislation alienates more feminists than it pleases. Still, censorship campaigns will always have considerable appeal. Like campaigns to reinstate the death penalty, they promise panaceas for profound social pathologies. They make their case by exploiting the wrenching anecdotal testimony of victims: politicians pushing the death penalty hold press conferences flanked by mothers of murdered children, just as feminists against pornography spotlight raped and battered women.

Rational argument is no match for highly emotional testimony. But it is wishful thinking to believe that penalizing the production and distribution of hard-core pornography would have much effect on sexual violence. It would probably have little effect even on pornography, given the black market. It would, however, complicate campaigns to distribute information about AIDS, let alone condoms, in the public schools. It would distract us from the harder, less popular work of reforming sexual stereotypes and roles, and addressing actual instead of metaphorical instruments of violence. The promise of the anti-porn movement is the promise of a world in which almost no one can buy pornography and almost anyone can buy a gun.

--- ■   ■   ■ ---

HARASSED AND ABANDONED

(*May 1995*)

"Is sexual harassment endemic to law firms?" journalists asked in
the aftermath of Rena Weeks's $7 million damage award in her
harassment suit against Baker & McKenzie. Does the culture of
the locker room still prevail, or was former Baker partner Martin
Greenstein's behavior anomalous? (He grabbed her breasts and
buttocks.) Have law firms ignored the problem of sexual harassment in the past, and will the Baker verdict (since reduced to
$3.5 million) scare them into addressing it in the future? Law-
yers, consultants, and commentators wondered. Meanwhile,
around the dinner table, less worthy discussions abounded. My
friends and I indulged in an unfeminist cost-benefit analysis:
How much harassment would you be willing to endure for $7
million? A lot, we all agreed. "If I had $7 million for every time a
man grabbed my breast . . . ," conversations began.

Of course, winning a seven-figure harassment judgment is a lot
like winning the lottery—a function of luck, not planning. It's
not as if women are given the choice of being harassed for an
agreed-on fee—$7 million or $7,000. Most women are harassed
for free. Lawsuits are hard to mount—both fiscally and emotionally draining—and hard to win. Many employers are not
such potentially lucrative targets as a multinational law firm.
Even at Baker, other women allegedly harassed by Martin Greenstein didn't sue, and the verdict won by Weeks may increase the

fear of sexual harassment lawsuits more than the suits themselves. Secretaries, receptionists, and other support personnel are even more vulnerable to harassment than relatively powerful professional women and may be less willing and financially able to seek redress for their rights in court.

Rena Weeks was a legal secretary; in fact, a majority of the women who reported being harassed by Martin Greenstein were part of the firm's support staff. Yet much of the commentary about sexual harassment in law firms that followed the Baker verdict (in the *American Lawyer,* the *New York Times,* and the *Wall Street Journal*) focused on the treatment of female attorneys. Secretaries were ignored. They were the women you didn't read about, with the problem that wasn't discussed, even though, says a former associate at two Wall Street firms, "most of the sexual gossip in law firms is about male attorneys and female secretaries." Attitudes toward sexual harassment have changed significantly in the past ten years, and the presence of female attorneys tends to inhibit the overt harassment of female secretaries. Men who harass their subordinates rely on the support of their colleagues and are deterred by their opprobrium; women naturally tend to be less tolerant of sexual harassment than men.

But if the harassment of secretaries and receptionists has abated and become less flagrant, it has not yet been eliminated. One male former associate at a California firm estimates roughly that secretaries are harassed "six times as often" as attorneys. Temporary secretaries report incidents of sexual harassment "on a regular basis," according to an associate at an employment agency that provides secretaries to major San Francisco firms. "We investigate the incident [and] talk to the client," the associate reports. "It depends on how far the temp wants to go. But most of the time, the problem is forgotten."

The harassment of secretaries "has gone on for such a long

time that it seems ingrained in the legal culture," says former Hildebrandt associate Carol Jordan. Now a business manager for the Law Offices of William L. Berg in Alameda, Jordan says that many incidents of harassment go unreported. "When harassment occurs, typically the secretary doesn't make an issue of it. She fears retribution." The fear is realistic, Jordan implies. "Secretaries are relatively powerless. Whom do they turn to? They are not income producers; if harassment becomes an issue, the secretary is typically the one who goes. There are strong lines of stratification at a law firm; secretaries are on the bottom." The award to Rena Weeks may encourage secretaries to report harassment, Jordan adds, but the risk of a lawsuit remains high. "The chance of being hired somewhere else is slim. You are under a black cloud. Employers don't want to hire someone who sues, even if the suit was justified."

The expectation that secretaries won't sue makes them more vulnerable to harassment. A man is more likely to harass a woman who seems less likely to speak up, Ellen Bravo stresses. Bravo, executive director of 9to5, National Association of Working Women, believes that female support staff suffer considerably more harassment than female professionals. A 1994 survey by *Working Woman* magazine suggested the contrary—that harassment is a particular problem for women in managerial and professional positions who pose particular threats to men. But this survey relied largely on self-reporting, which may have skewed the results if female support staff are indeed less likely to report harassment. In any event, as Bravo notes, the harassment of secretaries does not garner as much attention as the harassment of female professionals. "If Anita Hill were a secretary, we would never have known she existed," she says. With its focus on the treatment of female attorneys, commentary on Weeks's case has been an even stronger testament to what Bravo calls the invisibility of secretaries. (Male or female, the lower you are in a workplace hierarchy, the more likely you are to be faceless and the less individuality you're expected to assert.)

"No one wants to say anything about sexual harassment," one veteran legal secretary points out. "You've got to work, and it's tough to quit a job, because you don't know what you'll find," she adds, apparently not considering the possibility of reporting harassment and keeping your job. Harassment was particularly grievous in the 1950s and 1960s—"There was a lot of squirreling around"—and it continues to a lesser extent, although legal secretaries talk less about sexual harassment in particular than about bad bosses in general. "Usually my friends talk about what jerks their bosses are, how to get transferred to a better boss in the firm, or how to find a better job."

Kristen Flores, president of the San Francisco Legal Secretaries Association, doesn't present harassment as a priority or even as much of a problem. Flores stresses that her organization focuses on professionalizing secretarial work, offering such services as training classes and monthly speeches by attorneys on new developments in law. Wages, as well, are a perennial concern among the group's members. Flores minimizes the incidence of harassment, noting that she has never been harassed: "I've never been treated as anything but a professional." She suggests that secretaries themselves are responsible for the way they are treated by their bosses. "If I hear about sexual harassment, my first thought is to wonder, 'What was her conduct like?' . . . Some women tell certain jokes in mixed company. Maybe the situation went too far. It doesn't give someone permission to make an inappropriate or totally sexually suggestive remark, but if you carry yourself as a professional, you won't have a problem."

Rena Weeks would, no doubt, disagree. There was no evidence (not even an allegation) that she had provoked Greenstein's behavior. Flores doesn't question the finding of harassment in this case, but it did take her by surprise. She expresses "shock" that "in a firm of that stature, with a good reputation, this conduct would be going on."

The harassment in Weeks's suit may have shocked some, but it confirmed the long-standing suspicions of many others. Ann Guinn, a management consultant to law firms and a former legal secretary, remarks that "in any law firm of ten attorneys, there is one who crosses the line." Female attorneys do experience harassment, but Guinn, too, agrees that it is "more prevalent among staff people." She also speculates that "very few women over the age of thirty-five or forty have not experienced harassment, some of it very subtle, some of it outrageously overt." In her view, harassment hasn't abated all that much in recent years—the best she can say is, "I think it probably hasn't gotten worse." Women have been made more aware that "this is unacceptable behavior; we don't have to put up with it."

Even as more women speak out—and sometimes sue—when they are harassed, new economic realities are deterring harassment complaints from secretaries concerned about losing their jobs. Law firms are downsizing, Guinn stresses: "It's very common for three attorneys to share one secretary, and opportunities for change aren't as plentiful as they were ten or fifteen years ago." Female professionals as well as support staff view lawsuits as high-stakes gambles. Some women who work in law firms emphasize that protesting harassment and seeking an in-house remedy for it, much less initiating a lawsuit, may put your job and career at risk.

■   ■   ■

This dilemma confronts partners and first-year associates as well as secretaries. "There's nothing you can do; you have no recourse if you're harassed," a female partner at one of the state's larger firms remarks. "If you complain, you won't rise in the ranks, you won't get paid well, you won't be given good associates to work with. You aren't going to get clients through the firm. The only security you have is your own network of clients. Simply being a partner doesn't protect you at all. They can fire you in an instant."

Not all the female attorneys interviewed for this article reported experience with harassment; most of them complained about other, more subtle forms of discrimination—being patronized, excluded, or ignored. But every one of them insisted on anonymity. Many of the women are partners in their firms; several made partner years ago. Even for relatively powerful professional women, it is not politic to go on the record talking about sexual discrimination or harassment in the workplace.

Off the record, however, some female attorneys are apt to complain bitterly about the culture of law firms. Of course, you have to wonder about anyone, male or female, who works in a law firm and doesn't complain. For many women, however, the pressure to conform, the heavy workloads, and the abuses of power that generate the usual complaints are exacerbated by what they regard as old-fashioned sexism. Law firms are run "not just by men but by old-time men with no vision of the future," a partner of eleven years laments. They "put men in place to run the firm" and treat women as tokens or pawns "in puppet positions." The women who manage to rise within the hierarchy are even more vulnerable to discrimination. "As women get closer to power, they become more of a threat. I didn't experience any discrimination for the first ten years of my career. As I became a risk to men—getting business they thought they should get—then I felt discriminated against, left out, excluded."

Nowadays, a statement like this is bound to be dismissed by some as feminist victimism or the frustration of a woman who hasn't fulfilled her professional aspirations and needs someone to blame. But many attorneys confirm that law firms are not exactly hotbeds of sexual egalitarianism. Sometimes the problem is harassment; sexual harassment involves "control issues," and lawyers tend to be "very much into control," says Blane Prescott, director of Hildebrandt. But other forms of discrimination against female attorneys are more common—and a lot less likely to be addressed or even acknowledged by firm policy. Women are sometimes penalized for not conforming to male stereotypes of lawyering; they're presumed to be less competent than men; or they're not included in the social activities that cement professional relationships. They're left out of lunches, tennis games, or bull sessions at neighborhood bars. Prescott characterizes their exclusion as a kind of discrimination.

In other words, the problem is sometimes too little familiarity, not too much. (To the extent that they discourage fraternizing between the sexes, sexual harassment policies may be bad for professional women, some commentators suggest.) As Elizabeth Johnson, business manager for the Oakland firm of Kazan, McClain, Edises, Simon & Abrams, remarks, "Most real decisions are still made at ball games, restaurants, and other places where women are not welcome, like the after-dinner smoking room."

These forms of subtle, sometimes unintentional discrimination are harder to recognize and remedy than overt harassment, particularly in its cruder forms. How do you change a fact of life—that in our culture many men still enjoy greater credibility as lawyers merely by virtue of being men? Clients, in particular, may not regard women as "real" lawyers, some female attorneys report. Attitudes like this may well have discriminatory effects, but laws can change them only indirectly. You can require law firms to hire women, but you can't require partners, clients, or judges to like them. Nor can you easily apply employment discrimination laws to a firm's traditional gender-neutral policies that tend to disadvantage women. Female attorneys are "hurt more by the structure of law firms than by sexual harassment," San Francisco plaintiffs employment attorney Cliff Palefsky observes. "Law firms say they promote based on objective criteria—the number of billable hours and a book of business. But the use of these criteria hurts women. It's hard for them to get the business and the hours because of family obligations, client resistance to female attorneys, and the tendency of judges and juries to underrate women as attorneys."

The primary problems that beset women lawyers are, then, the problems of women who have taken on what used to be male roles. While women in traditional female roles—secretaries and receptionists—confront traditional problems, such as the expectation that they will be sexually available, attorneys struggle to succeed in a workplace that was not designed to accommodate them, and they argue about the role of the law in helping them. One woman who has been a partner at a California firm for fifteen years says she has limited sympathy for women who want to succeed without devoting themselves single-mindedly to lawyering. "I tend to be tough on attorneys who don't understand what it is to practice at a national law firm," she says. "You need to have a commitment, and if you can't deliver, you should leave." Many debates about regulating sexual discrimination focus on statements like this. They're debates about whether women should adapt to the workplace or the workplace should adapt to them. (Adaptation, of course, is required on both sides.)

Whether it is based in resentment of women's newfound power in the workplace or in exploitation of their old-fashioned powerlessness, harassment is controlled at most only partly by the response of its victims. It is an institutional, not simply an individual, problem. The business manager of one California firm points out that harassment will flourish in a law firm, or any other business organization, when senior managers fail to establish a culture that discourages it and when controlling harassment seems to threaten the bottom line. "If you've got one person who thinks it's cute to drop M&Ms down the front of a woman's blouse, and that person is a rainmaker, the partners will put up with his objectionable behavior" even if the firm has a sexual harassment policy in place, the manager says. (Martin Greenstein's harassment of female employees violated Baker & McKenzie's formal policy.) In California all businesses with more than one employee are required to have harassment policies, but "if you pop a pro forma policy in a manual and never pay attention to it, it does nothing for you."

The trouble is that the typical "model" sexual harassment policy may do less harm unenforced. Vagueness, overbreadth, and insensitivity to the free-speech rights of employees are common to prohibitions on harassment. Consider this definition of harassment, contained in the model policy distributed by the San Francisco Bar Association, which includes any "verbal (or) visual conduct of a sexual nature . . . that creates an intimidating, hostile, or offensive environment." This wording makes a single glance or offhand remark that one employee finds offensive an actionable form of harassment, even if it is not directed at her. (The policy does not require that offensive verbal or visual conduct target the complaining employee, nor does it heed a recent U.S. Supreme Court ruling that merely offensive speech is not harassment.) As examples of harassment, the bar association policy cites sexual jokes—which would make any number of women as well as men who discussed the Bobbitt trial at work guilty of harassment—and "derogatory" posters, which could easily include *Vogue* fashion layouts (condemned by many feminists) as well as the softest of *Playboy* pinups.

Cases involving expressive conduct (arguably rude, demeaning remarks) or visual displays (pinups) often involve a clash of free-speech rights with the rights of employees to a nondiscriminatory, nonhostile workplace. (The First Amendment may not be formally implicated in a private workplace, but employees retain a moral claim to free expression.) Sexual harassment claims often call for a difficult balancing of rights that can be made only on a case-by-case basis. But like other popular approaches to harassment control, the policy offered by the San Francisco Bar Association doesn't balance speech rights and equality rights; it chooses between them, effectively establishing a right to feel comfortable in the workplace that outweighs a right to express yourself. In a bar association or a law firm, this utter disregard for the speech rights of employees is stunning.

If it conflicts with free expression in the workplace, sexual harassment policy can also pose a challenge to the concept of workplace as family—a concept that entered the popular culture twenty years ago with *Mary Tyler Moore* and was solidified by *Cheers,* not to mention *L.A. Law,* which gave us a portrait of the familial workplace as contentious and often unhappy. The workplace may be a family only for fictional characters on TV (or actors in Walmart ads), but it is, for better or worse, a community in which adults spend a great deal of time. What do women want at work? Without having conducted or consulted any scientific surveys, I feel confident in saying that they want to be treated well and paid well; they also want friendships and casual conversations, if not romance. Sexual harassment policy must balance these wants, which sometimes conflict, for men and women alike; sometimes the price of friendship, conversation, and community is a willingness to tolerate discomfort, the capacity to take offense without being traumatized by it. Overbroad sexual harassment policies, which might be widely adopted and stupidly enforced in the wake of the Baker verdict, could discourage the friendly human intercourse so many law firms need.

I'm not suggesting that Baker & McKenzie and Martin Greenstein weren't guilty of sexual harassment and shouldn't have been liable for it. Nor am I saying that stupid reactions to the problem of sexual harassment by law firms intent on limiting their liability are inevitable. The verdict in Baker's case would chill relations between the sexes, several commentators opined: men are increasingly unsure about how to act around women in the workplace, particularly women in subordinate roles, and the award to Rena Weeks would scare some male lawyers into cutting off all inessential contact with female associates and support staff. This concern was overwrought. The harassment of Rena Weeks was grievous and unequivocal. Surely most men concerned about being charged with sexual harassment know the difference between asking a female colleague or subordinate to lunch to talk over a case, or having a friendly conversation with her about an issue unrelated to work, and grabbing her breasts. Any men who are confused about what constitutes acceptable behavior around a woman after the Baker & McKenzie verdict had to have been deeply confused before.

PORN AGAIN

(1993)

I was struck by the title of this panel, "Toward Safety, Equality, and Freedom," because it might easily be used as a panel title at a procensorship conference. We're all in favor of safety, equality, and freedom. Well, maybe we're not all in agreement about equality; the question of whether equality would make women safe and free has always been a divisive one for feminists. But surely we're all in favor of safety and freedom; antipornography feminists believe that censorship is the path to safety and freedom and, perhaps, some version (or perversion) of equality. More than moral superiority, many women seek safety in censorship.

The appeal of the antipornography movement is visceral, not intellectual; its arguments are primarily political, not legal. Despite all the academic theorizing about the clash of First and Fourteenth Amendment rights, the antipornography movement doesn't rely on legal theories about censorship; it relies primarily on political theories and political notions of sexuality. Catharine MacKinnon's great contribution to the antipornography debate has been to declare the First Amendment irrelevant to it, by declaring that pornography is not speech, but some sort of action. (Or, in her words, "Pornography is more act-like than thought-like.") MacKinnon's followers take this notion literally. I once appeared on a talk show with an antipornography activist who compared the production of pornography to the manufacture of unsafe cars. Like the infamous Pinto with the exploding gas tank, pornography was simply an incendiary device, she suggested, without even arguable constitutional protection. Her disregard for speech was consistent—she interrupted me incessantly, insisting that the First Amendment issue was a "red herring," because pornography was not speech and, therefore, antipornography legislation was not censorship.

But, more than indifference to the First Amendment, more than the sense that the First Amendment is not at issue in this debate, there is a great deal of hostility toward the First Amendment, at the heart of this debate. While anticensorship feminists regard the First Amendment as a path to safety and freedom, antipornography feminists regard it as a tool of male oppression.

So it is important to stress at the outset that this debate about pornography and censorship is not essentially a debate about legal theory; it is essentially a clash of values. It is a debate about values. Simply put, antipornography feminists do not value the First Amendment. They denigrate it, regarding it as just another privilege of the white male ruling class and a threat to women. What you can glean from Catharine MacKinnon's rather arcane academic writing (if you're motivated to decode it) is the suggestion that we replace the First Amendment with this principle: whatever is harmful to women and reinforces their subordinate position in society should be prohibited.

Who will decide what is harmful to women and what reinforces their subordinate status? Catharine MacKinnon, I guess, although given her view that society is simply an exercise in institutionalized sexism, it has never been clear to me why, as an acclaimed radical feminist, she might expect ever to enjoy discretionary power to interpret subjective legal principles, especially those involving the subordination of women. (I've always thought that the more you distrusted judges, in general, the more wary you'd be of legal subjectivism.)

But the perils of introducing more discretion into sex discrimination law are not seriously explored, and the hostility toward the First Amendment that pervades the antipornography movement is not always overtly expressed. Antipornography activists don't like being regarded as enemies of speech, any more than antiabortion activists like being regarded as enemies of choice. So, while academia may be rife with theories of democratic governance that seek to justify opposition to the First Amendment, antipornography activists have tended to focus on theories of sexuality to explain the First Amendment's irrelevance. They essentially argue that pornography is not speech because all men are beasts. Men are so essentially bestial, so unable to control their desires or urges, that, when exposed to misogynist literature or film, they are seized with an irresistible impulse to act it out. Under this view, it is the combination of men and pornography that's bad, because men are bad. You can, after all, expose women to pornography without fear that it will turn them into sex fiends.

The antipornography movement is founded, therefore, on a very traditional theory of gender difference—namely, the theory that men are naturally bestial, violent, and out of control, while women are pure, in control (if not repressed), and needful of protection. That has always been an appealing vision for men and women, and a recurrent theme for feminists. It is the vision that was at the heart of nineteenth-century moral reform movements. And it is also the vision that has been at the heart of sex discrimination—the laws and customs that have relegated women to a separate, secondary sphere.

Traditional notions about gender are shared by many revisionist feminists today, both inside and outside the antipornography movement. It's no coincidence that the antipornography movement was revitalized during the 1980s, at about the same time that theories about women's different voice were ascendant. Anticensorship feminists must understand this traditional vision of womanhood that fuels the antipornography movement and much of contemporary feminism. To oppose censorship effectively, we must offer an opposing view of sex and gender, an opposing view of human nature.

At the same time, we must be sensitive to the practical appeal of censorship during a period of public concern about an epidemic of sexual violence. Throughout our history, moral reform movements, like the campaign against pornography, have displaced women's anxieties about actual violence. Although in my view the moral reforms should be opposed, the anxiety that motivates them should be respected; it reflects the terror of actual sexual violence that has not been effectively addressed, just as the most repressive demands for law and order reflect anxiety about crime.

In some ways, censorship has the same relationship to sexual violence that capital punishment has to other violent crimes. It has enormous symbolic value. By demanding censorship, many women feel that they're taking action against rape and abuse. Joining a censorship campaign doesn't feel to them like playing the victim and asking for protection. It feels like fighting back, taking initiative on their own behalf. But like capital punishment, censorship would have very limited practical value. Censoring hard-core pornography (assuming we could adequately define the term), which is all that many antipornography feminists claim that they want to do, would have no more practical effect on the incidence of rape than several hundred executions a year would have on the incidence of murder.

Antipornography feminists essentially concede this conclusion when they target softer-core, mainstream "pornographic" images. When, for example, they rail against the "pornography" produced by Madison Avenue or Hollywood (which reaches millions more Americans than anything sold on Forty-second

Street) they are telling us that we live in a pornographic culture—sponsored by corporate America.

So, if you were to take the feminist critique of pornography seriously, you wouldn't stop with censoring low-rent, hard-core pornography. You wouldn't even start with it. You would start by establishing a national, feminist review board with authority to regulate all forms of expression that touch on sex or gender. You would censor everyone from Ernest Hemingway to David Mamet, from Larry Flynt to Calvin Klein, from *Cosmopolitan* to the *Ladies Home Journal.* You would probably also censor a great many fairy tales that celebrate female passivity. I suspect that "Cinderella" is destructive to more women than anything I've ever seen on Forty-second Street.

Concern about protrayals of sexuality in fairy tales, fashion magazines, or erotica is not exactly unique to the antipornography movement. I imagine that many women don't exactly see themselves in the images of women we would find down the block at Show World or in the pages of *Vogue.* And, while I deplore the strategies and ideals of the antipornography movement, I respect the fear and frustration it reflects. I doubt there is a woman in this room who has never feared being raped. It is a great mistake for anti-censorship feminists not to honor that fear. It is a great mistake to dismiss categorically the women engaged in the fight against pornography as being antisex, while presenting women engaged in the fight against censorship as prosex (just as it is a mistake for antiporn feminists to present themselves as antiviolence while labelling us pro-violence). Thus, although I agree that we should talk about the positive values of pornography and the benign ways in which some people use it, I think it is equally important to talk about rape.

Conceding the practical problem of sexual violence, however, we can still firmly oppose censorship, on practical as well as on

moral grounds. In my moral universe, censorship is more immoral than pornography. And as a practical matter, I have no
doubt that censorship would not work. Human behavior is a bit
more complicated than the simple cause-and-effect theories
about pornography and violence suggest.

You can't control behavior effectively by controlling speech,
except perhaps in a totalitarian society, in which the suspension
of free speech is matched by suspension of all other civil liberties and backed by an intrusive police state. For the state to
control private, personal attitudes and behaviors, its control
must be total and unrelenting. In our culture, the discrete,
minimalist forms of censorship that antipornography feminists
claim to be proposing would be imposed at an obvious cost to
the arts and the fight for reproductive choice, but would offer
no discernible benefit to the fight against sexual violence. The
single-minded scapegoating of particular forms of pornography
in what is labeled a pornographic culture—and what is indis-
putably a violent, well-armed culture—is a triumph of reductive reasoning.

The attempt to control antisocial speech overestimates the
power of words as much as it undervalues the right to utter them.
I don't mean to deny the existence of a relationship between
media and real-life violence. I'm not a fan of Arnold Schwarzenegger, and I'm glad to hear that he has been "born again" and
does not plan on making mindlessly violent movies anymore. But
I'm not holding my breath waiting for the world, along with his
movies, to become less violent.* The relationship between imaginary and actual violence is extremely diffuse and difficult to
isolate or quantify. It is an important subject for critics, artists,
producers, publishers, and philosophers, but an impossible one
for legislators.

* In fact, Schwarzenegger's conversion was short-lived.

As a writer, I like to think words matter, but they don't cast spells, at least not in a relatively free society in which people are encouraged to think for themselves. The more we value speech, the less we need to fear it, because the more we value speech, the more we value independent thinking. In a relatively free society, words are not incantations; we can resist them. (As a writer, I'm always struck by the ease with which people resist my words.)

Magical thinking suffuses the antipornography movement—and hate-speech movements in general. We are assured that if we just do away with the black magic of pornography, we will somehow do away with rape. But prohibiting sexist speech and name-calling will no more eradicate sexism, racism, and homophobia than prohibiting sex education will eradicate teenage pregnancy (much to Phyllis Schlafly's chagrin).

This exaggerated fear of images and ideas we don't like, this tendency to imbue them with magical power reflects, in part, a pervasive sense of victimization shared today even by the most privileged. "Women aren't free. Women don't have First Amendment rights," a Harvard undergraduate once told me. When a Harvard student tells you she is oppressed, you know you have just stepped through the looking glass.

A few years ago, as some of you may recall, women at Brown University wrote the names of purported sex offenders on bathroom walls. As Brown University professor Nancy Rosenblum says, that is the kind of action you take in a very repressive society, in which you have no official recourse for your complaints. While vestiges of official sexism may exist at Brown, there is also official concern about date rape, and there are procedures for dealing with it. Brown University, as Rosenblum points out, is not Czechoslovakia in 1968.

Nonetheless, at Brown, women's fear of rape and their sense of vulnerability apparently outweighed men's rights to confront their accusers, their rights to respond, and the possibility that

some of the accusations might have been false. Of course, the
possibility of false accusations is what we are not supposed to
consider. If all men are presumed to be victimizers and all
women presumed to be victims, the rights of individual men and
women do not matter nearly as much as does choosing sides.

At its most extreme, that is the logic of terrorism: devaluing
individuals and their rights, subordinating them to political
agendas, people put bombs on airplanes. I am not suggesting
that men are in danger of being blown away by women. I am not
even particularly concerned with the effect on men of the sexuality debates. I am concerned with their effect on women, and
with the resurrection of a feminist view of women as natural
victims, which the antipornography movement helps perpetuate.

What is reflected and reinforced by the sexuality debates is a
growing belief in women's fragility. We're so fragile that we are
assaulted by magazines; we're raped by rude remarks; we're
never merely offended; instead, we're emotionally disabled.
We're so weak than an unwelcome remark, or what might once
have been called an unwelcome advance, has the traumatic force
of a physical assault. Sometimes when women talk about date
rape and harassment, you have no idea what they are talking
about. Were they raped, or merely fondled (or "felt up," as we
used to say)? Were they chastised for not laughing at a dirty joke
or subject to sexual blackmail at work? The antipornography
movement has contributed much to this conflation of sexual
misconduct with sexual crime. It provides the underlying ideology that equates actual and metaphorical violence, which has
trivialized sexual violence and sexual discrimination, far more
than the Senate Judiciary Committee ever could.

Acknowledging this—that exaggerating the problem of sexual
violence also trivializes it—is difficult for many women who are
caught up in the sexuality debates, particularly privileged, college women. It means acknowledging that they are not so terribly

oppressed, at a time when they are encouraged to seek virtue in oppression and even a sense of identity. One great underlying challenge for anticensorship feminists, trying to inject some rationality into the sexuality debates, is the challenge that has always confronted civil rights advocates: how do we enlist people in a fight for institutional equality without overstating the institutional inequalities? How do we inspire people to seek liberation without instilling in them a crippling sense of how badly they are oppressed?

OF FACE-LIFTS AND FEMINISM

(*September 1988*)

"You have to suffer to be beautiful," my mother used to say, tugging at her girdle. Beauty, or the quest for it—like childbearing—was woman's burden, proudly borne. My mother dressed painfully, enduring high heels and a cinched waist, just as she endured her pregnancies.

Feminism was supposed to loosen beauty's hold on women. It was supposed to make being smart or competent or strong as important as being pretty. It was supposed to revalue women: we would no longer be defined or limited strictly by our looks. "What is a feminist?" I sometimes ask people. A feminist, they often reply, is a woman who burns her bra—which I like to think means that a feminist is a woman who is not a slave to appearances.

Still, like most women and many feminists my age (thirty-eight), I spend an inordinate amount of time thinking about how I look, worrying about what to eat and wear and whether or not to go gray. I've decided to dye my hair if it gets much worse.

"I'm not going to be gray before fifty," I assured my mother. "Fifty!" she exclaimed. "I'm not going to be gray 'til I'm eighty."

My mother is still suffering for her beauty. Two years ago, she had a face-lift. "Now I can age gracefully," she said when it healed. I visited her the day after the operation. Her head was wrapped in bloody bandages, her face was bruised, her eyes were swollen shut, and she moaned a lot. I managed not to say I told you so, and prayed I'd never care enough about looking young to let some doctor cut into my face.

I think cosmetic surgery is crazy and bad for women, and I worry about its increasing popularity. More than half a million cosmetic procedures were performed in 1986—24 percent more than were performed in 1984. Face-lifts, liposuctions to remove fat, and breast augmentations are becoming respectable among "postfeminist women," as well as prefeminist ones like my mother. Cher, newly sculpted and looking great, recently graced the cover of *Ms.* She's our new feminist role model, a "real" woman, *Ms.* proclaims, shaped by a surgeon's knife. Plastic surgery is a way of "reinventing" yourself, the editors gush; it's for women who "dare to take control of their lives."

In China, women once broke their feet, or had them broken, crushed, and bound in childhood. Between the ages of five and ten, the arches of their feet were wrapped and fractured by their mothers, in agonizing fits of feminine virtue. "My feet were on fire and I couldn't sleep; Mother struck me for crying," one woman remembered. "I was inflicted with the pain of foot-binding when I was seven years old. I was an active child who liked to jump about, but from then on my free and optimistic nature vanished." Maimed, in constant pain and practically immobilized, she was reinvented, too, because only hobbling women with tiny hoofed feet were beautiful. Only women who never strode but only swayed uncertainly were pleasing—icons of erotic delight.

"Take control of your life," ads for face lifts and liposuction exclaim, promoting plastic surgery as an exercise in self-esteem. But, like footbinding, it has always been an emblem of powerlessness. Plastic surgery is a way of ceding control, submitting to fears about aging or simply looking ordinary, risking your health to satisfy someone else's model of womanhood and the cruel equation of beauty with love and sexual pleasure. I imagine every face lift and tummy tuck making life a little harder for the plain, awkward, and imperfect women among us and for teenage girls who can't get dates.

I have a friend who is brilliant, successful, charming, and fat, and who says she expects never to be happy because of her lifelong weight problem. She's almost always alone—the girl no one asks to the prom. I think of her sometimes when I look at fashion magazines or see Cher on the cover of *Ms.* or remember my mother's old face. Not until women stop suffering for beauty will they stop suffering, too, for the lack of it.

CRASHING THE LOCKER ROOM

(July 1992)

In her thirteen years as a senator from Arkansas, Hattie Caraway, the first woman elected to the U.S. Senate, made only fifteen speeches on the floor. "And they say women talk all the time," she wrote in her diary, after listening to her colleagues' orations. A former housewife who inherited her husband's seat in 1931 and was reelected to it twice, Caraway was known as Silent Hattie or the Woman Who Holds Her Tongue. "I haven't the heart to take a minute away from the men," she explained. "The poor dears love it so."

Telling me this story at the outset of an interview, Nancy Kassebaum, a Republican senator from Kansas, at first seems like Hattie Caraway, less embittered than amused by the male monopoly on the Senate. Although she and the Maryland Democrat Barbara Mikulski are the only two women in the Senate today, she does not, she tells me, wish for more female senators so much as she wishes for more moderate Republican ones.* She calls herself a U.S. senator, not a female senator, in commenting on her vote in favor of Justice Clarence Thomas's nomination to the Supreme Court, and she says she has not felt disadvantaged by her sex in any of her campaigns or committee assignments. Kassebaum sits on the Senate Foreign Relations Committee,

---

*Today, in 1996, there are eight women in the Senate. Nancy Kassebaum is retiring.

overseeing a traditional male preserve. Still, she muses, men's voices do have more authority on foreign-policy issues. "There's an indifference to the contribution one can make," she says, only a little obliquely. "What I can resent is indifference"—which apparently extends even to areas in which women might be expected to have considerable expertise.

"I was never once asked by anyone at the White House or by any of my colleagues about how I reacted to Anita Hill's public allegations of sexual harassment or how I thought the allegations should be handled, which was kind of interesting," Kassebaum recalls.

Both Kassebaum and Mikulski, however, were invited to sit with the Judiciary Committee during the Thomas-Hill hearings. Both declined. "Barbara and I felt it would have been demeaning," Kassebaum explains. Mikulski, who voted against the Thomas confirmation, is a little more direct: "I was not on the committee. It was not my job to give an imprimatur to the hearings. It was not my job to prop them up or do a whitewash."

Precisely what other role the two women might have played on the committee was unclear. Their invitation was issued in haste, on the morning of Hill's testimony, when Mikulski called Senator Joseph Biden to protest the proceedings. (She previously had asked for a delay to investigate the allegations.) "It was fifteen minutes before the hearings began!" she exclaims. "I wasn't even in Washington; I was in Baltimore." Sometimes, as Nancy Kassebaum says, there's indifference.

That the Senate is indifferent to women's voices and concerns is the kindest interpretation of the Thomas-Hill hearings offered by many women. Male senators tended to ignore or trivialize the charges of sexual harassment—because, Bella Abzug, the former New York congresswoman, asserts, "they do it all the time." Abzug echoes a common refrain. "It's a way of life for them." Ellie Smeal, the founder of the Fund for the Feminist Majority, is blunter, recalling what a male lobbyist once told her about male legislators: "They fish together, they hunt together, they play cards together, and they whore together."

Whether or not outrage over the Thomas-Hill hearings is confined to politically active professional women, as some claim, whether or not that outrage will affect the upcoming election (it has already cost Alan Dixon, an Illinois Democrat who voted for Thomas, his seat, and may defeat Arlen Specter, of Pennsylvania, as well),* whether or not the public had its collective consciousness raised by Hill's story and the commentaries it engendered, the televised hearings provided an emotionally charged image of the Senate as an exclusive club for white males of a certain age. The judiciary committee looked like an aging former football team from some segregated suburban school.

Of course, the exclusion of women from Congress is not exactly news; it's history. Only fourteen women have ever served in the U.S. Senate, and the majority of them inherited their husbands' seats or were appointed for limited terms by governors with whom they had political or personal connections. (Two governors have appointed their wives to vacant Senate seats: Edwin Edwards, of Louisiana, in 1972; and Bibb Graves, of Alabama, in 1937.) Only 117 women have served in the House since its inception. Out of 11,230 people who have served in Congress, only 1 percent have been women. Today there are two women in the Senate and twenty-eight women in the House (out of 435 members). In other words, women constitute 5.6 percent of Congress, an increase of only about three percentage points since 1971.† Women have made considerably more progress at

* Specter, who survived a 1992 challenge from Democrat Lyn Yeakel, has since conceded that his interrogation of Hill during the hearings may have been too harsh.

†The number of women elected to Congress increased significantly in the aftermath of the Thomas/Hill hearings, not long after this article was published in August 1992. Today, with eight women in the Senate, there are forty-seven women in the house.

the state and local levels, suggesting that they face a glass ceiling in politics, as they do in corporate life.

But statistics are a bore; the Thomas-Hill hearings were enthralling, to partisans on either side. "I was as enraptured by the hearings as anyone," Secretary of Labor Lynn Martin recalls. "They were sirenlike." In a postliterate age the video images of the Judiciary Committee were also powerfully persuasive; they dramatized the homogeneity of the Senate more than statistics and polemics ever could.

Someday Clarence Thomas's most fervent opponents may thank him for his help in electing women to the Senate. As an organizing tool, the Thomas-Hill hearings may do for women politicians in the 1990s what *Roe* v. *Wade* did for the New Right in the 1970s. The dramatic upset primary victories of the senatorial candidates Carol Moseley Braun, in Illinois, and Lynn Yeakel, in Pennsylvania; the record number of women running for the Senate and the House; and record amounts of money pouring into women's campaigns have been among the biggest political stories of the year. Both Braun and Yeakel attribute their candidacies to the Senate hearings. Not only did the hearings make a lot of women angry but they "demystified the Senate," Braun says. "Instead of dignified men debating lofty issues, the public saw garden-variety politicians making bad speeches."*

The Problems Women Face

Why are garden-variety politicians invariably male? Why aren't more women in the Senate? You might also ask, Why aren't more women in corporate boardrooms, or at partnership meetings of major law firms?

You can usually predict the response to the question about women in the Senate (or the boardroom) if you know your

---

* Braun was elected to the Senate in 1992; Yeakel was not.

respondent's ideology. Liberal Democrats and feminists talk about the ways in which women have been kept out of power by bias. Conservative Republicans and other traditionalists are likely to say that women have opted out, following a natural inclination to stay home. Moderates tend to focus on "structural" obstacles to women's political advancement—the power of incumbency and the fact that having entered political life in significant numbers relatively recently, women are still making their way up the hierarchy; women lack "bench strength," they say inside the Beltway. (The same explanation is often given for women's secondary status in the corporate world.)

The structural explanation sounds appealingly objective and is no doubt partly true, but it takes you back to your starting point. Why weren't women more active politically thirty years ago? Were they kept out of power or did they opt out, naturally? Do we have any basis for asserting what comes naturally to women when their choices have long been so unnaturally constrained? The reasons for women's absence from the Senate are, of course, at least as complicated as the reasons for their absence from the upper echelons of most high-status professions. Socialization, custom, the division of labor within the home, access to contraception, some degree of choice, and, I suspect, considerable bias all play their roles. "The last time anything was simple, you were eight years old," Lynn Martin reminds me.

But to simplify just a little: Among political women and the experts who study them there is a clear consensus about the problems that women candidates have traditionally faced. Again, people perceive bias through the scrim of ideology. More-conservative female candidates are likely to present it as a relatively minor problem; more-liberal candidates are likely to present it as a major one. Talking to women from both parties, however, you hear complaints and observations about bias that are familiar to most professional women:

Women have a harder time than men establishing their credibility as candidates, because our traditional images of political leadership are male (along with our traditional images of trial lawyers and neurosurgeons). According to the Democratic pollster Celinda Lake, whose studies on female candidates are widely cited by Democrats, the credibility problem has "three prongs"—competence, electability, and toughness:

Men are presumed to be competent; women must prove they're competent. (Women internalize this message, some suggest, and think they have to be qualified to run; men just run.)

Women must also prove that they're viable candidates, capable of waging winning campaigns. This problem of proving electability is circular: women need to prove their viability to raise money, but they can't show that they're viable until they've raised money.

Women have a hard time proving that they're tough enough. Voters want candidates who will fight for them, but women who present themselves as fighters are likely to be considered strident, at best, or bitchy. Celinda Lake has observed, with apparently unintended poignancy, that a woman can effectively establish toughness by pointing to some personal tragedy she's managed to overcome.

In addition to these general credibility problems (which seem to be lessening), women candidates also cite particular, familiar manifestations of bias. They commonly complain that the press pays too much attention to a woman's appearance. Josie Heath, an unsuccessful 1990 and 1992 Democratic senatorial candidate from Colorado, notes that she can describe her wardrobe by reading her campaign clips. Women are also plagued by questions about their marital status, no matter what it is. That a husband can be a serious liability was clearly shown by Geraldine Ferraro's vice presidential campaign; Dianne Feinstein, the former mayor of San Francisco, and Josie Heath were also questioned about their husbands' finances. But the absence of a husband can be a liability too. Female candidates are "penalized by marriage," Barbara Mikulski says. "If you're married, you're neglecting the guy; if you're divorced, you couldn't keep him; if you're a widow, you killed him: if you're single, you couldn't get a man."

These problems of bias and the facts of family life underlie the primary structural obstacles to women's political advancement. Women tend to start their political careers later than men, after their children are grown, and so have less time to position themselves politically. Their place in the hierarchy and the presumption that women are not competent or electable make it difficult for them to raise money, and until recently fund-raising was cited as one of women's primary political problems. Fund-raising difficulties also reflect sex segregation throughout the job market (which is related, of course, to divisions of labor at home). Clustered in lower-paying jobs, women have less money to give to their candidates and causes. "Women tend to give in smaller amounts, and they give ideologically. They give for abortion rights or because they want to see someone fighting for Anita Hill," the Democratic consultant Nikki Heidepriem remarks. "Men tend to give for economic reasons, with an eye on the bottom line. The big money comes from entrepreneurs and corporate types who do business in Washington, and they tend not to be women."

The Parties as Locker Rooms

So what? Some men, and women, readers are probably impatient by now with these laments. Male candidates are not all well connected; they, too, have trouble raising money, challenging incumbents, and receiving what they consider fair treatment from the press. Appearance and image matter for men as well— graduate students in men's studies could write treatises on the politics of baldness. Minority men can probably point to at least as much bias as white women can (and have even less representation in the Senate). The generalizations about the special problems of female candidates are only generalizations. Each candidate has his or her own combination of advantages and disadvantages, involving not just sex and race or ethnicity but also geography, ideology, telegenicity, shrewdness, wit, personal history, and luck. Women complaining of bias don't deny this. They do claim that although the factors in each race are different, the balance of factors, particularly in statewide and federal elections, generally favors men.

The party apparatuses and operatives also favor men, particularly in the eyes of Democratic women. Republican women candidates don't as a rule offer much public criticism of their party, except perhaps on the issue of abortion. Democratic women don't as a rule offer much praise; instead, many scoff at the suggestion that their party is doing enough for women.

Levels of mistrust are high. Jane Danowitz, of the Women's Campaign Fund, is convinced that Dianne Feinstein would not have had a primary challenge in her bid this year for the California senate had she been a man. "Feinstein almost won the 1990 California gubernatorial race. She was the party's standard-bearer. Had she been a man, they would have cleared the field." Who's they? "You can start with George Mitchell [the Senate majority leader] and Chuck Robb [the head of the Democratic Senatorial Campaign Committee (DSCC)]. There is an old-boys' network that could have dried up the money for any other candidate entering the race." Kam Kuwata, Feinstein's campaign manager, dismisses this suggestion (as do a few other political women). The political director of the DSCC, Don Foley, stresses that the national party stays out of primary battles (as it is required to do). "They stay out officially but they go in the back door when they want," Danowitz charges.

The old boys, however, are beginning to change their ways, Danowitz adds. Since January of this year the DSCC has been holding unprecedented meetings with the women's political community and showing increasing concern for female candidates. Given the remarkable momentum of women this year, a resurgence of feminism, and a pervasive disgust for incumbents, it's fair to call this a foxhole conversion. Given the history of party politics, redemption may not be so easy.

Whether or not they believe that the party in effect conspires against them, women often describe it as a locker room. At the national level "both parties take a very conventional approach to recruitment," according to Anita Dunn, an aide to New Jersey Senator Bill Bradley and a former senior staffer at the DSCC. "They look at the governors and the visible congressmen. Recruitment is a very subjective process, depending on the same small, predominantly male circles. And if you're a Democrat, the conventional wisdom is that you shouldn't run a candidate who's perceived as liberal, as are most Democratic women in the House." Sometimes, Dunn adds, " 'liberal' is a code word for 'woman.' "

At the state level the locker room is smaller and perhaps even more firmly established. New Jersey Republican Christine Todd Whitman, who ran a surprisingly close race against Bradley in 1990, believes that if the party had thought it had any chance of defeating Bradley, it never would have nominated a woman to run against him.*

"All politics is local, and at the local level there's a group that says, 'We'll run Bob. He's my buddy,' " Colorado Congresswoman Pat Schroeder says. Schroeder recalls the party's "anointment" of Tim Wirth for the Senate seat that Gary Hart vacated in 1986. She had been in Congress longer than Wirth but, she says, was not even considered for the seat. "The party regulars said,

* Whitman was subsequently elected governor of New Jersey.

'We'll run Tim, he's our candidate, because it's so hard on him having to raise money to run for the House every two years'—as if it's easy for me."

The implication of bias in Schroeder's story may or may not be fair, but it indicates a pervasive view of the parties as men's clubs in which women are only tokens. That view has led at least a few Democratic women to demand affirmative action plans for candidates. "The parties say, 'We don't discriminate; women can run,' " Bella Abzug observes. "But we're running against the tide of history. It's not enough to say 'We don't discriminate.' " Women advanced professionally partly because of affirmative action, the argument goes; they may not advance politically without it.

In fact the Democratic Party does have an affirmative action plan for delegates; devising a plan for candidates is a bit more problematic (as well as extremely unpopular). Affirmative action plans for candidates may be feasible only in parliamentary systems, in which the parties run slates of candidates. But Abzug has a suggestion—or, rather, a demand. She has recently helped launch a campaign calling on the parties to nominate only women for open seats. "This may not be the idea that will do it, but I'm trying to get people to think creatively. I want people to be more creative and demanding."

Meanwhile, according to one Democratic consultant, "The Democratic Party has all it can do to get out of bed in the morning. You can say it's not doing much for women, but it's not doing much of anything at all. Apart from fund-raising, which is important, collecting some data, and holding an occasional conference, the best thing the Democratic Party can do is get out of the way."

The Republican Advantage

Whether or not the Democratic Party has the will to promote women, it lacks the means. "The Republicans have a recruitment budget; we don't," says Don Foley, of the DSCC. The political consultant Ann Lewis explains that the Republicans also have an organizational advantage when it comes to promoting women. "The Republican Party is a top-down hierarchy with centralized fund-raising. The Democratic Party is best understood as a federation of state parties. The only truly national Democratic operation is the presidential selection process. Everything else is run state by state, and some states are surer, swifter, and richer than others."

Because they had more resources and more control over their own system, Republicans made more progress recruiting women in the early 1980s, according to Lewis, who used to recruit for the Democrats. "My Republican counterpart would go to candidates and say, 'We'll get the nomination. We'll max on funding.' I'd say, 'Look, it's going to be a lot of fun, but you're going to have to fight for the nomination, and maybe I can get you a dollar.' "

Republicans also had more incentive to recruit women candidates after the gender gap appeared, in 1980, showing that women were more likely to vote Democratic. According to Kathy Wilson, a board member of the National Republican Coalition for Choice, "The gender gap scared them to death. The appointment of Sandra Day O'Connor was no accident. Republicans are shrewd, and they realize they need women to temper the Republican image." Republicans, because "they are better marketers than Democrats," are interested in fielding women, Ann Lewis says, summing things up. "Democrats think of politics as organizing. Republicans think of politics as marketing."

But Republicans have had the same problem marketing women candidates that Democrats might have had marketing SDI. The party has a credibility problem on women's issues. Running as a Republican can be a disadvantage to women candidates who seek support from women voters concerned with such issues as abortion rights, family leave, and health care. Claudine Schneider, a former congresswoman from Rhode Island who unsuccessfully challenged the incumbent senator Claiborne Pell in 1990, is convinced that she would have fared better as a Democrat. "Many women believe the myth that Republicans are bad for women and Democrats are good for them," she says. Lynn Martin, who lost a 1990 Senate race in Illinois to the incumbent Democrat Paul Simon, reports a similar disadvantage among women voters: "One group of voters won't vote for you because you're a woman; another group of women voters won't vote for you because you're a Republican." (Martin does not attribute her loss to bias; like Claudine Schneider, she was up against a popular incumbent.)

"The Republican Party is interested in the concept of promoting women, but they have an ideology problem," Ann Lewis says. During the 1980s the party's primary electorate became increasingly conservative—antiabortion and strongly in favor of "traditional" family roles—and resistant to electing women. Democrats have no similar ideology problem, but they have financial and organizational problems and, it seems, lack the requisite marketing skills—the ability to dramatize their message.

The Difficulty of Telling Their Own Stories

A campaign is a morality play, in the view of Larry K. Smith, a former manager of a presidential and several senatorial campaigns, and now counselor to the House Armed Services Committee. "A campaign is a contest over values and norms, not issues," he says. "Every campaign is a story about the candidate and the nation." The Democratic Party has distanced itself from voters, Smith suggests, by taking a "literalist" approach to campaigning, rather than a dramatic one. Instead of telling a first-person story about values, it has told a third-person story about issues.

Whether this is an accurate assessment of the Democratic Party in general (and not just of the Dukakis campaign), it does provide a useful perspective on women in politics. Women candidates have stories to tell different from men's, because, like it or not, they represent to voters different visions of authority and different values.

The primary storytellers in campaigns, however, aren't candidates but their media consultants—the majority of whom are men. They tend to imagine campaigns in ways that are inapposite to many women: their favorite campaign metaphors involve football and war; they tend to see themselves as hired guns. The consultant Wendy Sherman, a partner in the Washington firm Doak, Shrum, Harris, Sherman, Donilon and one of few women at the top of her field, suggests that the failures of male consultants to women are failures of imagination: "Consultants often get caught up in what is conventionally wise, and generally what's conventionally wise is what white men believe—because there are more of them inside the Beltway in positions of power."

That men's conventional wisdom sometimes misconceives women's political potential was demonstrated by Barbara Mikulski's successful 1986 Senate campaign. She was a popular congresswoman seeking an open seat in a contested primary, but "people inside the Beltway said she could not become a senator," Sherman, who was Mikulski's campaign manager in 1986, told me. "She didn't look like a senator, she didn't act like a senator, she didn't sound like a senator." For voters, however, that turned out to be the essence of her appeal. Sherman explained, "They looked at her and said, 'She's ours, and we may finally have a voice in the U.S. Senate, and we don't look like senators either.' "

The connection voters felt to Mikulski partly reflected her history of service in the House, Sherman added, but it also reflected and was strengthened by her sex. That female candidates seem more accessible to voters is indeed part of the new conventional wisdom; it's evidenced by the tendency to call women in authority by their first names.

Because women are expected to be more nurturant than men,

one of the biggest mistakes for a woman candidate, according to experts, is running harshly negative ads. A frequently cited horror story about a woman's campaign and a male consultant involves a series of negative ads that Bob Squier produced for Harriett Woods in her unsuccessful 1986 Senate campaign in Missouri—the "crying-farmer spots."

These were a series of interviews with a farmer and his wife suffering a foreclosure by an insurance company whose board included Woods's opponent, Kit Bond. Run as a dramatic three-part serial (like an AT&T commercial), the ad included a shot of the farmer breaking down and sobbing as he talked about losing his cows. It concluded with freeze frames of the farmer and Kit Bond, and attacked Bond for opposing a moratorium on farm foreclosures.

Woods and her staff initially opposed Squier's advice to air the spots early in the campaign. Then, against her better judgment, Woods says, she "caved in." She ran the ad, and it sparked a controversy that badly damaged her campaign. The local press was critical; the ad was deemed unfair and exploitative. Squier's partner, William Knapp, concedes that "the ad did not work as well as we would have liked," but believes that had Woods stayed on the attack, she would have prevailed. Instead, she fired Squier, her campaign seemed to be in trouble, and that became a story in itself. Woods believes that the image of an "inept" woman candidate who couldn't keep her own campaign in order resonated with voters and political elites.

Woods, now the president of the National Women's Political Caucus, does not believe that she lost the election simply because of the ad—"1986 was a year in which factory workers stayed home or voted Republican." She is no longer "brooding" about her loss, but in talking about Squier and the crying-farmer controversy, she stiffens with anger. Her mistake, she says, was not in firing Squier, as one spin on the story suggested; it was in hiring him. She was uneasy about his style and his understanding of her identity from the beginning: "I worried that he didn't care who I was; he could talk to me and never listen. So I arranged a lunch with him. I thought, if he knows who I am, I can trust him to translate it. We had the lunch, and he talked the whole time about himself."

Women's tales of male arrogance are legion in the political community, as they generally are in male-dominated occupations. You believe them or not, depending on your own experiences and sensitivities. The tales are hardly empirical evidence of bias, unconscious or intended. But they surely demonstrate that women perceive bias and that they encounter difficulties in telling their own stories and forging their own political identities.

Despite the horror stories and the litany of complaints, however, prospects for women candidates seem to be dramatically improving. Women have impressive new fund-raising networks, which enabled them to capitalize on outraged support for Anita Hill. Political outsiders are in vogue, and optimists expect women to gain at least fifteen to twenty seats in Congress this year. In the aftermath of the Thomas-Hill hearings, at the end of the cold war, in the midst of a recession, with battles over abortion rights looming in the states, the new conventional wisdom from the women's political community is upbeat. (It will sound a little pat, but that's part of its appeal.) This is what you're likely to hear today from politically active women, and some men, pollsters, organizers, consultants, and candidates, Democrats and quite a few Republicans alike.

Feminine Stereotypes

Women are perceived as being more honest than men, so they benefit from general concern about corruption. Women are outsiders, so they benefit from the anti-incumbency mood (women embody change, everyone says). Women are perceived as being more compassionate than men and better at dealing with the quotidian domestic problems—day care, education, and potholes—that are displacing concern about communism and national defense (which men are considered better able to address).

Republicans and Democrats differ as to whether the current climate favors Republican or Democratic women. The pollster Celinda Lake says that the combined strengths of Democrats and women on domestic issues are helpful; Kathy Wilson, of the National Republican Coalition for Choice, says that the combination of Democratic and presumptively feminine values is hurtful: "Too much compassion makes people clutch at their wallets." Republican women, she says, offer both compassion and fiscal competence—a quality that is particularly important to women. Sometimes women's advantage on domestic issues is said to be offset by a lack of credibility on fiscal matters. But the presumption that women don't understand budgets is usually said to be balanced by the presumption that they're honest. The media consultant William Knapp says, "There's a sense that a woman may not know how to fill out a general ledger sheet, but at least she won't steal." Ann Lewis remarks, "The stereotypes that used to work against us are now working for us."

It is probably not realistic even to hope that women might someday win or lose elections without being helped or hurt by stereotypes. Campaigning is the art of the superficial: it's about rhetoric, not policy; the manipulation of images, not the exchange of ideas. And, as everyone I interviewed reminded me, voters have different images of men and women: men are tougher and more stable in times of crisis. Women care more about their constituents; they're better housekeepers—and, as Jane Addams once suggested, government is "enlarged housekeeping" on a grand scale.

The use of feminine stereotypes to advance a feminist agenda is a central, historic irony of the American women's movement.

Late-nineteenth-century social reformers like Addams and Julia Ward Howe championed what were considered feminine virtues—honesty, compassion, and heightened concern for moral behavior—arguing that women, once empowered, would bestow good government and peace on the public. Stereotypes of femininity helped to fuel the suffrage movement, providing a rationale for women's participation in political life. Many women sought the vote not for its own sake, as a matter of right, but as a means of achieving womanly reforms. Listening to women candidates today, you sometimes hear a similar argument for electing women to high office: with their different voices, women will foster cooperation instead of confrontation in domestic and foreign affairs: as nature's housekeepers, women will clean up the environment.

The dangers of using stereotypes like these should be clear to generations of women who have had to prove their unfeminine ability and had to fight for the right to exercise power overtly outside the home, as well as covertly within it. By claiming "feminine" virtues, women may effectively deprive themselves of "masculine" strengths. Whether female candidates can exploit feminine stereotypes without ultimately being defeated by them is an unasked question at the heart of many women's campaigns.

Women can hardly avoid stressing the qualities attributed to them that voters find appealing, but they have to stress them carefully, in very particular ways. "If a woman runs for governor and says, 'I'm gentler, nicer, and like children better,' she sounds as if she's running for day-care supervisor," Ann Lewis remarks. "On the other hand, what she can say is 'I know what real life is like. I know what budgets are like, what it is like to pay hospital bills and try to make ends meet. And when I go to the governor's office, I'll bring that knowledge with me.' "

Voters of both parties are likely to be persuaded by this

message, Celinda Lake suggests, particularly during a recession; she observes in a 1991 report, "Winning with Women," that voters believe that women are better at "meeting the needs of the middle class." Lake surveyed about 1,160 voters, testing their reactions to "generic" male and female Republican and Democratic candidates. (She found, for example, that a generic Democratic woman would fare better than a generic Democratic man against a generic Republican man.) The trouble with this study, of course, is that neither campaigns nor candidates are generic; if all politics is local, then every race is unique, as is every candidate.

Some women also point out that previous predictions of victories for women did not come true. They said that women would win in 1990, the Republican pollster Linda DiVall recalls, but eight women ran for the Senate and seven lost. Claudine Schneider, who lost her 1990 challenge to Claiborne Pell, says that "for the first time," women's political future seems "foggy." Schneider says, "I still believed that with eight women running for Senate in 1990, at least half would be elected. When I lost, I was disappointed. When all the other women lost [except for the incumbent Nancy Kassebaum], I was devastated."

Congresswoman Pat Schroeder, too, is less than hopeful. She says, "The same women have been talking optimism for a long time, but here we are, in 1992, and we have only twenty-eight women in the House." Schroeder is also skeptical about assessments of the national mood and people's preoccupation with domestic concerns. "Something like the Gulf War rolls around, and the mood changes overnight. You could change the polls in two days if you suddenly got everyone in their flight suits bombing Qaddafi. The testosterone is flowing, and everyone's cheering—guys in the reserves put on their suits and they run the military hardware in the mall and crawl all over it. Great images."

At the national level, Schroeder adds, the electorate's focus shifts back and forth between domestic and international issues, and men are considered better able to handle both. In other words, men are less disadvantaged by stereotypes on domestic issues than women are on foreign policy. Schroeder says, "We'd look sillier than Dukakis in a tank."

Traditional images of women pose the stubbornest challenge on national security issues. The challenge comes from voters who don't trust women's capacity for military command and also from within the feminist community. There is a strong, historical strain of pacifism in the women's movement, embodied by Jeannette Rankin, the first woman elected to Congress. Rankin voted against the popular resolution to declare war against Germany in 1917, to the dismay of her constituents. She voted her conscience and lost her office; she was defeated in a race for Senate the following year. She never recanted her vote or her pacifism. Fifty years later she was marching to protest the Vietnam War. Rankin died in 1978, at ninety-two, having devoted much of her life to the peace movement. She is an American feminist hero; at women's rallies against the Gulf War last year, her name was invoked, along with the image of women as peacemakers.

Jeannette Rankin is, however, a problematic role model for women candidates. Not every woman will or should sacrifice her office for a symbolic vote of conscience. Not every woman will or should be a pacifist; and to advance in the Senate and into the White House, women will have to convince the voters that they're prepared to go to war.

That may seem self-evident, but within the women's community it is a highly controversial position, an unholy assertion of feminist machismo. "We would know we had the first woman candidate for president when we saw a female senator on a battleship, reviewing the troops," Ann Lewis recalls saying to a group of women. "And someone said, 'That's terrible. Do we have to repeat the military tradition?' And I said, 'No, you don't have to repeat it. You can vote for Mother Teresa.' "

This dialogue between pragmatism and purity is a staple of the women's community. In the Rankin tradition, significant factions of women have long practiced a politics of purity, promising to reform and cleanse the world in their own image, holding women candidates to higher standards than men, and seeking, in Lewis's words, "higher visions of ourselves."

The persistence and pervasiveness of this tradition and its broad implications for electoral politics are difficult to measure. Female candidates do commonly complain, however, that they are held to higher standards by voters than men are. The political double standard, like the double standard of sexual behavior, reflects both negative and positive stereotypes of women: voters tend to have lower expectations of women's ability and higher expectations of their intent. The suspicion that women are less competent than men gives them less leeway to make mistakes. The notion that women are more moral than men makes them more accountable for behavior that raises even minor moral questions.

In addition, women's funding networks are said by candidates and campaign managers to be tougher on their candidates than men's networks, according to a 1989 survey by Celinda Lake. And women candidates may have unrealistic expectations of their constituents, Lake suggests today. "I don't think women's interest groups are tougher; I think women candidates expect them to be easier. Running for office is a very isolating experience for a woman. Candidates want to believe they can go back to women supporters for nurturance."

In fact, in recent years the women's political community has become more "tough-minded" than nurturant. In Washington, at least, pragmatism has clearly displaced purity. Organizations like EMILY'S List, a Democratic fund-raising network, the National Women's Political Caucus, and the Women's Campaign Fund practice savvy, bottom-line politics, supporting only those candidates deemed to be electable. This practice is not universally acclaimed, however. Patricia Ireland, the president of the National Organization for Women, dismisses it as a "politics of scarcity" that deters qualified women from running. She prefers "flooding the ticket."

While organizations like EMILY'S List and the National Women's Political Caucus represent the new insider politics for women, NOW remains on the outside, along with Ellie Smeal's Fund for the Feminist Majority. Insider women—lobbyists and consultants—often deride NOW for obstructionist ideological purity, pointing out that politics is the art of the possible; but that may not be quite fair. Activists like Ireland and Smeal view the possibilities differently. "I think we're the ones who are pragmatic," Smeal remarks.

A Women's Party?

Patricia Ireland and Ellie Smeal advocate the formation of a third party, not just for women but, as Ireland says, "for all people excluded from power"—a rainbow coalition of the marginal. It's hardly surprising that insider feminist women prefer to put their faith in the Democratic Party, rejecting this idea, sometimes gently and sometimes with contempt. Lynn Cutler, the vice chair of the Democratic National Committee, calls creating a third party "the most self-destructive endeavor for women I can imagine." Pat Schroeder suggests that it's premature to talk about a third party, because "we don't yet have a second party."

Smeal isn't interested in reforming the Democratic Party, because of her firm belief that "the Republican boys and Democratic boys have more in common with each other than they do with a feminist agenda." The Democratic girls and Republican girls, she adds, have more in common with each other as well. Smeal puts her faith in sexual solidarity.

It's likely that the Thomas-Hill hearings generated sympathy for Smeal among women of both parties. Linda DiVall speculates that "as a long shot," women may cross party lines in November to vote for one another. Jane Danowitz, of the Women's Campaign Fund, suggests that the hearings have lessened party loyalties for Democrats particularly and have diminished the importance of ideology in campaigns: "Before the hearings, issues like reproductive choice were paramount over gender, and there was a feeling that good men were as good as good women. But those good men failed us. We'll come of age when we realize that a mediocre woman is as good as a good man."

Smeal says she learned this lesson and came of age more than a decade ago, when she unsuccessfully lobbied the Illinois legislature to pass the Equal Rights Amendment. "We were dressed in green and the STOP-ERA women were dressed in red. We were the cheerleaders and the guys were on the field, strutting around and guffawing at their stupid sexist jokes. I woke up and saw that this was a stag game and even the good guys play it."

Smeal recalls a male United Auto Workers lobbyist explaining to her, "It doesn't matter if they're Democratic or Republican. It doesn't matter if they're liberal or conservative. It doesn't matter if they're prolabor or antilabor. What matters to them is that there's a card game in the back room and you women don't know where it is. Democrats, Republicans, liberals, and conservatives are all playing cards back there. They're afraid if they let you in, you're going to find their card game and you'll say, 'You shouldn't be back here playing cards; you should be out there working,' because that's what wives and mothers always say."

Ellie Smeal's bleak image of sexual politics is powerfully depressing. (And I don't ever want her mad at me.) She articulates some of women's worst fears about male bonding, while the hope she offers of female bonding seems less compelling.

Smeal is convinced that once there are enough women in any legislature to form a critical mass, they will vote in the interests of their sex. (Accept for the sake of argument the questionable underlying assumption that those interests are clear.) She suggests, for example, that a moderate Republican, such as Nancy Kassebaum, would be more likely to promote a feminist agenda if she were one of thirty women in the Senate rather than one of just two. Kassebaum doesn't agree. "Women don't march in lockstep, nor should they," she asserts. "It diminishes women to say that we have one voice and everything in the Senate would change if we were there."

Each point of view has considerable support among political women. "If we had 50 percent women in Congress instead of 5 percent, we'd have family and medical leave," Patricia Ireland declares. "I don't want women there for the sake of diversity; I want them there because I think our issues would move faster." Madeleine Kunin, the former governor of Vermont, says she saw changes in the voting patterns of the Vermont legislature as women gained more seats. But Lynn Martin says: "You belong to your party. You don't just vote by sex. The ballot says Lynn Martin (Rep.), not Lynn Martin (Fem.)."

The debate about the importance of sex is constant. Are you a female candidate or a candidate who happens to be female or both? And how does sex interact with race or ethnicity in party politics? Carol Moseley Braun, the Democratic African American who successfully challenged Alan Dixon in Illinois this year, says that she will "play the gender card" in a campaign, indicating to women voters that she offers them a voice on their issues, but that she will not "play the race card," making a similar appeal to the black community. "Race is too divisive," she explains. Why is an appeal to sexual solidarity not divisive too? Perhaps because sexual loyalties have always been mitigated by race (and class) more than race has been mitigated by sex.

Do party loyalties also trump sex? It is axiomatic within the feminist community that if there had been more women in the Senate, the Thomas nomination would have been doomed. But half of the (two) women in the Senate voted to confirm him, and several Republican women who ran for the Senate in 1990 say they would have confirmed him too.

Probing the remarks of women from both parties, however, you find that there is more agreement about the importance of sex than first appears. Republicans who stress that women vary ideologically (usually meaning that not all women are feminists) also stress that women have perspectives different from men's, which reflect their different life experiences and maybe even something in their nature. Republican and Democratic women often say that they would devote more attention than men to issues involving children and family life, regardless of how they would vote to address those issues.

There is, finally, some empirical evidence that female legislators do have perspectives different from men's, which lead to different legislative results. According to *The Impact of Women in Public Office,* a study released by the Center for the American Woman and Politics, at Rutgers University, women are making a "profound and distinctive" difference in their legislatures, promoting popular feminist concerns: "Elected women are working to make the agendas of legislative institutions more responsive to women's demands for equal rights as articulated by the contemporary women's movement and more reflective of women's concerns stemming from their roles as caregivers in the family and in society." Based on telephone interviews with male and female state legislators, the CAWP study asserts that men and women tend to have different policy priorities. Women, it says, "were more likely to give top priority to women's rights policies" and to "policies dealing with children and families and health care."

The Gender Gap

It should go without saying, but probably doesn't, that regardless of how women would vote in the Senate, they have a right to be there. Women candidates should not have to earn access to the Senate as they once "earned" the right to vote, by promising to make the world a kinder, gentler place. Still, as a practical matter, candidates have to satisfy the expectations of their constituents. How does the electorate divide on women's issues and the need for more women in office?

Candidates often say that polling data indicate that equally small numbers of voters would or would not vote for a woman on account of her sex. The majority of voters say that they consider the issues. It's difficult to know, however, how these statements correspond to behavior. Many people probably wouldn't say that they vote on the basis of sex, and many people are probably affected by unconscious biases. Celinda Lake and several candidates report that the strongest support for women candidates comes from educated, professional women under forty-five; the strongest opposition comes from older women who have fulfilled traditional domestic roles. There seems to be little, if any, hard data about the accuracy of these generalizations as applied to different racial and ethnic groups.

Everybody knows there's a gender gap—differences in male and female voting patterns—but nobody knows how wide it is or how deep or reliable. As Eleanor Holmes Norton, the nonvoting delegate to the House from the District of Columbia, says, "We've been hearing about it, seeing evidence of it, for at least twelve years, and yet have been blown away by antifeminist men. At some point we ought to stop talking about the gender gap and try to understand it."

So what precisely do we know about the gender gap? According to Virginia Sapiro, a professor of political science at the University of Wisconsin, we know this: more women than men vote Democratic. We might also say, however, that more men than women vote Republican; and in fact, Sapiro says, the gender gap was caused by men leaving the Democratic Party while women stayed put. She adds, "When the discussion about the gender gap began, the question was 'What is it about women?'— reflecting an unspoken assumption that women are fickle. The question should have been 'What is it about men?'" Sapiro suspects that men became more conservative during the Reagan years partly in reaction to "the wimpiness of the Carter years," as typified by the hostage crisis. But, she cautions, this, too, is merely speculation.

So there is a partisan gender gap, for some reason or other, and since women register to vote in greater numbers than men, it can be said to favor the Democrats. But, as Linda DiVall says, the gap can be bridged: Republican men, for example, can sometimes win women's votes by attaching themselves to issues such as health care and social security. We know that there is also a gender gap on issues, as DiVall's strategy implies. Women are less likely to favor cutoffs in social spending, Virginia Sapiro says, and they're less likely to favor going to war.

The gender gap on issues is changeable, however, as Sapiro stresses. She says, "The gap on social welfare issues will lessen if men start losing faith in the economic policies of the last ten years." And the gender gap on issues is much more complicated than it first appears. For example, it is conventional wisdom that concern about the economy helps women candidates, but the truth of that hope, or fear, depends on how people analyze the economic crisis. Sapiro explains: "Everyone agrees the economy is a problem. Some will blame it on policies that favored the rich at the expense of the poor, and will talk about homelessness and the need to improve social services. Some will blame it on the deficit and the fact that we've been too wimpy with the Japanese. People aren't going to vote for women to stand up to the Japanese."

"Now, that's gender politics, that's a gender gap," Sapiro concludes. "But it's a lot more complicated, unpredictable, and interesting than the gender gap is usually supposed to be."

"There are a lot of pieces on this chessboard," Eleanor Holmes Norton remarks. The gender gap is also complicated by racial and class issues. It cuts across racial lines, Norton believes, but with varying degrees of incisiveness. Take women's reactions to the Thomas-Hill hearings: Sex interacted with race and class to divide public opinion every which way. Nonprofessional women seem to have found Anita Hill hard to believe, because they saw her as a woman with choices. Black women, Norton observes, were particularly troubled by the fact that Hill's allegations were made "at the last minute," because of a traditional concern within their community for procedural fairness, reflecting a history of unfair trials. "Blacks are very procedurally sensitive."

Still, many political women speculate hopefully that the Thomas-Hill hearings have activated diverse groups of women voters. Combined with anger over reversals of abortion rights, anger at the Thomas-Hill hearings may prove to have considerable political potency.

Or then again, it may not. Pat Schroeder is not sanguine. "I think women are feeling politically homeless more than empowered," she says. "You've got to win some now and again." Women in the House have just lost a battle on family leave, and Schroeder is contemplating powerlessness, including her own, and women's difficulties in confronting it. "Congresswomen aren't powerful. You get to the cloakroom and you're supposed to play ball. Women's issues aren't considered important. You're supposed to put them aside, not embarrass your colleagues, get with the program. 'Why don't you get on with something that matters?' they say. 'Why do you keep nagging us about family leave?' And when you protest caps on sex discrimination in the Civil Rights Bill, they say, 'Aren't you petty?' "

Most women do not want to hear this from her, Schroeder says. "It sounds too painfully familiar. Most women feel in their core so much more vulnerable than men. They don't want to hear from a Pat Schroeder that congresswomen don't get powerful."

Schroeder is probably voicing what many political women feel, at least on occasion—as do some men—for individual congressmen probably don't have much power either. Balancing Schroeder's pessimism with the official optimism of the professional political women's community, you may glean some sense of how much and how little women progress. Despite the proliferation of focus groups and polls, assessing women's political prospects is hardly a science, and it's less an art than a religion, grounded in instinct and faith. Assessments of the public mood are even more whimsical; often they reflect your own.

You can characterize the American public as fundamentally decent and fair, or you can characterize it as fundamentally cruel, biased, and ignorant; sometimes both characterizations seem true.

A lot of Americans are ready to elect more women to national and statewide office. And, as Pat Schroeder says, "A lot of Americans believe that Elvis is alive." Schroeder has been listening to talk radio, which is "vehemently antiwoman." She says: "I think they've decided to attack women with incredible vengeance because they're not afraid of us. They don't think we'll come and shoot them. Listen to hate radio for a week. Women who hope to break into the Senate had better be ready for trouble."

DIVORCE

(*February 1989*)

Twenty-five years ago, when déclassé lawyers wore shines on their suits, divorce lawyers shone only a little less brightly than ambulance chasers and criminal defense attorneys who hung around municipal courts hoping for assignments, happily processing pleas. Twenty-five years ago, divorce work "was what proctology is to medicine," attorney Raoul Felder likes to say. "It was the ass end of the law business, dirty and seamy." Adultery was the only ground for divorce, and it was more about sex than money. "For years it was some sleazy photographer bursting into a motel room trying to get pictures of two people doing it," attorney Bob Cohen recalls. "It was some guy who looked like Al Capone sniffing at motel rooms."

Today it's more likely to be some guy in pinstripes, or some woman in pearls, structuring deals. Divorce work has been gentrified: now it's more about money. Not only have the grounds for divorce been expanded, the amount of property it involves has been greatly increased. In 1980, New York adopted an equitable distribution law, defining marriage as an economic partnership and requiring the equitable distribution of marital property on divorce. Marital property includes, with few exceptions, essentially all property acquired during the marriage—not only houses, co-ops, and cars, but family businesses, pension rights, and professional degrees.

"Equitable distribution made this a very big business," Bob Cohen, managing partner of Morrison, Cohen & Singer, says. It made Mom and Pop split the grocery store, or the family chain of supermarkets, regardless of who holds title to it. They need accountants, appraisers, and tax experts to valuate property as well as lawyers to fight over it. They need emotional and economic stamina. "People walk into my office—I have to tell them I can't guarantee that they will be out of their marriage in less than two years, and it could take four," matrimonial lawyer Peter Bronstein says. "It could cost any number you want to put on it."

If you don't have a joint income of at least $250,000, you can't afford to get divorced, according to Bronstein. At least, you can't afford to get divorced by Bronstein. At $375 an hour, he represents "relatively wealthy" people, with marital estates worth at least $3 or $4 million and family incomes in the $400,000 to $500,000 range. Divorce may be a "financial disaster for all but the wealthy," as Bronstein asserts, but it's a financial blessing for the matrimonial bar, especially at the "high end," where Bronstein and Bob Cohen practice. Cohen refers to his cases as "partnership dissolutions" and claims they regularly involve $50 to $100 million dollars. "Between Fifty-seventh and Ninety-first Street, between First Avenue and Fifth, there's a lot of territory," he explains, "and at some point everyone out there is getting divorced."

Talking to high-end divorce lawyers is a little like watching *Dynasty* or even *The Philadelphia Story.* Interviewing Peter Bronstein in his office, overlooking the territory, his press agent quietly present, I imagine his clients—glossy, coiffed wives, Ivanas and Krystles in spangles and furs, elegant wives, Dina Merrills in fine leather pumps and handbags to match, and a parade of pinstriped husbands. I imagine a world in which marrying well is a respectable job for a woman and divorcing well means she'll never have to go to work again. A "successful divorce," Bronstein explains, can turn a housewife into something like an heiress.

Bronstein was born into the world of successful divorces. His father, Eli Bronstein, who died in 1979, established the law firm of Bronstein, Van Veen & Bronstein. In the competitive, high-profile, and lucrative business of divorce, Peter Bronstein seems at home. He's unabashedly Ivy League (his vision of an ideal world is one in which everyone gets a Harvard education), and he's a brawler: "Matrimonial lawyers are a rough and tumble bunch," he explains. You have to be something of a street fighter. You can't be a white-glove matrimonial lawyer cause you're gonna get killed. I pride myself on getting along with other matrimonial lawyers, but if someone mistreats you, you remember. You have a long memory."

Bronstein's press release claims his "soft-spoken manner" conceals an "aggressive courtroom demeanor," and I believe it. I can see him going in for the kill. Like a law professor, he speaks in fluent hypotheticals, about stockbrokers, heiresses, and very big businessmen. But like a trial attorney, he always looks you in the eye.

In his office at the end of a day, uninterrupted by calls, Bronstein is in a friendly, only slightly professorial mode. Everyone likes being interviewed (and hates the way they're described), and, sitting back, Bronstein has a lot to say about the follies of divorce. He thinks there is too much of it and too much puritanism about adultery:

"You know, in French culture, a man having a mistress does not signal the end of a marriage. It's accepted as something that's a part of life . . . as long as he doesn't treat the mistress any better than the wife. And I don't mean to be sexist about it." French women have lovers too, he adds, without breaking up their marriages.

Perhaps. Whether or not France has a single standard of fidelity, the stereotypical French man and woman have a sophisticated pragmatism about sex and marriage, whereas Americans, Bronstein suggests, are still stuck on romance.

"We have this concept that we marry for love. But marriage is a long road. [Bronstein has been married for eighteen years.] Sometimes economics are better, sometimes love lives are better. Sometimes other people intrude and create tension in a relationship. . . . You have to fight through some of that." Some of his clients are in terrible, abusive situations they should not endure ("the woman's being battered or people are being insulted in some way that's unbearable"), but, in general, Bronstein does not approve of divorce, or, at least, he doesn't have much faith in it:

"People tend to think that divorce is gonna be some sort of panacea, and it's not in many cases. . . . People tend to think that a change is gonna make them happy. I'm not convinced that a change in the marital situation always does. Frequently we sit here and explain to people that they shouldn't be divorced—that they can't afford divorce or that the ignominy they're suffering in their marriage is something they have to deal with as a condition of their lives."

Divorce lawyers are "amateur psychiatrists." You have to find out what the client wants, Bronstein says, but "sometimes you have to tell them what they want." Sometimes you can only sell them what they don't want. "Some people aren't happy about the divorce," Bronstein notes. Some don't want to "get on" with their lives. "If you're talking to a sixty-year-old woman who's been married for thirty-five years, she really has no desire to get on with her life. She's been on with her life for thirty-five years, and now her husband's flirting with his secretary.

"I recall returning to my office with a client after a trial in which I did a wonderful job, asking 'Are you happy with the result?' And he looked at me forlornly and said: "Absolutely not. I really want to be married to this woman.' "

"Clients adore me," Bronstein admits. "I have a wonderful relationship with my clients. But it's amazing how few of those relationships continue after the divorce. They never want to see me again as long as they live." Matrimonial lawyers learn too much about their clients. "You see people at their worst. . . . You see a part of people that has not been doctored up and presented in some public way." It's interesting, he says. "It's like being a cancer surgeon."

■   ■   ■

"It's quite painful," attorney Betty Levinson says. "We spend more money on tissues than a psychiatrist does." Levinson, who surveys New York from a lower vantage point, five floors above Twenty-sixth Street and Fifth, represents people with family incomes in the $100,000 range—the people Peter Bronstein says can't afford to get divorced. A former legal aid lawyer, now a partner in a small, general litigation firm, she has been practicing matrimonial law for about thirteen years. At $200 an hour, her fees are "moderate."

She doesn't have a press agent and is harder to track down for an interview. Squeezing me into her morning, she keeps careful track of our time. She doesn't have a banker's desk, and, in a denim skirt and sweater, she doesn't quite have the look of a lawyer. It's not hard to imagine clients, especially women clients, relating to her as a friend, and Levinson has had to learn to assert her professional distance: "As a young lawyer, I used to offer clients cookies and tea," she recalls, and "often they would mistake my desk for my kitchen table." People still want her to make "life decisions" for them, and Levinson is wary of the tendency of matrimonial lawyers to mirror their clients: "Sometimes at a conference, I'm sitting there with the wife, and he's sitting there with his lawyer. In a different setting, we could be friends, sisters, and they look the same too."

"I think there's a transference between an attorney and client in a divorce case as there is in a therapeutic relationship," she explains. "Clients want to feel protected. They want to feel liked. They want to feel that their interests are being asserted in every way possible, and often people choose lawyers who are in some sense alter egos, or reflections of what they would like to see in themselves."

Whether or not women lawyers are, in general, especially sensitive to the psychodynamics of divorce work or the needs of their clients is a question for the women's magazines to decide. It's clear that Levinson empathizes with her clients (empathy is a slippery slope for a lawyer; you end up representing yourself). But she also has a political commitment to serving them. Divorce is "dismal" for middle-class people, she says, and it's especially dismal for women.

Equitable distribution was supposed to be good for women, and compared with New York's old law, it hasn't been too bad. It gave wives unprecedented rights in what had long been considered their husband's property. When title determined ownership, women had no right to share in "his" business, "his" law practice, "his" stock portfolio, and other property in his name (until he died). What they had was a right to be supported during marriage, which was difficult to enforce, and a derivative right to alimony, which was difficult to collect. The old law was based on a view of women as dependents in a hierarchal relationship. Equitable distribution made them partners in a marital enterprise.

But it did not make them equal partners, to the chagrin of some feminists. Equitable distribution does not entitle women to one-half of the marital property; it entitles them to whatever share in it the judge deems fair, under the circumstances, considering the length of the marriage, the contributions of each spouse, their "probable future financial circumstances," and ten other factors. In long-term marriages, women homemakers have been receiving up to about one-third, not one-half, of the marital property, which, depending on your view of the marriage relation, is either small recompense or a windfall.

The equitable distribution law vests considerable discretion in the courts: it's a law that's as good as the judges applying it. Judges have the power to award women half shares in their marital estates; what they apparently lack is the inclination to do so. Awards to women are said to be slowly increasing, but whether or not the law should mandate a fifty-fifty property split, leaving it to either spouse to prove it's unfair, is a controversial question. How you answer it depends not just on your gender biases but on your view of judges.

Peter Bronstein, who believes the law has been fairly applied, likens women demanding equal instead of equitable distribution to "lobbying groups" demanding "subsidies for milk production." He does not approve of an across-the-board rule: "There are homemakers and there are homemakers," he explains, comparing "the woman who has four kids and lives in a walk-up in Brownsville . . . doing somebody else's laundry on the side to make ends meet" to "some Park Avenue lady with three in help, with only one kid, who's wearing ermine and going off to Aspen to ski every Christmas."

But the woman in Brownsville probably doesn't have a marital estate worth fighting over; the Park Avenue lady can manage on one-third of $50 million if she must. What about the women in the middle? Leave them to the "hardworking judges who are out there trying to put a number on what's fair and what's right."

Hardworking judges, however, are likely to be middle-class males. They come to work with their own biases, and, Betty

Levinson says, "they don't like to stick their necks out": Judges won't necessarily award women fifty percent of the marital property simply because they've earned it. First, "the legislature has to give everybody a pat on the head and say it's okay."

Still, as Peter Bronstein points out, "life's not fair:" women face other problems on divorce that may not readily be solved by legislative intervention. Like most laws, equitable distribution works best for people who can afford to make sure it's enforced. Women tend to be poorer than men and are more likely to lack the resources to litigate. Counsel fees are difficult to obtain while an action is pending, so an uncooperative spouse, with more money, can effectively negotiate a settlement by blocking discovery proceedings, sitting back, and letting the meter run.

Women make more compromises, Levinson suggests, partly because they're at an emotional as well as a financial disadvantage on divorce. They're blackmailed by threats of custody disputes, and they like to "make peace," often for the sake of their children. Women "need to connect," she says, echoing feminist psychologist Carol Gilligan and lots of women's books and magazines. "They feel isolated and terrified and dysfunctional when they're disconnected and not communicating." They're more likely to settle than "fight it to the end."

■   ■   ■

Talking about divorce, you almost always end up talking about gender stereotypes and gender roles, whether or not you believe in them. (It's a lot like talking about marriage.) Divorce in the 1980s looks sadly anachronistic. Divorce lawyers describe a prefeminist world in which women are either predators or victims, Park Avenue ladies or hardworking homemakers, callously discarded. "Women suffer more and feel their troubles more acutely," that brilliant old misogynist Balzac said, an assertion with which some feminists and unrepentant chauvinists sometimes agree.

Raoul Felder, a very visible and (at $450 an hour) very expensive divorce lawyer, counsel to such luminaries as Robin Givens, Lisa Gastineau, and Nancy Capasso, calls himself "more Victorian than a feminist." He does not approve of "this equality business" in divorce courts and probably does not share Betty Levinson's vision of sexual justice. But he agrees that women are more hurt by divorce and they feel the loss of marriage more acutely.

A woman has more invested in marriage, he says: "It's her whole life. Divorce is less "disruptive" for men because they "maintain dual and triple lives." They're also less likely to be satisfied with family life and more likely to stray: "Men live in this Tom Ewell dream world of the seven-year itch."

Some men, he might have added, and maybe even some women. Committing to a relationship and suffering the loss of it are not exclusively female activities, like childbirth and menstruation. Some men share what Felder considers a feminine ideal of raising a family and coming home to it every night. "Did you ever consider getting divorced?" I asked a man who has been married nearly fifty years. "What for?" he laughed. "What for?"

But Felder probably doesn't see many men like this. What he apparently sees instead are men who stay married out of spite. If women are terrified by divorce, he suggests, they're also "terrorized" into not divorcing: "I see it all the time, you know. 'Nobody will want you. What are you gonna do out there? You'll be back in the Bronx with one pair of bloomers.' "

Even economically independent women are "pushed around" by their husbands. "You'd be shocked at what goes on in their home lives," Felder says. "They're nothing but Geisha girls in their home lives. . . . It's part of the institutionalized terror that women undergo in our society."

Institutionalized terror? Maybe he suspects he's talking to a feminist. Maybe he's being chivalrous. Felder is courtly, courteous, and very accessible. He has been profiled in *GQ, Vanity*

Fair, and *People* and poked at in *SPY;* he writes his own column for *Fame* and surely does not want for publicity. But he sets aside two and a half hours in the middle of a day for an interview and is eager to talk about issues—"Women's problems, children's problems, the crisis in the courts . . . the expense, the delay, the perversion of the system by lawyers; they've made an orgy out of discovery."

Felder is known less for his stand on the issues than for his eccentricities—a penchant for posing in safari suits and collecting expensive slippers—and for his celebrity clientele. He wants to be "number one" in his very competitive and acrimonious profession ("Divorce lawyers are among the most suspicious, quasi-paranoid, and hostile people," he says, but "who wants to be number 622?"). Still, Felder complains about being regarded as a "lawyer/celebrity," instead of a lawyer. He doesn't want to be known simply for "after-dinner stories," and he doesn't tell me any. "It's a pleasure not being asked how many slippers I have," he says when I leave.

Law is a dissonant profession. Lawyers are supposed to represent people they don't like who take actions of which they don't approve, and Felder has his share of contradictions. If his flashy image (surely cultivated) cloaks concern about substantive issues, it contrasts sharply with his essential conservatism. Divorce has made him rich and famous, but Felder views it as a sort of moral failure. Married for twenty-three years to Myrna Felder, a prominent appellate lawyer, he views marriage as "something that has to endure."

"The worst marriage is better than the best divorce, putting aside physical brutality," he says, because every divorce "is built upon the bones of failure." Even a bad marriage represents "some constancy in life." His own parents had "not a good marriage," Felder says, but he is grateful they did not divorce and believes that "by the end of their lives," they were too. "I don't think many couples end up as two hateful people cursing each other across wheelchairs," he explains.

Felder worries about marriage becoming "a transient state of grace, an institution with thinner walls around it." He does not believe law should facilitate divorce and does not like the trend toward no-fault. It is a "breakdown" in moral standards "to say you can get in and out of a marriage. . . . Cardinal Cooke and I were the only ones who favored the old law. I would keep fault in the law. In life, there is a right and wrong."

In marriage, there are many, but rights and wrongs are becoming increasingly irrelevant to divorce. Fault may still limit your right to get divorced in New York (if your spouse doesn't agree to a divorce, you need grounds to obtain one), but it does not affect the distribution of property, except when it's particularly aggrievous. (What is aggrievous fault? Only "extraordinary" and "uncivilized" acts, like hiring someone to murder your wife, according to a leading New York case.) Mundane abuses and infidelities are not relevant to the distribution of property. There are no price tags on betrayal and bad faith in marriage.

How could there be, attorney Katherine Thompson wonders. Thompson shows me her tissue box and tries to describe the emotional devastation of a sudden, unwanted divorce.

Imagine this: You've just celebrated your fifth anniversary with a bottle of Verve Cliquot and a toast to your fiftieth. You've bought your first co-op. You're smiling at babies on buses. Your spouse falls in love with someone else.

"Unless you've experienced it, I don't think you can imagine the devastation," Thompson says. "Somebody you thought was the greatest thing in the world says, 'I no longer love you.' You thought forever was forever. What remedy can you get?"

What you get, if you're lucky and have a good lawyer, is a fair share of the marital estate and a layer of cynicism about love. What you don't get is recognized by law as a person in pain.

"I have a couple of cases in which the husband is leading a double life," Betty Levinson says. "There's another relationship in another city, another apartment. . . . It's absolutely devastating. And you know what's more devastating? To say to the woman who didn't know, it just doesn't matter. Who cares? The judge doesn't care. The lawyer doesn't care. Nobody cares."

Levinson believes the spouse at fault, who wants the divorce, should pay for it. Peter Bronstein suggests that New York has got fault the wrong way 'round; he proposes no-fault divorce and a fault-based distribution of property, ensuring "economic compensation for someone who's been wronged."

Economic compensation for essentially incompensable injuries is familiar enough in tort law. Courts have long put prices on arms and legs and children's lives. People are regularly required to pay for the devastation they cause. Should adultery, mental cruelty, and other sorrows they inflict on their spouses be treated as torts? If there is no justice for an injured spouse (no remedy for being unloved), there might at least be some revenge.

But courts are anxious to get out of the business of determining guilt and innocence in marital relationships, and many lawyers are too. "Who cares?" attorney Bob Cohen asks. "What some woman says about her husband—he didn't pay attention to me after my operation—who cares?" And who can quantify the pain of being ignored? "The emotional and psychic damage in a marriage is very hard to prove," Raoul Felder says. "Subtleties are not within the wherewithal of the courts. Courts love broken fingers."

No-fault divorce was appealing precisely because it relieved the courts of assessing psychic damages and deciding who did what to whom. It could not, of course, relieve the agony of divorce for people in the midst of it. But, ideally, no-fault divorce is reasonably dignified and rational. Ideally, each side is well represented, courts make fair property settlements, and injured spouses can find more appropriate forums in which to rage.

"Courts have no business in the divorce business at all," Raoul Felder believes, despite his opposition to no-fault and his view of divorce as a moral issue. "They're mucking about in the business of the human heart. . . . This is a barbaric way to resolve a dispute between a husband and wife, in divorce court."

There are probably no gentle ways to divorce, only relatively civil ones, like mediation. But mediation works only for people who agree to agree. It also works best in simpler cases, lawyers suggest; they claim that mediators often lack the resources and expertise to structure complex settlements. The less barbaric way preferred by lawyers is the way of prenuptial agreements, which are essentially agreements to disagree.

Like most high-end divorce lawyers, Raoul Felder prepares a lot of prenuptial agreements, intended partly to stop courts "mucking about" in divorce. Prenuptials are private marriage contracts, sanctioned by law. (Postnuptials are permitted too.) If you don't like the rules governing property distribution and maintenance the state has written, you can write your own, as wealthy people often do. At the high end, divorce has been privatized.

Prenuptials don't eliminate litigation, but they do limit it. An angry spouse can still "shlep you around in court," challenging the validity of an agreement, Felder says, but either an agreement is enforceable or it's not, and courts in New York favor enforcement. "Courts like finality," Bob Cohen says. "If you sign a prenuptial knowingly, willingly, with all the dressings, you're stuck with it."

Felder calls prenuptials the "wave of the future. Everybody should have one," middle-class couples as well as rich ones. Middle-class people "can least afford divorce," and, he adds, they may not be middle class forever, or so they hope: "Everyone believes, like Tiny Tim, he has prospects. This is America. . . . Nobody wants to start with the proposition he's gonna be a waiter all his life. He thinks he's gonna own the restaurant."

There is a caveat, Felder notes: "Prenuptials are pretty much exploitation devices for men against women," since men who have money usually demand them of women who don't. But women are free not to marry men intent on exploiting them, as some discover: engagements break off over prenuptials. They cause "a lot of rancor," they're disquieting for the "nonmoneyed spouse," attorney Katherine Thompson says. " 'Trust me,' people say. 'Marriage is based on trust.' "

Not completely. Marriage is based on law, governed by law; it's an economic partnership under law. When you marry, you sign a contract you've probably never read, written by the state. Why not write your own?

"People don't find it romantic," Thompson says. "Men think 'If I tell her I want a prenuptial, she'll think I don't love her.' " People don't like prenuptials, Betty Levinson says, because "love and law don't mix"; but neither, sometimes, do love and marriage.

Love is a private mystery and marriage a very public institution. You marry to protect your children and establish property rights—to make sure you have a claim to your apartment if he leaves, or dies, and social security benefits as a surviving spouse. One price you pay is privacy, and you pay it when the partnership dissolves. Divorce is a painful ritual of public recriminations.

It's always been difficult to reconcile ideals of love and marriage with matrimonial law. The notion that the state should not interfere in family relationships is fundamental. But families break down. When they do, familial autonomy is superseded by the state's interest in regulating conflicts between family members—protecting children and battered women, or writing rules about divorce.

The rules have changed considerably in the past ten years, partly because of feminism, partly because the rise in divorce during the 1960s and 1970s made it visible, transforming broken homes, displaced homemakers, and their children into pervasive public problems for law to solve. Law can alleviate some of them, by introducing some justice into divorce, equitably dividing property, and somehow deciding custody. Justice ought to determine divorce's economic consequences, but it deals clumsily, or not at all, with its emotional ones.

Divorce is still a private disaster as well as a public problem, the end of a love affair as well as a marriage. Everybody knows a dreadful divorce story—her own or someone else's. Being lied to and left after five years or thirty-five is devastating. (Lawyers talk a lot about devastation.) Leaving a bad marriage is wrenching. Being suddenly alone is terrifying. Fighting over your children is only less awful than losing them.

Everybody knows a divorce story. Divorce is a mundane affliction, the subject of a million self-help books. Divorce is an industry, for therapists, writers, and talk show hosts, as well as lawyers. People learn to "mourn" their marriages, to "share," and "communicate" their pain; but in the end they're left alone with it. In the end, they're scarred and mystified. "All women are sadists or masochists," a divorced man I knew once said, as if sex determined character, as if there were a simple explanation for emotional intrigues, unholy alliances, and the occasional horrors of human relations.

LAYING DOWN THE LAW ON SEX

(*March 1982*)

The French prostitute strike began in Lyons on June 2, 1975. Angered and frightened by the brutal murders of several local prostitutes and increased police harassment of women on the street, more than one hundred Lyons hookers quietly entered and began occupying the Church of Saint Nivier. They sought sanctuary from prison, an end to the issuance of fines for soliciting, and nothing less than a change in the public's attitude toward the women who worked at prostitution. "We are mothers talking to you," they said in their first statement. "If we are prostitutes, it is not because we are depraved; it is the way we have found to deal with the problems in our lives."

In six days, the strike had spread to Paris; prostitutes in Marseilles, Grenoble, Toulouse, and Cannes were occupying churches, demanding the right to work. The media and the feminist community responded eagerly: journalists, film crews, and women's groups converged on Lyons (Simone de Beauvoir paid a visit in support of the strike). The women at Saint Nivier debated their issues with the public, gave interviews, and issued statements. The government response was less sympathetic: one week after the strike began, it was ended by police, who raided the church and dragged the women back onto the street.

Prostitutes: Our Life begins with this account of the strike; it includes autobiographical monologues by six of the women who occupied Saint Nivier and supplementary statements on the rights of prostitutes from the English Collective of Prostitutes and COYOTE. The book is an uneven, hybrid collection of confessional conversation and political rhetoric: prostitutes talk about their personal backgrounds, their work experiences, their feelings about themselves and the men they service; prostitute/organizers state their doctrine on the rights of women to control their own bodies and earn the livings of their choice, insisting that women turn to prostitution out of economic necessity and, of course, that prostitution is no different from waitressing, office work, or wifehood.

Fortunately, between the memoirs and the manifestos there is straightforward information about prostitution laws; and laws regulating private, consensual sex that are directed almost exclusively against women speak for themselves of injustice. The book succeeds, finally, as a passionate argument for decriminalization: filled with the righteous anger of women wronged and the poignant appeals of the Lyons strikers for personal recognition and social acceptance, it makes clear the awful, intrusive effect of the law on the lives of female prostitutes.

Whatever may be said about prostitution—that it is sexual bondage or sexual liberation—it is, after all, a job that women have a right to choose. What the women at Saint Nivier demanded was their civil right to work without being isolated and stigmatized for what they do: "Being a prostitute is a way of being seen as different, being rejected." "We're like people's bad consciences." "People want prostitutes to exist, but they don't want them to have the means to work. They don't want to see us in their field of vision, in everyday life."

In France, prostitution itself is not against the law; women are, instead, prosecuted for "any act leading to its practice": soliciting is a crime punishable by fines or incarceration, but prostitutes are not permitted to advertise their services in newspapers or magazines. They are not permitted to rent hotel rooms, apartments, or even cars for use in their work. Once convicted of soliciting, a woman is booked and forever labeled a "known prostitute": she loses her social status and, sometimes, the custody of her children; she cannot enter into relationships or spend her money as she chooses (any man or woman with whom she lives or shares her "immoral earnings" risks prosecution for pimping). She cannot live, work, or even walk where she chooses: one Saint Nivier woman tells of being evicted from her apartment because she is a prostitute and "morally unacceptable" to her neighbors; prostitutes are not permitted even to enter certain neighborhoods, whether or not they are soliciting.

These are laws that lend themselves to arbitrary, harsh, and heavy-handed enforcement. What exactly does any woman on the street have to do to "incite" a man "to debauchery" and be guilty of soliciting? (What does a woman on a New York City street have to do to indicate to a police officer that she is "loitering for purposes of prostitution"?) At the very least, "known" prostitutes will be arrested or fined for simply appearing in public:

"In the evening in Lyons, all the cops and all the squads come and make their little rounds. It's hunt the fine. It's their big game, their hobby, their idea of fun. They cart us off on the slightest pretext, pin fines on us even when we're at home, stick them on our windows."

"Two, three, four times a day, cops . . . would hunt down their prey. For them it was precisely a hunt, they were playing cowboys and Indians. 'We have to collect at least thirty fines a day,' a young inspector admitted to some prostitutes. . . ."

In Manhattan, prostitutes are routinely rounded up by police officers assigned to the Public Morals Division (PMB—the "Pussy Squad"). In 1980, in midtown Manhattan alone, more than one thousand women were arrested for prostitution or loitering for purposes of prostitution; arrest for these women generally means a day or so of prearraignment detention, plea to a boilerplate complaint, and a fine (the cost of doing business) or, occasionally, a prison sentence.

There are no reliable estimates of the cost to the criminal justice system of processing these cases, but the folly of prosecuting prostitutes in criminal court has long been officially recognized. In 1979, a Special Committee of the Association of the Bar of the City of New York recommended decriminalizing prostitution, noting that 10 percent of all arrests in New York County were prostitution related: the committee called these arrests a "futile exercise" in "turnstile enforcement," and suggested that the system's resources would be better spent on violent crimes.

Today, in New York, prostitution is popularly considered a quality-of-life crime, a violation of some vaguely defined right to walk down the street in peace and a dangerous nuisance in residential neighborhoods. The bar committee cited the "severe impact" of prostitution and soliciting on many of the city's business and residential communities and suggested exploring alternative ways of regulating it, through zoning, public health, and safety laws. Presumably, they were talking about legalization (not decriminalizing, but regulating prostitution), which has always seemed such a good, "progressive" alternative for the rest of us.

For prostitutes, however, legalization is a nightmare: restrictive zoning and prohibitions on soliciting effectively deprive them of the right to even walk through certain neighborhoods; licensing and registration requirements, mandatory medical examinations, and consignment to legal brothels feel to them like a kind of sexual bondage—"just like the army." "We'd become workers"—for the state—"skilled workers of sex."

The Lyons women prefer working the street, risking fines and imprisonment, to working in brothels. On the street, they're free—to choose and refuse their own clients, set their own prices, and keep all the money they earn. Brothels, they say, are like prisons, where they are "at the mercy of the client and the madam." Their indictment of brothel life is persuasive:

"In a brothel you can't stop for a minute, like you can on the street. . . . I must have done over one hundred clients a day, I worked fifteen hours a day."

"You couldn't refuse a guy. . . . You felt you were gradually turning into a sex machine, a robot, you stopped thinking. . . . You no longer existed."

Most brothels work on a voucher system, so that the women never see the money they earn, of which they receive only a small cut. Germany's legal "Eros Centers," described as "hooker supermarkets," slick showcase complexes where women employees are displayed, are examples of "high-powered . . . industrialized pimping." The state taxes the brothel management, which in turn taxes the women workers: "Everyone divides up the cake, almost scientifically, like an industry, with the smallest share going to the girls, of course."

Formulating an alternative to criminalizing prostitution that respects both the rights of individual prostitutes and the concerns of residential neighborhoods is a formidable, practical challenge. But isolating the governing legal principle is easy: it is simply not the business of government to regulate private, consensual sex. We should hardly have to romanticize or defend prostitution to recognize that prostitutes have rights to work, for themselves, and to walk where they choose. Legalization, involving the exclusive confinement of prostitutes to legal brothels, is assembly-line sexual exploitation of women, state-sanctioned pimping on the grand scale. Criminal prohibition of prostitution and soliciting, leading to the arrests of thousands of women each year (and virtually none of their male customers), is criminal sexual harassment. It is also a senseless and cynical waste of time and money; no one expects the criminal law to deter or effectively control prostitution.

The implacable resistance to changing a system that is almost universally acknowledged to be completely ineffectual, as well as expensive, is telling: prostitution, like pornography, abortion, and other sex-related issues, is rarely debated with any sense or objectivity. Laws regulating or prohibiting prostitution rarely serve legitimate public interests; they are designed to punish women who charge for their services and keep them in their place. Prostitution laws are not conceived with any rational purpose; they will not be changed by any rational argument.

What's interesting is that the intellectual dishonesty and defensiveness that has shaped public policy toward prostitution is, in some ways, shared by prostitutes themselves. It is evident in this book that the rhetoric with which they justify themselves, comparing their work to other female service jobs, does not reflect what they feel. Being a prostitute is *not* the same as being a secretary; the voices of the Lyons women attest to the differences, and to the line a woman crosses when she sells herself not metaphorically, but in fact:

"The first time you tell yourself, 'Well it won't kill me,' and you try and make light of it. You tell yourself that if other women have done it you must be able to do it too. . . . You make light of it, you try to condition yourself to it inside, and yet the first time it really is horrible."

"It was something impossible, something you'd never do, out of bounds. It was like diving off the deep end."

It is, after all, relatively easy for a secretary to separate herself from her work—her typing, shorthand, or even coffee-making skills. For a prostitute, it's a deeper and more destructive struggle to "hold back my own body, my own body, the one that's real":

"Gradually it becomes routine, so you find ways of distancing yourself from it. You find escape routes, blinkers, drugs. . . . Everyone finds their own way of coping, but you never really get used to it. Sometimes on the street or with a client you have awful, painful moments."

The women in this book who talk about their experiences as prostitutes give the lie not only to their own political rhetoric but also to the rhetoric of much pornography, which sells prostitution as the ultimate in sexual liberation. Prostitutes do not do it for pleasure. ("It kind of kills you but it's over fast.") Most of them talk about the need to develop a "second skin" for their work. Generally, they have nothing but contempt for their johns; they get nothing but contempt back:

"Some days, I just don't understand what they've come looking for; it takes four minutes, it's over and done with very quickly. Then I think I'm selling thin air, that what they've bought is the fact of going to bed with a prostitute. What they've bought is being able to pay us, a piece of degradation, our degradation."

There is a sad irony to the prostitute's demand for her legal right to "control" her own body, when it is such a burden to her. "I don't feel free with my body," says one woman. "I feel bad about it. I feel self-conscious. I don't really feel like my body's alive. I think of it more as bruised, as a weight."

The feminist response to prostitution has been, inevitably, both angry and confused. Prostitution is terribly threatening to women: it is too easy to imagine; it is the worst of what feminism struggles to overcome. The rhetoric with which prostitutes defend themselves to other women is provocative because the metaphoric truth of it is profound. When prostitutes insist that they are like other women, that their work is the work of all women, they touch off our deepest fears about ourselves—about what we are or might become. Kate Millett, in *The Prostitution Papers,* summarizes the enmity straight women feel for prostitutes in one line: "You're selling it. I could too, but I won't."

The sexual politics of prostitution are confusing, divisive for legislators, feminists, and prostitutes themselves. Prostitution will always be offensive and disturbing to many—it may even demean urban life. But laws are supposed to protect rights, not sensibilities, and we cannot so readily sacrifice the right of a prostitute to appear on a public street to the outraged demand for a better class of street life. Women are used to being routinely accosted on the street by men who expect to get it for free. Surely, we, at least, can learn to tolerate the mere commercial solicitings of other women.

"It's true that prostitution must disappear but I think that so many things are needed to bring that about that we won't see it happen and neither will our children," one prostitute remarks. "So people could at least try and accept prostitutes. They could at least be ready to look them in the face and acknowledge them. It's the least they could do."

So much law is wishful thinking. Prostitution laws do not even begin to address the problems of prostitution—of systematic sexual and economic exploitation of women, of sexual violence and guilt. The problems are profound; they might at least be debated with some honesty, intellectual integrity, and a little logic, and without confusing public and private questions of what is or ought to be legal and what is or ought to be.

SECOND THOUGHTS ON THE
SECOND AMENDMENT

(January 1995)

Calmly, patiently, with considerable bravery, the instructor at the shooting range shows me how to fire the submachine gun, a MAC 11—the first real gun I have ever held. It jams repeatedly. "That's why they call it a jam-o-matic," someone says. Finally, anticlimactically, like an idiot, I am shooting up the floor (the instructor told me to aim down). Seven or eight men standing behind me await their turns.

The MAC 11—small, relatively lightweight, with little recoil—is less intimidating than the semiautomatic rifles, which I can't quite bring myself to use. I am anxious enough around the handguns. "Lean forward," the instructor keeps telling me, while I lean back, trying to get as far away from the gun as I can. How do thirteen-year-olds do this, I wonder, trying not to hurt myself with the huge, heavy revolver. I jump every time a shot is fired (and can't wait for the guys to stop playing with the machine gun). I can barely get the slide back on one of the semiautomatics. But I'm pleased when I hit the target with the nine-millimeter Glock, the only one of these guns I can imagine being able to use. And when someone offers me a casing from the Walther PPK I've just shot (James Bond's gun, everyone points out), I pocket it.

I've been invited to the shooting range to "observe and try out the right to bear arms in action," along with about fifteen other participants in a two-day seminar on guns and the Constitution, sponsored by Academics for the Second Amendment. Funded partly by the National Rifle Association, Academics for the Second Amendment isn't exactly a collection of academic gun nuts—most of its approximately 650 members aren't academics, and its president, Joseph Olson, an NRA board member and a professor at Hamline Law School, in Minnesota, seems a rational, open-minded man. But the organization is engaged in a genteel lobbying effort to popularize what many liberals consider the gun nut's view of the Second Amendment: that it confers an individual right to bear arms, not just the right to bear arms in a well-regulated militia.

Since it was founded, in 1993, Academics for the Second Amendment has held three invitation-only seminars for academics who share its beliefs about the Second Amendment—or might be persuaded to adopt them. Last year I asked permission to attend this conference but was turned down; this year I received an unsolicited invitation, apparently in response to an article in which I had questioned the effectiveness of traditional approaches to gun control.

Don Kates, a San Francisco lawyer, gun aficionado, and the author of numerous articles on guns and the Constitution, leads the seminar energetically, taking only a little time out to show us baby pictures of his parrot. His approach is scattershot, or spray and pray. Ranging over legal, moral, and practical arguments for private gun ownership, he discusses the correlation between guns and crime; self-defense and the alleged deterrent effect of an armed citizenry; difficulties of enforcing gun controls; bigotry against gun owners; and, finally, constitutional rights. Comments by participants are sometimes sensible and occasionally insane: one man proclaims that mothers should give guns to children who attend dangerous public schools.

"What would you do if you had a fourteen-year-old kid who felt he needed a gun for self-defense?" he asks me repeatedly.

"I'd take him out of school before giving him a gun."

"You can't take him out of school, that's against the law," he responds—as if giving a fourteen-year-old a gun to carry were legal.

"I'd join with other mothers in the district to demand that the school install weapons detectors and hire security guards."

He shakes his head and smiles.

Why should a good kid give up his gun while the bad kids are still carrying? To some advocates of gun ownership, gun prohibitions are, at best, naïve demands for unilateral disarmament. When you're talking about fourteen-year-olds, considering the blind impulsiveness of adolescents and increasing juvenile gun violence, this reliance on mutually assured deterence is Strangelovian. MAD requires what frightened children lack—the sobriety and self-control not to destroy yourself in order to destroy your enemy. But, even among putative gun nuts, there is relatively little support for the rights of juveniles to own guns, or opposition to juvenile gun bans. Opposition to gun prohibitions focuses on attempts to disarm more or less sane, law abiding adults, deemed endowed with both natural and constitutional rights to self-defense against criminals and despots, as well as a practical need to bear arms.

Like moral and legal claims about gun owners' rights, the practical consequences of widespread gun ownership are highly debatable. No one can say with any certainty whether it increases violence or decreases crime. Don Kates speculates that magically reducing the estimated 200 million firearms in circulation to five million would have virtually no reductive effect on the crime rate: According to a 1983 National Institute of Justice (NIJ) funded study by James D. Wright, Peter H. Rossi, and Kathleen Daly, about 1 percent of privately owned firearms are involved in criminal activity, arguably suggesting that eliminating 99 percent of the nation's guns would not ameliorate crime. Or would it? Philip Cook, an economist at Duke University and a leading researcher on gun violence, considers Kates's speculation about the uselessness of reducing the number of guns "patently absurd." We can't predict which guns will be used in crimes, even if a relatively small number are used feloniously overall, he notes, and reducing the availability of guns would raise their price to adult felons as well as juveniles. Even if a drastic reduction in the number of guns wouldn't necessarily decrease crime, it would decrease fatalities. Guns are particularly lethal, Cook has stressed: the "fraction of serious gun assaults that result in the victim's death is much higher than that of assaults with other weapons." Since not all gun homicides reflect a clearly formulated intent to kill, Cook reasons, access to guns can increase the lethality of assaults. A decrease in the use of guns, however, may lead to an increase in nonfatal injuries. Robberies committed with guns tend to involve less violence because the victims are less likely to resist. (Victims who do resist robbers armed with guns are more likely to be killed.)

Further complicating the relationship between guns, crime, and violence are the possible deterent effects of armed victims and the use of guns by crime victims acting in self-defense. A 1986 survey of felons, by James D. Wright and Peter H. Rossi, suggests that many avoid attacking victims perceived to be armed, and many opponents of stringent gun controls believe that gun ownership actually keeps the crime rate down. Deterrence, however, is extremely difficult to measure, partly because it can't be measured by counting the number of known attacks: at issue are attacks that never occurred. The incidence of self-defense is also unclear. Estimates of the number of people who successfully use guns to protect themselves against crime vary wildly. Using government crime surveys, Philip Cook determined that firearms are used in self-defense in 78,000 incidents annually. Using private surveys that ask people about their defensive use of guns, Florida State University criminologist Gary

Kleck reported that some 700,000 people armed with guns ward off would be attackers every year.

Cook's estimates may be too low, according to the National Research Council, because the government surveys he uses exclude and undercount certain crimes. Kleck's figures may be too high because, like surveys of sexual behavior, surveys of people who use guns in self-defense rely on self-reporting. People probably lie about their adventures with firearms as much as they lie about their adventures in bed, either bragging about what they view as exploits or concealing what they fear are transgressions. Or they make mistakes. You can swear that you've never committed adultery if he never told you he was married, just as you can insist that you successfully defended your family against a burglar when you heard a noise late at night, ventured outside with your gun, fired a shot in the air and chased off a querelous squirrel.

Debates about gun ownership and gun control are driven more by values and ideology than by pragmatism—much less empirical research, which is complex and inconclusive. Wright, Rossi, and Daly reported that there is not even any "suggestive evidence" showing that "gun ownership, among the population as a whole is, per se, an important cause of criminal violence." Evidence that guns deter criminal violence is equally insubstantial, they added, as is evidence that additional gun controls would reduce crime. Many are already in place and barely, if ever, enforced; or they make no sense.* In 1983 Wright, Rossi, and Daly concluded that the "probable benefits of stricter gun controls in terms of crime reduction are at best uncertain, and at worst close to nil."

Empirical data is irrelevant, or at least peripheral, to legal debates about the existence of constitutional rights. But the paucity of proof that gun controls ameliorate crime is partic-

---

* The federal ban on "assault weapons," for example, applies to a select group of semi-automatic rifles that differ only cosmetically from rifles to which the ban does not apply.

ularly galling to people who believe they have a fundamental right to bear arms. In theory, at least, we restrict constitutional rights only when the costs of exercising them seem unbearably high. In fact, we argue continually about what those costs are: Does violence in the media cause violence in real life? Did release of the Pentagon Papers clearly endanger the national security? Does hate speech constitute discrimination? In the debate about firearms, however, we can't even agree on the principles governing restrictions on guns, because we can't agree about the right to own them.

How could we, given the competing values at stake—the right of self-defense and demands for public safety—and the opacity of the constitutional text? The awkwardly drafted Second Amendment doesn't quite make itself clear: "A well-regulated Militia, being necessary to the security of a free State, the right of the people to keep and bear Arms shall not be infringed." Is the reference to a militia a limitation on the right to bear arms or merely an explanation of an armed citizenry's role in a government by consent? There is little dispute that one purpose of the Second Amendment was to ensure that the people would be able to resist a central government should it ever devolve into despotism. But there is little agreement about what that capacity for resistance entails—armed citizens acting under the auspices of state militias, or armed citizens able to organize and act on their own. And there is virtually no consensus about the constitutional right to own a gun in the interests of individual self-defense against crime, rather than communal defense against tyranny. Is defense of the state, and of the common good, the raison d'être of the Second Amendment or merely one use of it?

■　■　■

The Supreme Court has never answered these fundamental questions about the constitutional uses of guns. It has paid little attention to the Second Amendment, providing little guidance to the gun control debate. The two late-nineteenth-century cases involving the Second Amendment are more about federalism than about the right to bear arms. *Presser* v. *Illinois,* decided in 1886, involved a challenge to a state law prohibiting private citizens from organizing their own military units and parades. The Court held that the Second Amendment was a limitation on federal, not state, power, reflecting the prevailing view (now discredited) that the Bill of Rights in general applied only to Congress, not to the states. A hundred years ago the Court did not apply the First Amendment to the states either. *Presser* followed *U.S.* v. *Cruikshank,* which held held that the federal government could not protect people from private infringement of their rights to assemble and bear arms. This ruling, essentially concerned with limiting federal police power, invalidated the federal prosecution of participants in the lynching of two black men. Decided in 1876, *Cruikshank* is virtually irrelevant to Second Amendment debates today, although it has been cited for the proposition that an oppressed minority has a compelling need (or a natural right) to bear arms in self-defense.

The primary Supreme Court decision on the Second Amendment was *U.S.* v. *Miller,* a less-than-definitive holding cited approvingly by both sides in the gun control debate. *Miller* involved a prosecution under the 1934 National Firearms Act. Jack Miller and his accomplice had been convicted of transporting an unregistered sawed-off shotgun across state lines. In striking down their Second Amendment claim, and upholding their conviction, the Court noted that no evidence had been presented that a shotgun was, in fact, a militia weapon, implying that the Second Amendment could protect the right to bear arms suitable for use in a militia.

Advocates of gun control or prohibition like the Miller case because it makes the right to bear arms dependent on at least the possibility of service in a militia. They cite the Court's declaration that the Second Amendment was obviously intended to "assure the continuation of and render possible the effectiveness" of state militias; they place less emphasis on the Court's apparent willingness to permit private citizens to possess military weapons. Citing *Miller,* a dealer at a gun show told me that the Second Amendment protects ownership only of such devices as machine guns, stingers, and grenade throwers. But advocates of gun ownership don't generally emphasize this awkward implication of *U.S.* v. *Miller* any more than their opponents do: it could lead to prohibitions on handguns. They like the *Miller* decision because it delves into the history of the Second Amendment and stresses that for the framers, the militia "comprised all males physically capable of acting in concert for the common defense."

This view of the militia as an inchoate citizen's army, not a standing body of professionals, is central to the claim that the Second Amendment protects the rights of individual civilians, not simply the right of states to organize and arm the National Guard. And, in fact, fear and loathing of standing armies did underlie the Second Amendment, which was at least partly intended to ensure that states would be able to call up individual citizens in defense against a tyrannical central government. (Like the Bill of Rights in general, the Second Amendment was a response to concerns about federal abuses of power.) James Madison, who authored the Second Amendment, invoked the potential force of a citizen militia as a guarantee against a federal military coup:

> Let a regular army, fully equal to the resources of the country, be formed; and let it be entirely at the devotion of the federal government: still it would not be going too far to say that the State governments with the people on their side would be able to repel the danger. To (the regular army) would be opposed a militia amounting to near half a million of citizens with arms in their hands, officered by men chosen from among themselves, fighting

for their common liberties and united and conducted by governments possessing their affection and confidence. It may well be
doubted whether a militia thus circumstanced could ever be con-
quered by such a proportion of regular troops. Those who are best
acquainted with the late successful resistance of this country
against the British arms will be most inclined to deny the possibility of it. Besides the advantage of being armed, which the
Americans possess over the people of almost every other nation,
the existence of subordinate governments, to which the people are
attached and by which the militia officers are appointed, forms a
barrier against the enterprises of ambition, more insurmountable
than any which a simple government of any form can admit of.

This passage from the *Federalist Papers* is enthusiastically cited
by advocates of the right to bear arms, because it supports their
notion of the militia as the body of people, privately armed; but
it's also cited by their opponents, because it suggests that the
militia is activated and "conducted" by the states, and it stresses
the "attachment" of citizens to their local governments. The
colonial militia was "an organized military force, not an ad hoc
group of armed individuals," Dennis Henigan, a handgun control advocate, has argued.

That Madison's reflection on the militia and the Supreme
Court's holding in *U.S. v. Miller* can be cited with some accuracy
by both sides in the debate testifies to the hybrid nature of
Second Amendment rights. The Second Amendment presumes
(as did the framers) that private citizens will possess private arms;
Madison referred offhandedly to "the advantage of being armed,
which the Americans possess." But Madison also implied that the
right to bear arms is based on the obligation of citizens to band
together as a militia to defend the common good, as opposed to
the prerogative of citizens to take up arms individually in pursuit
of self-interest and happiness.

■ ■ ■

The tension at the heart of the Second Amendment, which makes it so difficult to construe, is the tension between republicanism (marked by commitment to the general welfare) and liberal individualism. (Put very simply, republicanism calls for the subordination of individual interests to the public good; liberalism focuses on protecting individuals against popular conceptions of the good.) A growing body of scholarly literature on the Second Amendment locates the right to bear arms in republican theories of governance. In a 1989 article in the *Yale Law Journal* that helped animate a Second Amendment debate, the University of Texas law professor Sanford Levinson argued that the Second Amendment confers an individual right to bear arms so that, in the republican tradition, armed citizens might rise up against an oppressive state. Wendy Brown, a professor of women's studies at the University of California, and David C. Williams, a law professor at Cornell University, have questioned the uses of a republican right to bear arms in a society that lacks republican virtue—namely, the willingness to put communal interests first. Progun activists don't generally acknowledge the challenge posed by republicanism to the individualist culture that many gun owners inhabit. They embrace republican justifications for gun ownership, stressing the use of arms in defending the community, at the same time that they stress the importance of guns in protecting individual autonomy.

Advocates of the right to bear arms insist that the Second Amendment is rooted in both collective and individual rights of self-defense—against political oppression and crime—without recognizing how those rights conflict. The republican right to resist oppression is the right of the majority, or the people, not the right of a small religious cult in Waco, Texas, or of a few survivalist tax protesters in Idaho. They have individual rights against the government, state and federal. (Both the American Civil Liberties Union and the NRA protested the government's actions in Waco and its attack on white separatist Randy Weaver and his family.) But refuseniks and refugees from society are not republicans. They do not constitute the citizen militia envisioned by the framers, any more than they stand for the American community; indeed, they stand against it—withdrawing from the body politic, asserting their rights to alienation and anomie or membership in exclusionary alternative communities of their own. Republicanism can't logically be invoked in the service of libertarianism. It elevates civic virtue over individualism, consensus over dissent.

Nor can social contract theory readily be invoked in support of a right to arm yourself in a war against street crime, despite the claims of some gun ownership advocates. The right or power to enforce criminal laws is precisely what you give up when you enter an ordered civil society. Self-help is the price of the social contract. "God hath certainly appointed Government to restrain the violence and partiality of man," John Locke wrote. A person may always defend his or her life when threatened, but only when there is no chance to appeal to the law. If a man points his sword at me and demands my purse, Locke explained, I may kill him. But if he steals my purse by stealth and then raises a sword to defend it, I cannot use force to get it back. "My life not being in danger, I may have the *benefit of appealing* to the Law, and have Reparation for my 100 pounds that way."

Locke was essentially drawing a line between self-defense and vigilantism, which many gun owners would no doubt respect. Others would point to the inability of the criminal justice system to avenge crimes and provide reparation to victims, asserting a right to engage in self-help. Social contract theory, however, might suggest that if the government is no longer able to provide order, or justice, the remedy is not vigilantism but revolution; the utter failure of law enforcement is a fundamental breach of trust. And, in fact, there are large pockets of disaffected citizens who do not trust the government to protect them or to provide impartial justice, and who might be persuaded to rise up against it, as evidenced by the disorder that followed the 1992 acquittal of police officers who assaulted Rodney King. Was Los Angeles the scene of a riot or an uprising?

Injustice, and the sense of oppression it spawns, are often matters of perspective—particularly today, when claims of political victimization abound and there is little consensus on the demands of public welfare. We use the term "oppression" promiscuously, to describe any instance of discrimination. In this climate of aggrievement and hyperbole, so many acts of violence are politicized. How do we decide whether an insurrection is just? Don Kates observes that the Second Amendment doesn't exactly confer the right to resist. "It gives you a right to win."

The prospect of armed resistance, however, is probably irrelevant to much public support for gun ownership, which reflects a fear of crime much more than a fear or loathing of government. In the belief that the police can't protect them, people buy guns to protect themselves and their families—not to overthrow or even to thwart the government. Recognizing this, the NRA appeals to fear of crime, particularly crime against women. ("Choose to refuse to be a victim," NRA ads proclaim, showing a woman and her daughter alone in a desolate parking lot at night.) And it has generally countered demands for tougher gun controls not with radical individualist appeals for insurrection but with statist appeals for tougher anticrime laws, notably stringent mandatory-minimum sentences and abolition of parole. There is considerable precedent for the NRA appeal to state authority: founded after the Civil War, with the mission of teaching soldiers to shoot straight, in its early years the NRA was closely tied to the military and dependent on government largesse; until recently it drew considerable support from the police. Today, however, statist anticrime campaigns are mainly matters of politics for the NRA and for gun nuts in general; tough sentencing laws for the criminal use of firearms defuse demands for firearm controls. Personal liberty—meaning the liberty to own guns and use them against the government if necessary—is their passion.

Gun nuts are apt to be extravagantly libertarian when the right to own guns is at stake. At heart many are insurrectionists—at least, they need to feel prepared. Nothing arouses their anger more, I've found, than challenges to the belief that private gun ownership is an essential check on political oppression.*

■　　■　　■

During the two-day seminar held by Academics for the Second Amendment, we argue equanimously about nearly everything—crime control, constitutional rights, and the fairness and feasibility of gun controls—until I question whether, two hundred years after the Revolution, citizens armed with rifles and handguns can effectively resist the federal government. I ask, if Nixon had staged a military coup in 1974—assuming he had military support—instead of resigning the presidency, could the NRA and the nation's various unaffiliated gun owners have stopped him? For the first time in two days Don Kates flares up in anger; the room is incandescent.

"Give me one example from history of a successful government oppression of an armed populace," he rages. The FBI raid on the Koresh compound in Waco, Texas, doesn't count, he says, because Koresh's group was a small, isolated minority. The Civil

*After this article was written in January, 1995, the Oklahoma City bombing brought to light the fierce anti-government fervor of the militia movements.

War doesn't count either. (I can't remember why.) Neither do uprisings in Malaysia and the Philippines. (Nobody mentions Chechnya, which had yet to fall.)

People like me think it is possible to oppose the government only with nuclear weapons, Kates rages, because we're stupid; we don't understand military strategy and the effectiveness of guerrilla warfare, and we underestimate the hesitancy of troops to engage in armed conflict with their fellow citizens. Millions of Americans armed only with pistols and long guns could turn a bloodless coup into a prolonged civil war.

Perhaps. I am almost persuaded that Kates might have a point, until he brings up the Holocaust.

Gun nuts sometimes point out that the Holocaust was preceded by gun control laws that disarmed the Jews and made it easy to round them up. (In an article in *Guns and Ammo,* Jay Simkin, the president of Jews for the Preservation of Firearms, argues that gun control causes genocide. Today he says, "Genocides can be prevented if civilians worldwide own military-type rifles and plenty of ammunition.") Kates doesn't go nearly this far, but he does point out that genocides are difficult to predict. At the turn of the century, you would not have predicted the Holocaust, he reminds me, and today you can't predict what holocausts may occur in the next fifteen or fifty years. I give up. "If millions are slaughtered in the next fifty years because of gun control laws," I declare, exasperated, "let their deaths be on my head."

"It's very interesting that you say that," Kates concludes, a bit triumphantly, as if, in all seriousness, I have acknowledged that regulating the private ownership of guns risks genocide.

Kates apologizes later for his outburst, and in a subsequent phone conversation he acknowledges that "the Holocaust was not an event where guns would have mattered; the force was overwhelming." But guns might matter to a Serbian woman who shoots a Bosnian soldier breaking into her house, he suggests;

and if there were a Second Amendment in Serbia, it would protect her.

Zealots in the progun camp (Kates is not exactly among them) seem to identify with the Serbian woman defending her home. They fear attack by the federal government. "Using a national epidemic of crime and violence as their justification, media pundits and collectivist politicians are aggressively campaigning to disarm private citizens and strengthen federal law enforcement powers," proclaims a special edition of the *New American,* a magazine on sale at a gun show. After gun control, the editors suggest, the greatest threat to individual liberty is the Clinton plan for providing local police departments with federal assistance. "Is it possible that some of those who are advocating a disarmed populace and a centralized police system have totalitarian designs in mind? It is worth noting that this is exactly what happened in many countries during this century."*

This can be dismissed as ravings on the fringe, but it captures in crazed form the hostility toward a powerful central government that inspired adoption of the Second Amendment right to bear arms two hundred years ago and fires support for it today. Advocates of First Amendment rights, who believe firmly that free speech is both a moral imperative and an instrument of democratic governance, should understand the passion of Second Amendment claims.

They should be sympathetic as well to the more dispassionate constitutional arguments of gun owners. Civil libertarians who believe that the Bill of Rights in general protects individuals have a hard time explaining why the Second Amendment protects only groups. They have a hard time reconciling their opposition to prohibitions of problematic behavior, such as drug use, with their support for the prohibition of guns. (Liberals tend to de-

* Rhetoric like this surfaced publicly after the Oklahoma City bombing.

monize guns and gun owners the way conservatives demonize drugs and pornography and the people who use them.) In asserting that the Second Amendment provides no individual right to bear arms or that the right provided is anachronistic and not worth its cost, civil libertarians place themselves in the awkward position of denying the existence of a constitutional right because they don't value its exercise.

The civil-libertarian principles at issue in the gun debate are made clear by the rhetoric of First and Second Amendment advocates, which is strikingly similar, as is the rhetoric of their opponents. Pornography rapes, some feminists say. Words oppress, according to advocates of censoring hate speech. "Words Kill," a Planned Parenthood ad declared, following the murders of clinic workers. And all you can say in response is "Words don't kill people; people kill people."

To an antilibertarian, however, the literature sold at gun shows may seem as dangerous as the guns; at a recent gun show I bought *Incendiaries,* an army manual on unconventional warfare; *Exotic Weapons: An Access Book; Gunrunning for Fun and Profit;* and *Vigilante Handbook,* which tells me how to harass, torture, and assassinate people. Should any of this material be censored? If it were, it would be sold on the black market; and the remedy for bad speech is good speech, First Amendment devotees point out. According to Second Amendment supporters, gun control laws affect only law-abiding gun owners, and the best defense against armed criminals is armed victims; the remedy for the bad use of guns in violent crime is the good use of guns in self-defense.

Of course, guns do seem a bit more dangerous than books; but none of our constitutional rights is absolute. Recognizing that the Second Amendment confers an individual right to bear arms would not completely immunize guns from regulation; it would require that the government establish a necessity, not just a desire, to regulate. The majority of gun owners, Don Kates suggests, would be amenable to gun controls, such as waiting periods and even licensing and training requirements, if they didn't perceive them as preludes to prohibition. The irony of the Second Amendment debate is that acknowledging an individual right to bear arms might facilitate gun control more than denying it ever could.

But it will not facilitate civic engagement or the community that Americans are exhorted to seek. The civil-libertarian defense of Second Amendment rights is not a republican one; it does not derive the individual right to bear arms from republican notions of the militia; instead it relies on traditional liberal views of personal autonomy. It is a communitarian nightmare. If the war against crime has replaced the cold war in popular culture, a private storehouse of guns has replaced the fallout shelter in the psyche of Americans who feel besieged. Barricaded, mistrustful of their neighbors, they've sacrificed virtue to fear.

MURDER MOST FEMININE

(*November 1980*)

Murder is not ladylike. The classic prototypical feminine crime is shoplifting—a furtive snatch off a counter, an item quickly secreted in a large handbag. When women are bad, according to prevailing stereotypes, they get sneaky, and their crimes are nonviolent crimes of deception. Violence and aggression are commonly identified as uniquely masculine characteristics; women who kill deviate from sexual as well as moral codes of behavior.

Ann Jones begins *Women Who Kill* with the thesis that "the story of women who kill is the story of women," and she has written an intelligent, scrupulously researched account of women murderers and murder suspects in America from the colonial period to the present. It is primarily a study of murder within the family: as Jones notes in her foreword, "we women usually kill our intimates: we kill our children, our husbands, our lovers." And, she maintains, in chronicling scores of cases that span three hundred years, men have never really understood why. To admit that a sane, ordinary women has a motive to kill her husband or children is to admit that something is wrong; and to acknowledge that a woman may commit a premeditated murder in her own self-interest is to acknowledge that women will try to take charge of their lives by whatever awful and desperate means are left to them.

Jones suggests that many women have killed to extricate them-selves from unbearable domestic circumstances—to escape mar-riage or motherhood—because neither the law nor their communities would protect or assist them. Historically, there has been no place in society for a poor woman with an illegitimate child, no remedy for a wife beaten or raped by her husband, no opportunity even for divorce. *Women Who Kill* contains a com-pelling indictment of the institution of marriage and the family, highlighted in a quoted passage from a nineteenth-century radi-cal feminist analysis of marriage as the "haphazard" coupling of men and women in often "intolerable" unions of constant physi-cal intimacy, from which the only escape was death. Jones agrees that "the very structure of the institution might make the people within it murderous."

Domestic crimes by women are, in this view, an inevitable outgrowth of their domestic subjugation, and Jones blames the sins of women on patriarchy. Her analysis raises obvious ques-tions about individual responsibility and the morality of violence as a defense or weapon against oppression; at some point, despite our personal and social histories, our acts become our own. But the murders Jones describes sound like futile snatches at sur-vival, and her account of women who commit crimes is also a persuasive account of crimes committed against women.

Infanticide is, perhaps, the most frightening murder of all, the clearest violation of a presumed natural order. Infanticide was apparently not uncommon in colonial America, particularly among poor, unmarried women and girls who sometimes killed their children at birth—a crime for which many of them were hanged. Jones demythologizes the act, without judging it: under colonial law servants were forbidden to marry, and female ser-vants, often impregnated by their masters, faced additional years of servitude and public whippings for bearing out-of-wedlock children; rape was hardly uncommon, birth control was nonexistent, and an out-of-wedlock child was born into a social limbo.

These are the easy cases: a sixteen-year-old "bound" girl who hides alone in a barn to give birth, and smothers her newborn infant, seems almost as much a victim as her child. Not all the homicides described in *Women Who Kill* can so readily be put down to the perpetrator's oppression, and the political perspective of this book does, sometimes, leave more to be said. Take the case of Lydia Sherman, who poisoned six or eight of her grown children and three husbands in a period of seven years, from 1864 to 1871. She killed them because life was hard and they had no money. She killed them when they got sick, to end their suffering. She killed because she was intolerably overburdened, and killing seemed to her the only way out.

It is not enough to suggest, as Jones does, that Sherman was one of a number of women who "put themselves first merely to survive." She appears more like a morally and emotionally stunted woman whose murders seem a child's attempt to make her problems disappear. What is most disturbing about her is the calm, matter-of-fact way in which she dispatched entire families, because she simply did not know what else to do. It seems that for Jones the latter is the point, that Lydia Sherman was not a monster of her own making.

Certainly, women have been treated like children throughout history—denied the right to vote, pursue male professions, enjoy equal rights under the law—and many have learned to play the submissive roles expected of them in order to survive. There are cases reported here in which women, apparently guilty of murder, were acquitted against all the evidence, because, once on trial, they acted like children—like weak, reactive victims of unbearable circumstance, often beset by a sort of temporary insanity. We're told that seduction and insanity became common defenses in nineteenth-century courtrooms for women accused of murdering their husbands or lovers, with the insanity defense often tied to menstruation (women, of course, were naturally hysterical, and the victims even of their own bodies). The most compelling cases described in *Women Who Kill* involve arguably justifiable homicides in which women on trial could not, on pain of certain conviction, stand up in court like rational, adult human beings to admit and explain their acts.

Today, things are supposed to have changed, and a few judges and juries have recognized that a woman may kill a man, justifiably, in self-defense: Joanne Little, in a headline case, was acquitted of murdering the jailer who allegedly raped her; Yvonne Wanrow, who killed and wounded two men to protect herself and her children, was allowed to plead guilty to manslaughter with a promise of probation; and Francine Hughes, a battered wife, was acquitted, by reason of temporary insanity, of murdering the husband who had threatened to kill her (a rather equivocal victory for feminists) who believe that killing an abusive husband is an act of sanity and self-defense.

Jones notes that the publicity surrounding these and similar cases, and an increased awareness of domestic violence, are often presumed to have afforded women new, preventive legal remedies against abusive husbands, so that, unlike Francine Hughes, they will not have to turn to murder to save themselves. But there is little the police can ever do to protect anyone, man or woman, from the threat of violence, and Jones records a backlash against battered women who fight back, reflected in the emergence of claims of allegedly battered husbands—those mythic henpecked men with their fat, rolling-pin-wielding wives. Moreover, she notes, few women are actually acquitted for killing their assaultive spouses, even in the most grievous cases: Bernadette Powell, a battered wife, was recently convicted of second-degree murder in New York State for shooting her ex-husband in a struggle over his gun, while he was holding her hostage in a hotel room. (The district attorney who prosecuted Powell had been divorced by his own wife, in an uncontested proceeding, for brutal and periodic assaults on her.)

We are left with an image of women battered by the law, and Jones asserts, finally, that traditional legal formulations of self-defense should not be applied in cases involving the killing by a woman of her male assailant. She cites the remarkable jury instruction given in the Yvonne Wanrow case, in which the court ruled that, in assessing the reasonableness of Wanrow's perception of danger, the jury had to consider not only the greater physical strength and prowess of her attackers but the effect on her of a "long and unfortunate history of sex discrimination."

This presumably proceeds from the sensible premise that a woman may have a reasonable anticipation of harm when a man does not, because of a history of subordination and physical abuse. Yet, as *a matter of law* it is a troublesome precedent. Social and cultural conditioning undeniably shapes the ways in which men and women interrelate, but it is not a phenomenon for which the law may readily account if it is to maintain standards of individual responsibility. Jones unwittingly advocates, in effect, a system that would assign varying degrees of guilt to people who have committed the same act, according to their historic rank in society. Sex is, after all, only one element in a matrix of pervasive inequalities. How should we juggle all the other variables of race, ethnicity, wealth, and even physical and mental well-being in trying to determine whether someone is guilty of a crime?

Incorporating these considerations into an initial determination of guilt, as she suggests, confuses the trial and sentencing processes. A criminal defendant's personal, racial, or class history may well be appropriately reviewed in fixing a fair and compassionate sentence—but if we look to these criteria in establishing standards of guilt for a jury to consider in reaching a verdict, we may end with no standards at all. Women, as one oppressed class, will be among the first victims of an ad hoc system of justice that defines crimes according to the status of the person accused.

Jones would perhaps counter with the correct assertion that women have often been punished for acts that are perfectly legal or socially acceptable if committed by men. Prostitution laws are a clear example of our double standards—notwithstanding the "John law," women are harassed, arrested, and jailed for selling sex that men are permitted to buy. But to suggest the converse— that women should not be prosecuted as harshly as men for the same acts—is to ask for special "protection" under the law that is the flip side of discrimination.

Unspoken questions of individual guilt and public account-ability underlie every case in *Women Who Kill*. How should the law treat any of these women, given the facts of their case, their social and economic histories, their mental and physical health? Jones does not address this issue directly; instead, she circles around it in an intriguing discussion of the effects of class, sexism, politics, and individual circumstance in each case she presents. Alice Crimmins, a working-class woman, publicly con-demned for "sleeping around," is compared to Candace Mossler, the "beautiful" "lissome blond" whose notorious sexual esca-pades did not prevent her acquittal on the charge of murdering her millionaire husband. Lizzie Borden—who, Jones suggests, was in the end protected by a patriarchal society because it would not bear to admit that a respectable woman of property could murder her father—is compared to Bridget Durgan, an epileptic, half-crazy servant who murdered her mistress in a fit and was hanged for it.

Ann Jones does not judge any of these women, presumably because to her they are all victims, first and foremost; at the heart of this book is a controlled rage against institutionalized injustices perpetrated against women. Still there are lingering questions. What would Jones say about Patty Hearst, jailed for bank robbery in spite of her class, her passive, girlish malleability, and her brainwash defense? What sort of coercion should mitigate criminal responsibility? How do we reconcile the cases of Inez Garcia, cleared of murder charges for killing the man who allegedly raped her, some time after the attack, and John Spinkelink, executed for shooting the male companion who had apparently abused him sexually, stolen his money, and threatened his life? Spinkelink may have been, in part, the victim of death penalty politics that finally demanded the execution of a white male; but perhaps we can also say that because he was identified as a homosexual, Spinkelink was treated by the state as if he were a woman.

NOT A LOVE STORY

(*June 1982*)

*Men have died from time to time and
worms have eaten them, but not for love.*

—*Wm. Shakespeare*

It is not easy to talk about Bonnie Garland's killing. It was a bloody, awful act. You want some distance from it. She was bludgeoned to death in her sleep by her boyfriend Richard Herrin, in the bedroom of her parents' home, five years ago. He broke her skull with a hammer ("Her head split open like a watermelon," he said), and he smashed her larynx—she had been a talented singer.

They had been together for three years in a relationship that should never have been more than a melodrama about rebellious young love. She was rich—the daughter of an upper-class suburban family, a twenty-year-old senior at Yale when she died. He was relatively poor, a Mexican American from East Los Angeles who attended Yale on a full scholarship. Her parents didn't like him. He wanted to marry her. He loved her. He killed her because she wanted to sleep with other men.

Richard sought out a priest several hours after the killing, surrendered to police, and signed a full voluntary confession the

236

following day. His friends from the Yale community and the Catholic Church immediately formed a highly effective defense fund for him, secured his release on bail, and hired a lawyer. Richard pleaded not guilty to murder by reason of insanity or, in the alternative, extreme emotional distress; the second defense would reduce his crime to manslaughter. He was characterized by the defense as a good but troubled boy who had been too much in love with Bonnie and couldn't bear to lose her: he had snapped under stress. He was acquitted of murder, convicted of manslaughter, and sentenced to eight to twenty-five years. Richard and his supporters believe the sentence was excessively harsh for a first offender. Bonnie's parents are outraged and embittered by his acquittal for murdering their daughter.

Crime and punishment like this have the feel of a moral tale. There ought to be a lesson in it for the law and a hidden truth that Conrad would reveal about "the strength, the power, the horror, of human emotions." It should have been a novel by Thomas Hardy, bloodless and imagined. The dramatic force of the story and the questions it raises about criminal justice and responsibility have inspired two new and very different books: *The Killing of Bonnie Garland,* an analysis of "Questions of Justice," by psychiatrist Willard Gaylin, and *The Yale Murder,* a docudrama about a "Fatal Romance," by journalist Peter Meyer.

Meyer tells a sometimes lurid story from beginning to end. Read *The Yale Murder* for the plot line, and for its simple, straightforward account of the trial, including some illuminating postverdict comments by jurors. Meyer takes only a cursory look at the underlying questions about Richard's culpability, the dynamics of his relationship with Bonnie, and his successful psychiatric defense. This is a thorough but not always thoughtful reporting job.

Gaylin addresses the moral and legal questions about psychiatry and the law and the "rights" of a victim in an anatomy of the murder and trial. The story of Bonnie and Richard emerges piecemeal, through interviews and profiles and excerpts from the trial transcript; he tells the story only to get to its moral. *The Killing of Bonnie Garland* is a complex and troubling book, distinguished by an understanding of the trial process and motivated by Gaylin's concern that something went wrong in this case. He does not believe that psychodynamic theories should determine questions of legal guilt and has an outraged sense that Bonnie was too soon forgotten in a misplaced rush of compassion for Richard—as if she were the incidental casualty of his emotional distress. Gaylin wants us to remember this as her tragedy, not his.

The sympathy and support that flowed forth for Richard when he turned himself in was extraordinary. "You couldn't say, 'Richard how could you do this terrible thing?' It never occurred to me," recalls one of his staunchest supporters, a New Haven nun interviewed by Gaylin. "We were involved in being horrified with him, not judging him. The girl is dead." This was the theme of Richard's supporters: something terrible has happened and Bonnie is dead; ". . . having lost one life, we do what we can to salvage another." Suffering and repentant, Richard was embraced by the Catholic community, notably the Christian Brothers who gave him a home when he was released on bail. They forgave him; they would help him learn to forgive himself.

Perhaps this is an appropriate response from the church. We are all sinners in the sight of God ("I can see myself losing control and doing practically anything," one of the brothers tells Gaylin, who does not believe him), and Bonnie's death was no doubt part of some grand and holy design. But if we are all capable of evil, we may also all be saved. You do not punish the sinner, you rehabilitate him.

The traditional psychoanalytic response to crime can be oddly compatible with this: we may not all be capable of evil but we are certainly all capable of being sick. The seeds of pathology are planted from birth; sometimes they flower like sin. Psychiatry, Gaylin notes, is grounded in a particularly deterministic view of human behavior. The role of a psychiatrist is to understand, not to judge—to treat, not to punish.

Should these ideals govern the legal response to crime? This is Gaylin's question and, put very simply, the theme of his book. His answer is that the law must serve society, not the individual; its purpose is to enforce objective codes of conduct and hold us accountable for our acts—to preserve the public order, to protect and even avenge the innocent.

This will sound like knee-jerk law and orderism to some, and it will surely appeal to popular demands for "tough" laws and sentences. But Gaylin is not so thoughtless, and his analysis raises serious questions about the basic function and limits of law. The "Object" of an "official inquiry," says Marlowe in *Lord Jim*, is not the "fundamental why, but the superficial how, of [the] affair." "You can't expect the constituted authorities to inquire into the state of a man's soul. . . . Their business [is] to come down upon the consequences." Can a trial be a search for the truth of the human heart?

Questions of how and why have, however, always been inextricably bound in our legal system by the doctrine of criminal intent. The notion that you have to know what you do and have some conscious capacity to control your acts in order to be convicted of a crime is basic to the criminal law. The question of legal intent is not a question of legal sanity; eliminating the insanity defense, deferring a decision on a defendant's mental health to the time of sentence, could limit the use of psychiatric testimony and effect standards of mental culpability, but juries would still have to probe a defendant's state of mind to discover the nature of his intent.

Richard Herrin was not acquitted of murder by reason of

insanity but convicted of manslaughter because his emotional stress mitigated his intent to murder. Under New York law, he had only to prove that he had broken under stress and should not be held responsible for murder. The question before the jury was not would anyone break under these circumstances, but, given his history and psychological profile, did Richard break. Gaylin objects to the formulation of this defense (it is too subjective a standard of culpability) and to the use of psychiatric evidence to establish it. He believes this carries individualized justice to a dangerous extreme. Richard was judged by who he was, not what he'd done.

But how do you separate character and deed in putting the question of guilt before twelve live jurors confronted with a live defendant? Is it required by a common sense of justice to allow a defendant to explain himself? This might have been Bonnie's tragedy, but it was Richard's trial, and his background and personality would determine his guilt.

Richard's father deserted the family when he was three; his mother remarried when he was seven. His stepfather was unaffectionate, his mother worked and sent him to nursery school, "interfering," according to a defense psychiatrist, with his "wholesome development." He wet his bed, and developed an embarrassing case of eczema on his legs as a young boy that forced him to wear girlish knee socks and sandals. This was cited by the defense as a troubled childhood that left Richard with a terrible fear of being abandoned by his mother. Afraid of expressing anger, he developed an "ingratiating" personality; he was a "model" boy who worked for his stepfather, studied hard, and performed well in school.

Richard entered Yale in 1971, a high school honors student on a full scholarship. He did not prosper there. Ill at ease in an "elitist preppie" atmosphere and with intense academic competition, he was a poor, completely disinterested student who spent most of his time eating, drinking, and hanging out with his friends. He is remembered by one of his friends as a "great guy, real low-keyed and laid-back."

For several years, he was a great guy in search of a girlfriend. Richard was sexually inexperienced; he had dated one girl his junior year and fantasized a "romantic" relationship with her after a few dates. (He spied on her when she began seeing someone else and still speaks of her with hatred.) He met Bonnie his senior year, when she was a freshman. It was the first sexual relationship for both of them, and they were said to be inseparable their first year together. Their relationship was commonly described as "symbiotic," but Gaylin suggests that after an initial infatuation, Bonnie was much less attached to Richard than he was to her. She was a seventeen-year-old virgin when they met; she seems to have spent the next and last three years of her life growing up and away from him.

Richard was intensely possessive and, in Gaylin's words, "pathologically dependent" on Bonnie. He did not want her to pursue a music career that would take her from his side and discouraged her from seeing a psychiatrist because she might learn she didn't need him. His fears intensified when he left New Haven the year after they met and entered a graduate program at Texas Christian University. She carried on a life of her own at Yale; he spent most of his time alone in his room, eating and watching TV game shows, and thinking about Bonnie. He called and wrote her constantly, worried obsessively about her holding hands with other men, partly because he was afraid people would think less of him if she were seen with someone else. He fantasized about mutilating her sexually for being unfaithful. They had been secretly engaged when he left New Haven, and he wanted desperately to marry her.

He killed her when she returned from a Yale singing tour of Europe; she had written that she was dating another man. Richard visited her at her parents' home in an attempt to win her back. The night he killed her, she had fallen asleep with Richard sitting at her side (she'd turned her back to him, he recalls to Gaylin). The "idea" of killing her "came" to him while he was reading a magazine. A defense psychiatrist said it "intruded upon his consciousness." He methodically went downstairs and found a hammer.

You can react to this story with compassion for Richard or contempt; you can describe him and his crime in a way that suits your purpose. This is what trial attorneys do. They make up scenarios and spin out summations that will fit the facts they can't dispute and win the jury's sympathy. They interpret and characterize and try on alternate theories about what happened and why, settling on one that will help their client and trying to manipulate the jury into believing it.

Gaylin understands that all good lawyers are good "storytellers," and he is adept at analyzing the particular story told by the defense in Richard's case. You can reconstruct it yourself, from excerpted portions of the trial transcript, including statements by defense and prosecution psychiatrists, and an interview with defense attorney Jack Litman:

Richard had always been a good boy who loved his mother and had loved Bonnie so much: he felt his life depended on her. Her threatened abandonment of him set off childhood fears of being abandoned by his mother and years of accumulated rage. He was not himself when he killed her; the idea invaded his consciousness and he was unable to resist it—he was under so much stress at the time. The Richard Herrin who killed Bonnie was not the Richard Herrin his friends and family had known and loved and he is not the Richard Herrin you see before you today.

Richard asked the jury to befriend, not to judge, him, and was turned from criminal to victim by the defense's skillful use of psychiatric testimony, myths about romantic love, and a bit of misogyny. "Because of Herrin's personality, people believed that for him this was a stressful situation," recalls a juror interviewed by Peter Meyer. "He loved Bonnie so much . . . this was the extreme emotional disturbance . . . no one ever doubted he was deeply in love. It was really so sad."

The story of Richard's love painted a romantic, even noble, gloss over what might otherwise have been considered pathological behavior that would have alienated the jury. His tendency to fixate on women he barely knew, his insistence that Bonnie belong to him, his dreams of sexual mutilation, and the depressed solitary year he spent in Texas became if not normal, at least acceptable, behavior patterns in a boy who "loved not wisely but too well." Juries don't feel sorry for people who scare them. Richard's great love, along with the traumas of his youth, explained and defused his conduct.

It is hard to imagine a woman being acquitted of murder in a parallel case. How would a jury with eight men react to a woman defendant who had fantasized about castrating the man she eventually killed? They would hardly see her as a tragic romantic heroine. Richard's lawyer offered the jury a subtle version of a battered spouse defense that would never have worked for a woman: Richard had been battered emotionally by Bonnie. He was faithful, totally devoted, and very vulnerable, and she was about to desert him. Defense attorney Litman told Gaylin that "it was important to taint [Bonnie] a little bit." He had to make her appear more worldly than Richard and a girl who, in the words of a defense psychiatrist, "was not living up to the idealized image he had of her." She was a sweet girl who had made what Litman called some "critical mistakes" and, in a sense, brought this tragedy on herself. Gaylin is deeply troubled by the defense attack on Bonnie and the failure of the prosecutor to bring her back to life for the jury. He suggests, rather melodramatically, that Bonnie was killed a second time at Richard's trial.

It should be clear at the outset that a defense attorney's responsibility is to his client. Litman could hardly have characterized Bonnie in a way that would have hurt his chances for an acquittal or a manslaughter conviction. It is much more difficult to define a prosecutor's responsibility to the victim. Crimes are supposed to be prosecuted in the interest of the community, not to serve or avenge the victim. But is the victim somehow a part of the crime? Gaylin believes the prosecutor in this case should have memorialized Bonnie and made the jury "mourn for her. . . . She should have been brought back to life so they could have appreciated the enormity of her death." The increasingly popular belief that a victim should be made a presence at trial has at first a certain commonsense appeal, but its legal implications are troubling. Bonnie's "vivacity" and "delightful sense of humor" had nothing to do with the question of Richard's guilt. "Beautiful red hair and . . . a beautiful soprano voice" are not legal elements of homicide. Should Richard have been convicted of murder because he killed a charming girl the jury would have liked? If she had been mean and stupid and boring, would it have been less of a crime?

Still, the absence of Bonnie's personality at this trial is remarkable because Richard made his the linchpin of the case. He was acquitted of murder because the jury felt sorry for him, accepted his version of their love, and decided he was basically a nice boy. Bonnie's character was part of the truth of their relationship and the nature of that relationship was central to the defense. There should have been ways for the prosecutor to bring her to life just a little.

Richard had a right to depict Bonnie any way he liked and a right to make his own character an issue, to explain the why of what he did and ask for mercy. The prosecutor's job was to tear apart Richard's case, to make the Richard and Bonnie story sound like a lie, to challenge psychiatric evidence of insanity and emotional distress. He had to make the jury sneer at Richard's traumas and distress, portraying him as weak and dangerous, but not crazy. But the prosecutor, says Gaylin, did not attack Richard's manslaughter case, seeking only to establish his legal sanity, ensuring at least that he would not be acquitted for being crazy. He even allowed testimony of his own chief psychiatric witness to be used by the defense to establish Richard's emotional distress. There is one short and very simple answer to Gaylin's question about what went wrong in this case: the defense attorney did a better job than the prosecutor; he put on a better show and told a moving and convincing story that the prosecutor failed to refute.

This is not to minimize the familiar problems of using psychiatric testimony in a criminal trial. There may be something inherently unreliable about a diagnosis fashioned by a psychiatrist to suit a defense or prosecuting attorney's theory of a case, and jurors may not always have the expertise or common sense to evaluate opposing opinions of expert psychiatric witnesses. Psychoanalysis will sometimes offer explanations for behavior that some of us would not want the law to recognize: not every form of suffering or sorrow can be made an excuse for crime. But these are problems for judges, lawyers, and, ultimately, jurors to address in every case.

It is also easy to overstate the practical problems of a psychiatric defense and the extent to which the law can be said to favor the individual over society. Most criminal defendants don't raise insanity or diminished capacity defenses, and those who do are not often successful. Most criminal defendants are never even tried.

Bad cases make bad law. Gaylin would change the rules of the game because he is not happy with the way one extraordinary case was prosecuted. His outrage is understandable: he was greatly moved by an image of Bonnie; her letters, he says "break your heart," there was "richness and promise" to her life. He does not like Richard or believe that the traumas he suffered as a boy excuse his act ("Eczema, bed-wetting, and a second father do not represent a Dickensian childhood. . . . It is not Oliver Twist. It is not even David Copperfield"). He does not believe Richard appreciates the "enormity" of his crime or that he is truly repentant. (His first "year or two" in prison was punishment enough, he says. He has now served about half of his eight-year sentence and believes that his life is being "wasted" needlessly: he can't bring Bonnie back.) But it is a great leap from Gaylin's feelings about Richard and his dissatisfaction with the prosecution of this case to the assertion that we should forswear the use of psychiatric testimony and abandon concepts of individualized justice.

You chase your tail around the lessons of a case like this. It tells all the troubles of a psychiatric defense and then teaches us not to engage in what is probably a futile attempt to eliminate it. Courts will always inquire into character as well as conduct to determine criminal intent. Jurors will always be swayed by their emotional responses to a defendant or victim and won over by the lawyer who looks them in the eye and tells a better tale. Jurors look for morals too. Every lawyer knows no jury is impartial, and every lawyer strives to break the jury's heart. This trial-by-jury system of ours is "the palladium of our liberties," wrote Mark Twain. "I do not know what a palladium is, having never seen a palladium, but it is a good thing no doubt at any rate."

---- ■ ■ ■ ----

THE AVENGERS

(*January 1984*)

Why do we imprison people, or execute them, and by what right? How do we determine their sentences? Should the punishment fit the criminal or the crime? Are there moral or simply utilitarian reasons or both for a criminal justice system? Legal scholars, criminals, victims, and interested bystanders have been asking these questions for years, and arguing over a litany of answers: *Punishment is purely practical.* It incapacitates the criminal and deters others with similar predilections. It protects the rest of us from those who are too dangerous to roam free. It may even help rehabilitate them. *Punishment is a moral imperative*: Every civilized society must enforce a moral code of behavior. Criminal sanctions are legitimate expressions of public outrage, and society has the right and responsibility to exact a pound of flesh for every transgression, to punish for punishment's sake.

Deterrence, self-defense, rehabilitation, and revenge—these ideals shape our institutions of criminal justice. To balance and even choose between them is not an idle academic exercise. The overwhelming practical problems that beset our court and correctional system today are exacerbated by confusion about its underlying purpose. Although that confusion is framed most dramatically in headline cases involving insanity, it also surfaces in the most routine cases. The same questions are asked every day in the criminal courts—When should character mitigate a

crime? When should retribution be tempered with mercy?—and
as the answers vary, so do the dispositions of related cases.
Different defendants draw different punishments for similar
crimes not just because they draw different prosecutors, defense
attorneys, and judges, but because there is no consensus about
why they are being punished. To design a fair and effective
system of law enforcement we need a clear idea of what we want
it to do and why. What precisely do we mean by justice?

This is the grand question Susan Jacoby asks in *Wild Justice:
The Evolution of Revenge,* a work of rare intelligence and informed convictions. In an ambitious analysis of the force of
revenge in literature, law, and religion, from Classical Greek and
early Judeo-Christian cultures to our own, she enunciates a
model for a criminal justice system. Here is a system of "proportional retribution" in which revenge, limited by compassion and
common sense, has a place. The purpose is to settle accounts
fairly and in public, to satisfy and restrain the impulse toward
revenge.

Jacoby's central thesis is that revenge must be validated and
institutionalized if it is to be contained. In her view, the primary
task of civilized society throughout Western history has been to
"suppress" private acts of vengeance by providing public redress
of wrongs inflicted. This may be a reductive approach to the
history of the world, but it expands our understanding of the
evolution of revenge and clarifies the failure of our society to
systematically seek and exact retribution for the crimes of its
members.

It is this failure that Jacoby has set out to explore; for her it
represents unwillingness to recognize revenge as a legitimate
reason for imposing punishment. The most grievous example,
she says, is the public response to Holocaust survivors who
demand prosecution of Nazi war criminals; accused of being
vindictive, obsessed with the past, they are exhorted to "bury

their dead" and forget about what happened some forty years ago. We have "tabooed" revenge, Jacoby argues, and, in so doing, forced it underground. Denied a place in the courtroom, it surfaces in a movie like *Death Wish,* which celebrates blind and bloody vigilantism. She attributes this taboo to psychiatry's influence on prevailing theories of justice; in the post-Freudian world, revenge has been stigmatized as an "immature" emotion. We are expected to forgo retribution and forgive criminals who are said to be only the victims of their own psychosocial histories.

Surely revenge carried to extremes was considered a kind of disease long before Freud, and in a cogent analysis of revenge literature from the Oresteian trilogy to *Othello* to *Moby-Dick* to last year's detective stories, Jacoby makes clear that revenge has always been viewed as a potentially dangerous and disruptive emotion. But she also points out that in Classical Greek and Elizabethan cultures, there was a place for revenge in the public sphere. It was not just the prerogative but the responsibility of duly constituted authorities—monarchs acting in God's name or the gods themselves—to provide public redress for individual wrongs. The message of the great revenge tragedies, she maintains, is that a system that does not accommodate the need for vengeance will only unleash its destructive fury. Medea was driven to murder her children because she had "no legal means of redressing [her] grievances." *Othello* is, in part, a play about vigilante justice gone wrong, vengeance unchecked by "a formal proceeding to establish guilt or innocence." Hamlet's tragedy was that he was asked to shoulder by himself the burden of avenging the murder of his father.

The moral Jacoby draws from history is that private revenge threatens the social order; public revenge is part of justice, and the primary function of criminal law is to punish, not to understand or forgive. Justice is a system of public accountability; forgiveness is a private matter among victim, offender, and God.

This analysis of revenge and forgiveness rests on a careful distinction between public and private spheres, between the secular and the divine. As Jacoby suggests, "A sin . . . is not always a crime but crime is always a sin." Law should proscribe only those acts that violate a common morality and present a danger to the community at large. Crimes are prosecuted in the name of the community, and any willingness of the victim to forgive does not affect the community's need to punish for communal harm. If this seems like a theoretical distinction, consider the case of a nun who declined to prosecute the men who had brutally beaten, knifed, and raped her, choosing instead to forgive them. How was the damage to public safety and faith in public justice mitigated by her private act of forgiveness? Conversely, a sin that endangers only the soul of the sinner and not the social order isn't a social but a religious concern, which is why "victimless" crimes, by definition, should not generally be considered crimes at all.

In practice, however, the question of what constitutes harm, individual or communal, is not always easily resolved. That crime and sin sometimes converge is illustrated by the controversy surrounding the prosecution of crimes within the family and the battle over abortion. Jacoby devotes a chapter to sexual crimes, noting that revenge in such cases has always been considered "beyond the law," a tribal or familial matter. The traditional failure of police and the courts to prosecute cases of domestic violence reflected the view, she says, that these were "private disasters" and not "public crimes," as if there were nothing uncivilized about the rape of a wife by her husband, as if it did no real damage to her or to a civilized community. It took the feminist movement to make clear that this was a matter of public concern and that abortion was, perhaps, a private one. In Jacoby's view, abortion is a religious, medical, emotional, and feminist issue, but not necessarily a legal one that "inflicts the kind of social damage that demands retribution." Still, whether you believe abortion is not a private act but a public one that does indeed inflict harm on another depends on whether you believe a fetus is an independent human being, deserving of public protection. It is clear that abortions neither can nor should be prohibited as long as there is no consensus on when life begins. Perhaps in a pluralistic society there can never be agreement on a matter that generates such profound metaphysical disputes. But what if there were?

Jacoby does not directly address the underlying problem of identifying crime and sin. How do we define harm to others? Is there such a thing as a crime that affects only the "quality of life"? Should the law proscribe public nuisances or acts that violate a commonly accepted moral code? Does unredressed moral indignation by itself ever present a danger to society? The age-old debate about legislating morality hinges on whether victimless acts that provoke widespread moral outrage threaten the social fabric, making them the business of law. Jacoby suggests that they do not, that there ought to be "external evidence" of harm, and she would probably agree that there are countervailing rights of privacy and conscience that outweigh objections to "immoral" behavior. But if the demand for retribution in such cases is vehement and broadly based, must the law exact public retribution to keep faith with prevailing ideas of justice, for the sake of preserving order? What determines the need for criminal sanctions—the actual physical damage wrought by an act or the depth and scope of the outcry against it?

But assuming it is possible, in fact, to distinguish between crimes against God and crimes against men and women, Jacoby is clear and convincing on the dangers of using the machinery of state to enforce a set of religious beliefs. Law works as a safety valve for vengeance, as a vehicle for the reasonable and limited expression of it, precisely because its quest for justice is, ideally, uncomplicated by the personal animus of a private vendetta. When it aligns itself with religion, it loses this relative objectivity empowering and releasing the revenge impulse in all its fury. Revenge motivated by religious belief has been a "bloody leit-motif" of history, Jacoby observes: persecution of the Jews for the mythic role of their ancestors in the crucifixion is one of the bloodiest and most "devastating" examples and, perhaps, "the longest running revenge tragedy of Western civilization."

Throughout its history, Western religion has had a paradoxical relationship with revenge. Religion has controlled the urge for vengeance by preaching forgiveness within the fold while committing some of its worst excesses by giving the state the right to punish rebels and nonbelievers in God's name. The executions of Protestant heretics by Catholic states during the Reformation and the witch trials of Puritan New England also demonstrate the dangers of mixing "sacred injunctions" with "secular power." The agents of God are not likely to be swayed by voices of compassion and moderation in taking His revenge. How can we measure retribution with reason and contain it when the state takes sides in a holy war?

Justice in this world is an exercise in moderation, tempered by an awareness of human fallibility and the destructiveness of vengeance uncontained. This is why Jacoby opposes capital punishment, while recognizing some legitimacy in the underlying demand for retribution. Life imprisonment is retribution enough, she says, and an equally strong deterrent; retribution, the expression of moral outrage, is in fact a kind of deterrent to the extent that it defines a moral code and shapes our social conscience. Executions are also "unseemly"; there is something ghoulish about public fascination with them, and it's simply "absurd" to express outrage against one murder by committing another. Proportional retribution does not mean payment in kind: a civilized society is not supposed to engage in the atrocities of its most uncivilized members, and for the most heinous crimes, there are no proportional responses. How do we exact an eye for an eye from a mass murderer, she asks. What punishment could ever fit the crime of the Holocaust?

Jacoby is a relativist seeking a "middle ground" of retribution based on her understanding of the difference between justice in this world and the next. She opposes capital punishment for the same reason she opposes the use of a psychiatric standard of guilt or a doctrine of Christian forgiveness in the courtroom. To forgive a crime because we understand why it was committed or because we are only human serves neither the purposes of secular justice nor the limits of a secular court. Whether or not we are all ultimately responsible for what we do, we have to act "as if" we are.

What's interesting is that she's defensive about this attempt to legitimize revenge and afford it a place in the criminal justice system. She is indeed refuting a common moral ideal—that the best part of us seeks forgiveness and the worst revenge—and she does so convincingly. " 'Do good to them that hurt you' is an ethic for saints, and it may sound hard," she says; still, "there are some actions that ought never to be pardoned by society." In defending revenge, Jacoby writes as if she were pitting herself against the entire liberal intellectual establishment. This might have been true in the 1960s or early 1970s, when the more fashionable liberal view of punishment was that deterrence or self-defense was its only justification. But this view has been supplanted in recent years; revenge has gained renewed respect among the populace. The victims' rights movement, which Jacoby doesn't discuss, is a direct demand for restitution and recognition of, at least, the moral claims of victims to a measure of revenge. It is also an extremely popular movement—victims' rights are something of a motherhood issue. Advocates of capital punishment now talk less about deterrence and more about revenge, without apology. The quest for vengeance is not nearly as taboo as Jacoby makes it appear.

Vigilantism and the confusion about revenge and forgiveness that she attributes to a "taboo" also reflect a desire for absolute justice—for some, proportional retribution is not enough—and an unwillingness to confront the crimes of the past. Support for capital punishment is based not only on the system's failure to punish but on the mistaken belief that there is indeed an adequate punishment for every crime, that if we simply do to the criminal what he or she has done to another, we can make the victim whole and heal the community. The most Draconian punishments designed to fit the worst of crimes foster this comforting illusion: by imposing a punishment that is said to make up for a crime, we can forget that it ever occurred.

It's clear that we are conflicted about revenge. The blood-thirsty allure of the *Death Wish* or Dirty Harry movies exists alongside a pervasive sense of vulnerability that turns us away from the survivors of crime. No one wants to hear from Julie Patz about the mysterious disappearance of her six-year-old son, Etan; as Jacoby observes, we would prefer that she "mourn in silence." Perhaps this unease arises from a revenge taboo— the belief that it's not healthy to fixate on the past and not nice to be vengeful. But it also denotes fear that if one child can disappear so can another.

This is the kind of fear that blames the victim: if Julie Patz had walked her son to his school bus, people say, this crime would never have happened. The increase in street crimes and anonymous murders has made the need to forget as strong as the need to avenge. It is this conflict that distorts our attitude toward vengeance, as much as the notion that the impulse to forgive is somehow a higher and healthier emotion. It is painful to dwell on the kidnapping or murder of someone down the block, and more painful still to be reminded of mass murders and genocide.

Wild Justice begins and ends with the specter of the Holocaust. In some ways it is a tribute to bearing witness. Forgiving and forgetting is not justice, not in this world. Justice is a way of remembering.

THE WRONG MEN

(*December 1992*)

If movies mirror popular opinion, many Americans believe that innocent people are sometimes presumed guilty of crimes. The idea of an innocent man caught in a web of circumstance that implicates him in a murder was most artfully exploited by Alfred Hitchcock and has long been a Hollywood staple. Yet a majority of Americans also support the death penalty, presumably in the belief that the average inmate on death row belongs there.

In Spite of Innocence painstakingly demonstrates that real people convicted of murder are sometimes as innocent as film heroes, if rarely as appealing. Michael Radelet, a professor of sociology at the University of Florida; Hugo Adam Bedau, a professor of philosophy at Tufts University; and the journalist Constance Putnam chronicle more than four hundred wrongful capital convictions, from the early 1900s to the present. Most are murder convictions, but a few involve rape. (The Supreme Court invalidated the death penalty in rape cases in 1977.) Most vulnerable to being executed for rape were black men accused by white women.

The cases described here, in considerable detail, range from the notorious to the obscure. They include the case of the Scottsboro Boys, nine black men who "spent a total of 104 years in prison for a [rape] that never occurred," and the Randall Adams case, made famous by Errol Morris's documentary *The Thin Blue Line*. Adams, recently released from prison after twelve years, had been convicted of killing a police officer on the basis of perjured testimony, in a trial marked by prosecutorial misconduct and defense inexperience. In a less publicized, 1974 case Jerry Banks spent six years on death row for a murder conviction reflecting grossly incompetent defense counsel and the falsification of evidence by a sheriff's detective. In a 1956 case James Foster was convicted of murder on the basis of a mistaken eyewitness identification, which may have resulted from police failure to conduct a proper lineup. Foster spent two years on death row and was released only after the actual murderer confessed.

What went wrong in these cases? The authors point to perjured testimony by prosecution witnesses and mistaken eyewitness identifications as the most frequent causes of error. But probably the most disturbing cases, as they observe, are those involving shoddy or bad-faith police work, prosecutorial misconduct, and racism—all of which bring into question the integrity of the justice system itself.

The criminal justice system delineated by the cases in this book is one in which people are not proved guilty of crimes so much as chosen to be found guilty: the police and prosecutors light on a suspect because of prejudice or circumstances or in response to public pressure for a quick conviction. They interpret or distort evidence in a way that supports their case and suppress evidence against it. If this is not typical of law enforcement work, there are too many documented cases of police and prosecutorial misconduct to dismiss it as a fluke. And after all, there is no reason to assume that police officers and district attorneys as a class are more honest than the rest of us.

Nor are they necessarily more competent. At best, the system described here is less malevolent than arbitrary. As the authors point out, it is "fickle good fortune rather than anything having to do with the rational workings of the criminal justice system" that eventually exonerates some people. In southern states, they note (quoting from a *National Law Journal* report), "justice in capital murder trials is more like a random flip of the coin than a delicate balancing of the scales." Contrary to what we want to believe about criminal justice, this is not a system in which character is fate.

Proponents of capital punishment vigorously question this critique, and many dismiss it as political. In fact, an earlier version of this study, published in the mid-1980s by Radelet and Bedau, generated an aggressive response from The Department of Justice and exchanges of op-ed pieces and law review articles. A 1986 Justice Department memo by the assistant attorney general Stephen J. Markman attacked Radelet and Bedau's findings by questioning their political sympathies. The authors discussed more than three hundred cases, but the fact that they chose to include Sacco and Vanzetti, the Rosenbergs, and Bruno Hauptmann (none of these is much more than mentioned in the book), Markman wrote, "makes it clear that this 'study' is, more than the authors would admit, a polemical tract rather than a serious and fair-minded inquiry." Equally damning was the fact that the study had been funded partly by the Unitarian Universalist Society, which "has provided financial support to many liberal groups seeking to change national policies on social issues."

In addition to the authors' nefarious political ties, however, Markman addressed the substance of their study, notably the assertion that the convictions they described were wrongful. But he is not persuasive. Radelet, Bedau, and Putnam's work is thoroughly documented, and 90 percent of the cases they report involve official acknowledgment of error.

A less frivolous line of attack is that these wrongful convictions are anomalies. The authors, however, contend that the cases they describe are typical of hundreds or perhaps thousands of others. Readers will be guided by their own instincts and experience in deciding whether this claim is true. The authors do suggest, persuasively, that coerced confessions are a particular problem in capital cases: people plead guilty out of fear of receiving the death penalty. They also point out that in questionable cases, investigations of guilt and innocence are rarely pursued after an execution has been carried out. Except for the occasional cause célèbre, like the Rosenberg case, people's cases die with them.

Finally, some statistical evidence indicates that capital punishment is not fairly applied. Practically all the more than two thousand defendants currently on death row are poor; many have received less than competent defense counsel at trial, particularly in states that rely on court-appointed private attorneys, who may have little criminal litigation experience, instead of seasoned public defenders. There is also much evidence that the system is racially biased, particularly with regard to the race of the victims, suggesting that the lives of white people are valued more within the system than the lives of blacks. Of the 231 victims whose convicted killers have been executed since the death penalty was reinstated, 194 were white.

It's difficult to predict how supporters of capital punishment would react to statistics like this if they were publicized, say, on *Oprah*. Some might lose faith in the system; others might question the reliability of the statistics or dismiss their implications. The Supreme Court has held that the greater statistical likelihood of being sentenced to death for killing a white person "does not demonstrate a constitutionally significant risk of racial bias."

Support for capital punishment requires leaps of faith like this—a willingness to believe, in spite of the evidence, that the system is fair or, at least, can readily be made fair. In Massachusetts, Governor William Weld, seeking to enact a death penalty bill, has answered charges of racial bias in the criminal justice system by promising to eliminate it, which is a little like justifying abortion prohibitions by promising to eliminate sex. Radelet, Bedau, and Putnam do not believe that errors in the system can be significantly reduced, partly because the human beings administering the system are fallible; so they advocate reducing the risk of error by eliminating capital punishment instead.

Would this eliminate deterrence as well? It might in a rational world—a world in which criminals carefully considered the consequences of their actions, keeping their emotions, not to mention their psychoses, under control. But in this world the assertion that the death penalty deters murder is not supported by the evidence, as the authors point out (and even Assistant Attorney General Markman conceded). In the absence of proof of the death penalty's deterrent effect, Governor Weld, for one, says that on the question of deterrence he is guided by his gut.

Debates about capital punishment usually come down to the viscera. Regardless of rational arguments about inequitable application or deterrent effect, the concept of capital punishment is deeply satisfying to many people who are, with good reason, fearful of crime and furious that it is out of control. Until opponents of capital punishment offer alternative ways of honoring legitimate demands that murders be avenged, they will futilely contribute rational arguments to a highly irrational debate. Many people, after all, don't need to be persuaded that lawyers and courts can't be trusted. Many think the judicial system can't prosecute traffic tickets fairly, much less rapes and homicides, and in fact their anger at the system's breakdown fuels the demand for executions. There is a lot of cognitive dissonance in the capital punishment debate: so many people are eager to grant so much power to a system in which they have so little faith.

MORALITY—THE NEWEST DEAL

(*September 1993*)

Michael Lerner, alleged guru to Hillary Rodham Clinton and editor of *Tikkun,* a progressive Jewish journal of opinion, and William Bennett, conservative philosopher prince and former Reagan administration drug czar, are debating morality, meaning, and government on *Larry King Live.* Asked to define his elusive catchphrase, the "politics of meaning," Lerner explains, "We need a politics that encourages rather than discourages moral behavior, a move away from selfishness . . . a move away from the disrespect that people face in their daily lives and towards a valuing of human beings, not for how much money they make . . . but for their intrinsic worth as human beings."

I am grappling with a bad attitude. I am trying to forget what a perceptive college professor said about my senior thesis: "Perhaps Miss Kaminer should declare a moratorium on her use of the word 'meaningful.' " I am trying hard to sympathize with Lerner's plea for goodness, which is, after all, unassailable in its generality. Then something horrifying happens. I find myself agreeing with William Bennett:

"This is the same government that has trouble delivering the mail . . . and now it's going to be in the meaning business," Bennett snorts. "I do not want new feelings of meaning from Bill Clinton. What I'd like to see him come up with is a reasonable budget."

Lerner is such an easy target. Vague, verbose, and platitudinous, his sermons about the politics of meaning are extended greeting cards. The more he writes, the less he says. Hillary Clinton, too, has been easily lampooned for her starryeyed, Oprahfied rhetoric about sharing and caring and connectedness, and her ambitious demand that we "remold society by redefining what it means to be a human being." Posing for the cover of the *New York Times Magazine* in a pure white suit and pearls, blond hair swept back, hands clasped before her, posture picture-perfect, she begs to be called sanctimonious.

Still, after the cheap shots are fired, there remains a stubborn question about what role government plays in a pluralistic society in promoting particular ethical and religious values, as well as a not so incidental question about the morality of individual rights. The culture wars—over gender roles, abortion, homosexuality, censorship, creationism, and school prayers—continue. Even, maybe especially, William Bennett, who owes his own political ascendance to Republican success in addressing conservative Christian concerns about values, should concede that these questions may be worth revisiting.*

As every schoolchild is supposed to know—and perhaps at one time did—the disestablishment of religion was one of the founding principles of the Republic, enshrined in the First Amendment. Right-wing religious leaders bemoaning the absence of prayer in public schools like to deny that there is supposed to be a wall between church and state, but that is precisely what Jefferson and Madison erected. They believed that religious integrity would be protected by religious independence and freedom of religion would be secured by religious diversity—what Madison heralded in the *Federalist Papers* as the competition of a "multiplicity of sects."

---

*Since his attack on Hillary Clinton's appeal for a politics of meaning, William Bennett has become the nation's unofficial virtue czar.

So, it is axiomatic that government stays out of the trans-cendent-value business, as Hillary Clinton has acknowledged. Or, at least, government's role in our pursuit of transcendence is only indirect, she suggested to *Washington Post* reporter Martha Sherrill: "There are things government can do that are more likely to create a condition for more people to be secure enough to take responsibility for themselves and therefore participate fully in this search for meaning."

Is that clear? What exactly does the creation of "meaningful" conditions entail? You might say that government makes the trains run on time; it maintains order, protects national security, and enhances economic productivity (with regulation or lack of it), enabling individuals, families, and religious groups to seek and supply their own meanings.

But you might also point out that government administers public schools that can't help but impart values; imposes tax laws and domestic politics that favor some families and religions over others; enforces criminal laws that make express moral judgments about individual behavior; and promulgates civil rights laws to combat the evils of discrimination. When govern-ment creates a condition in which individuals, families, and churches can flourish, it doesn't simply get out of their way; it establishes the boundaries of private space and decides who may inhabit it. The refusal to recognize polygamous or homo-sexual marriages denies Mormons and gays access to private space reserved for family life and whatever spiritual sustenance it affords.

There is nothing, then, particularly controversial about the suggestion that government play a role in establishing moral and, in some sense, religious values. Public policies naturally reflect and enforce public morals, and most Americans ground their morals in religion. Law cannot be entirely agnostic (it's simply supposed to be nonsectarian), and the great legal reforms of the past hundred and fifty years—abolition, the progressive income tax, women's suffrage, and the 1964 Civil Rights Act—have all been moral reforms, often infused with religion. The expectation that the president and first lady provide moral leadership is equally unremarkable. Indeed, the primary criticism leveled against George Bush and Bill Clinton was that each lacked a "moral center." Perceived as too quick to compromise or essentially untrustworthy, each was accused of practicing a politics of expediency.

This is what neither Hillary Clinton nor Michael Lerner seems to understand: the only candidate generally invested by his followers with moral leadership in the last election was Ross Perot. Faced with a failing economy, people voted against an apparently befuddled incumbent, either by casting an impassioned protest vote for Perot or taking their chances with Clinton's mantra-like promise of change. Hillary Clinton's exhortations about being and doing good presume a moral authority that neither she nor her husband was awarded and that neither can win simply by making speeches.

Barbara Bush was better positioned to talk about morality. Hillary Clinton, firmly identified as a liberal feminist and grounded in a 1960s politics of rebellion, will have a harder time establishing herself as a preacher of moral values, which many Americans still associate with the prefeminist nuclear family and, preferably, Protestant religiosity. Of course, this conservative monopoly on "values" is precisely what Hillary Clinton is trying to combat. She has the advantage of her own, apparently sincere, dignified religious faith (although she may risk that advantage by forging a spiritual alliance with a Jewish intellectual like Michael Lerner, who might not play well in the heartland). She ought not to underestimate the disadvantage of her liberal past or her feminism.

Nor should she overestimate the appeal to liberals of her

mortal exhortations. It's not that liberals are afraid to talk about
values or morality: They led the fight to introduce new social
values into the public schools, particularly through sex education, and they have always presented anti-discrimination laws as
moral imperatives. But at least some liberal feminists and most
civil libertarians will find Hillary Clinton's implicit disparage-
ment of individual rights unpalatable.

The rhetoric of the politics of meaning being employed by
Hillary Clinton and Lerner is the rhetoric of communitarianism,
which accuses traditional liberals of excessive reliance on rights
and calls for a new ethic of responsibility. Communitarianism
associates rights with selfishness, the acquisitive eighties, anomie,
and the destruction of community. Rights are considered inimical to sharing and caring and insensible to duty and virtue: An
assertion of smoker's rights is, for example, a violation of a duty
not to pollute the communal environment. Production of a pornographic film or utterance of a racist joke violates a duty not to
offend.

Of course, people don't always exercise their rights virtuously,
partly because it is a linchpin of democracy that not only virtuous
people have rights. Reduced to untempered assertion of individual desire, individual rights can easily be labeled selfish. But civil
libertarianism is not simply permission to assert your rights; it's a
mandate to respect the rights of others. Individual rights are
essential ways of enforcing social responsibilities: the right to be
hired without regard to race or sex enforces a social obligation to
treat people fairly and with respect.

The antirights rhetoric of communitarians is a shortsighted
effort by liberals to regain the moral high ground of "responsibility," which conservatives have dominated in recent years,
particularly in the welfare debate. But conservatives tend to talk
mostly about individual responsibility. Liberals should clarify

their focus on social responsibility. Put very simply, the message is this: "Americans don't just take care of themselves; they also take care of each other, partly through their common government." That's the message requiring the embrace, not the abandonment, of individual rights.

In fact, Lerner's politics-of-meaning "platform" is essentially a traditional, liberal, rights-based agenda dressed up in the rhetoric of responsibility: a more humane workplace (in other words, worker rights, a cause of the ACLU); unrestricted health care (patients' rights); an end to poverty, homelessness, and hunger (welfare rights, which liberals demanded more than twenty years ago); respect for children (children's rights). "It's not because they are the owners of 'rights' that children ought to be respected," Lerner points out, and all you can say is "obviously." But it is only when children have rights that they will be respected.

This is not rocket science. The role that individual rights play in inculcating social virtue is clear, particularly in the aftermath of the civil rights movement. Law cannot eradicate prejudice directly, but it can establish as a guiding principle that prejudice is wrong. Why, then, are individual rights so consistently denigrated by communitarians as obstacles to community?

The communitarian movement is rooted, in part, in liberal discomfort with the women's movement. Equal rights feminism—the feminism represented by Ruth Bader Ginsburg's assault on sex discrimination and the demand for gender-neutral laws—has long been associated by communitarians with narcissism, selfishness, a careerism that leads women to place their own interests above the interests of their children and communities. The popular communitarian book *Habits of the Heart,* by the sociologist Robert Bellah, warned that "equality of women could lead to a complete loss of the human qualities long associated with 'woman's sphere.' " (I always thought that men had human qualities, too, and surely one premise of feminism is that human qualities, like compassion and a capacity to nurture, ought not to be confined to a "woman's sphere.")

It is most telling that equal rights feminism is regarded as a cautionary tale about selfishness by many communitarians, while the civil rights movement is lauded as a model of community: both were communal movements to acquire individual rights. But, as any woman old enough to remember the antiwar movement knows, sexual equality can be as threatening to liberal males as racial equality is to closet white supremacists.

Of course, communal life has been significantly altered by feminism. The increased participation in the workforce of middle-class women with young children and the professionalization of the female workforce have greatly reduced the number of women volunteering in their communities. This is particularly true in middle class white communities, since black women have a history of combining paid work and volunteerism. Anxiety about community among white liberals began, in part, anxiety about feminism. Who would lead the Girl Scout troops or run the Meals on Wheels programs or the local crafts fair? (Surely not men, who have insufficient "human qualities.") How could feminists be so selfish as to abandon their social responsibilities for individual, equal rights?

During the past decade, many feminists have begun asking themselves similar questions in a frenzy of revisionism. "Rights talk" is no more fashionable among progressive feminists (particularly in academia) than it is among communitarians. It has become conventional feminist wisdom to suggest that women care more about responsibilities than rights, although I know no woman who has offered to abdicate her rights under federal equal employment laws or *Roe* v. *Wade* for the sake of her community. And it has been at least ten years since feminism might be characterized as a campaign for equal rights. Many feminists today advocate special protections for women instead of rights.

It would, therefore, be inaccurate and unfair to suggest that Hillary Clinton's use of communitarian rhetoric is an abandonment of feminism; I doubt it even represents an abandonment of equal rights. Indeed, since she is probably irrevocably identified in the public mind as a feminist, and since feminism is still identified as a selfish quest for rights, if she were somehow to succeed in representing herself as a paragon of civic and maternal virtue, she would perhaps help soften feminism's image. But this would also soften feminism's demands and undermine its cardinal claim for rights-based equal justice. If, as a feminist, Clinton is interested in restoring communal virtue, she'd do better to illuminate the virtue of rights.

Franklin Delano Roosevelt, the great liberal practitioner of a politics of meaning, was not afraid to talk about rights at the same time that he appealed to a longing for community. (Read the Fireside Chats and you begin to understand what a true politics of meaning might be.) In 1944, near the close of World War II, Roosevelt proposed an Economic Bill of Rights for all Americans, which would include the right to work and the rights to food and health care. FDR called for new economic rights to match the country's traditional political rights, in order to ensure the survival of democratic community: "People who are hungry, people who are out of a job, are the stuff of which dictatorships are made." In the same speech, he called for a national service plan to mobilize manpower and capital, relying on the "obligation of each citizen to serve his nation."

Roosevelt delivered some thirty Fireside Chats between 1933 and 1945—informal radio addresses to the nation in which he spoke simply and intimately, using the first and second person. In those prepsychobabble days, he spoke concretely, explaining in lay terms the various financial and international crises facing the country and outlining his proposed solutions. He didn't pontificate about spiritual needs; he implemented programs that gave people hope and an abiding sense of common purpose.

One constant theme in all his talks was the strengthening of community in America. He stressed interdependence and a sense of expansive, enlightened self-interest. In one preelection speech, on the eve of Labor Day in 1936, he explained that the interests of farmers and urban laborers were tied, if only because they bought each other's goods: "Thus city wages and farm buying power are the two strong legs that carry the nation forward." He spoke of the power of collective action, "of everybody doing things together"—the idea at the heart of his New Deal programs.

He emphasized that democratic governance was collaborative and talked of sacrifice, but described it as a privilege, an opportunity to participate in the community: "The United States does not consider it a sacrifice to do all one can, to give one's best to the nation," he said as the country went to war with Japan. "In time of crisis when the future is in the balance, we come to understand, with full recognition and devotion, what this nation is, and what we owe to it."

Of course, any dictator might use similar language to inspire troops and civilians on the eve of war. That's the trouble with the politics of meaning: it's a politics of emotionalism, not rationality; it easily reduces to demagoguery. America in the 1930s was lucky to have a leader who practiced a politics of meaning so benevolently, with empathy and the willingness to acknowledge uncertainty:

"I can hear your unspoken wonder as to where we are headed in this troubled world," Roosevelt assured the nation during the recession of 1938. FDR didn't scold people; he comforted them.

He didn't demand unselfishness so much as inspire it: "There is placed on all of us a duty of self-restraint. . . . That is the discipline of a democracy."

He was, of course, paternalistic (that was part of his appeal), and a great many Americans saw him as their savior. He could have used his power quite perversely. My father, an iconoclast who taught me always to question authority, shocked me when I asked him what listening to the Fireside Chats was like—I've never heard him sound so reverential. "We felt like we were listening to our father," he told me. "His words were gospel. We felt he was a man who had the public at heart."

"He was the president," my mother adds, wondering why I ask such silly questions. "He was the president, and he was talking to us, and he was going to get us out of trouble."

What is most striking to me about my parents' recollections of Roosevelt, however, is not their adoration of him but rather their persistent use of the collective "we" and "us." Not "he cared about me" but "he cared about us." Not "I listened to his words as if they were gospel" but "*we* listened."

■　■　■

Hillary Clinton talks about connectedness without connecting. She poses charismatic questions—about what it means to be a human being—without charisma. Michael Lerner says that the Clintons "model" the politics of meaning. Even if that's true, they need to *embody* meaning, as Franklin and Eleanor Roosevelt did, as Martin Luther King, Jr., did, as charismatic leaders always do. They address spiritual needs by fulfilling them.

Introducing existential meaning into political life is a dangerous business—after all, Hitler was a charismatic, too. But if in an ideal world people wouldn't seek spiritual sustenance in political leaders, in this world they do. I suspect that Hillary Clinton has some intellectual understanding of the charismatic political role, but neither she nor Bill Clinton is equipped to play it, at least not yet. I fear that Americans in the 1990s are less likely to find meaning in the earnest, popular therapeutic nostrums of Hillary Clinton than in the calculated demagoguery of a Ross Perot.

WHEN FREEDOM OF SPEECH
MEANT NOT SAYING THE PLEDGE

(*June 1990*)

Elementary school mornings always started for me with the Pledge of Allegiance and the New York State school prayer. It was simple, nonsectarian, and patriotic—"Almighty God, we acknowledge our dependence upon thee and beg thy blessings upon us, our parents, our teachers and our country"—but I always associated the prayer with Christianity. We said different prayers in temple, so I assumed this was what my neighbors said in church. The pledge felt equally alien to me. What, after all, did "indivisible" mean? And if this was a country of liberty as well as justice for all, why was I required to stand and recite pledge and prayer in unison with my classmates? Compulsory recitation never made me feel free.

So, in the seventh grade, I decided to stop pledging allegiance. The Supreme Court had recently declared school prayer unconstitutional, and I was enjoying the freedom not to pray. Knowing very little about the First Amendment, I sensed that free speech included the freedom not to pledge.

My homeroom teacher disagreed. When I refused to stand and pledge, explaining that, "it's not right to make somebody say something," he called me a Commie. Red-faced with fury, he proclaimed that people who didn't love this country should go back to Russia, a country that my grandparents had happily escaped and that never had appealed to me. Lacking the power to deport me, he sent me to the principal's office.

The principal, Francis Xavier Driscoll, asked me if I was a Jehovah's Witness. (The Supreme Court had relieved them of the obligation to pledge in 1948, in respect of their religious beliefs.) I was not a Jehovah's Witness, but Mr. Driscoll persisted. Was there anything at all in my religion that forbade me to say the pledge, he asked hopefully, seeking an easy way out for both of us. When I told him I thought it was wrong to force people to pledge, he called my mother.

"So say the pledge. What would it hurt?" she said to me.

"So let her keep quiet. What would it hurt?" she said to the principal. "Just ignore her. Don't aggravate yourself."

My mother, a practical woman and a peacemaker, managed to fashion a compromise. I could remain silent and keep my right hand at my side, not over my heart, if I stood up with my classmates and wasn't "disruptive." Assured that order would be maintained, Mr. Driscoll agreed, and I felt vindicated: I was willing to acknowledge the school's interest in crowd control. Teachers could tell me to stand up or sit down or get in line, as long as they didn't tell me what to say.

My homeroom teacher was enraged and felt betrayed by the administration. He thought I should have been suspended, at least, for "subversion." He warned the class against me, explaining that I would not say the pledge because I had no respect for the values that made this country great—values that apparently did not include free speech. People like me were a threat to the Free World, he suggested; I was weakening our defenses against the Russians.

But the Red Army never did roll into Elmont Memorial High School, even though I never again recited the pledge. It's true that the Berlin Wall went up the year after my insurrection, but I swear that wasn't my fault. The country survived my refusal to pledge allegiance, just as it survives occasional flag burnings. The Berlin Wall came down in spite of them. The Soviet Union loosened its hold on Eastern Europe despite last year's Supreme Court decision affirming the First Amendment right to burn a flag.

Questions about flag burning have wound their way back to the court, which will soon decide the constitutionality of the Flag Protection Act passed by Congress in response to the Court's controversial 1989 flag-burning decision (involving a state flag desecration law). If the Supreme Court persists in upholding the First Amendment and strikes down the new federal flag law, Congress will once again be confronted with proposals for a constitutional amendment prohibiting flag burning, which my seventh-grade homeroom teacher would no doubt support. He would have hated flag burners as much as he hated me, as much as he loved the flag and feared the freedom to honor it voluntarily.*

---

*The Supreme Court has confirmed that flag burning is constitutionally protected speech. A proposed constitutional amendment that would allow for the criminalization of flag desecration was recently defeated by the U.S. Senate (in December, 1995).

CHURCH & STATE, INC.

(September 1984)

Religion is supposed to occupy a cheerfully anarchic place in American life. According to Supreme Court Justice William Brennan, the First Amendment envisions a "benign regime of competitive disorder among all denominations." Given the routine invocation of God in our courts and legislatures, America is not quite a secular country, but it's supposed to be a nonsectarian one. We may write "In God We Trust" on our money, but not "Christ Died for Your Sins."

At least not yet. A recent Supreme Court decision permitting the city of Pawtucket, Rhode Island, to erect a creche at Christmas suggests that government need not remain strictly neutral toward religion; instead, it may enter the fray among competing sects, on the side of the majority. Justice Brennan voiced his concern for accommodating all denominations in his dissent to the Pawtucket case, which arguably holds that America is, by God and the Constitution, a Christian country. Along with the endless debates about school prayer and abortion, this case reflects the considerable influence of conservative Evangelicals on the nation's self-image as well as the deep dissatisfaction of many with the "competitive disorder" of nonsectarianism. Where in all the clamor is the voice of God, the Word, the comfort of some one and only road to heaven?

The emergence of the fundamentalist road as a main street in

American culture is expertly explored in *Redemptorama: Culture, Politics and the New Evangelicism* by journalist Carol Flake. A native of rural Texas who recalls with some fondness her own "preteen piety," Flake combines understanding and affection for rank-and-file faithful with a sharp critique of the political and commercial exploits of their leaders. This is not the first book charting the rise of the New Right (Flo Conway and Jim Siegelman's *Holy Terror* details the fundamentalist assault on "America's freedoms"), but *Redemptorama* offers the best, the most balanced and informed account of how faith coupled with fear— of change and disorder—was transformed into a quest for power.

American Protestantism has a history of involvement in social and political affairs, which Flake deftly summarizes: it was at the center of nineteenth-century reform and temperance movements, abolition, Progressivism, and the modern civil rights movement. Conversely, the American political scene has had its share of Protestant preachers, from Cotton Mather to Jesse Jackson. But evangelicals have generally been outside the mainstream of society, at least in this century, having turned back from activist, reformist trends of late nineteenth-century Protestantism to develop what Flake describes as an insular subculture of their own.

They reemerged, with a vengeance, in the 1960s; fueled by anticommunist fervor and the permissiveness of a decade that began with the prohibition of official school prayers, evangelical churches grew in membership, while liberal Protestant ones declined. Anxious to impress their vision of Godliness on mainstream America, evangelicals moved into the marketplace in the late 1970s, using the tools of mass communications and the products of popular culture. The genius of New Right leaders and preachers, Flake suggests, was not only their development of a direct mail network but the masterful way in which they used the trappings of a secular culture to transform it into a sectarian one. Christian capitalists marketed Jesus bumper stickers and comic book bibles; they bought TV and radio stations and began presenting popular Christian entertainment, and built glitzy new church complexes modeled after shopping malls. They published a Christian yellow pages and, to rival Jane Fonda, Christian workout records for women, called "Firm Believer" and "Believer-cise."

Flake provides a witty and insightful guide to the growth of an evangelical counterculture, facilitated in part by a drive to preserve the traditional nuclear family and the traditional sex roles that went with it. The model Christian woman is a Total one, the model Christian man an athlete. The Total Woman, as Flake notes, is a pornographic counterpart to the Victorian True Woman; the born-again athlete continues a tradition of muscular Christianity dating back to the formation of the YMCA and the Boy Scouts. Fear of feminism and of male effeminacy were highly effective weapons in the hands of New Right leaders of the 1970s—most notably Phyllis Schafly.

Fear was what newly politicized preachers like Jerry Falwell played on, says Flake, fear and the hunger to be saved, both individually and as a nation. Without condoning the intolerance and presumptive self-righteousness that infect fundamentalism, she writes with considerable compassion of the fear and frailty behind it. For her, the villains of the piece are men like Pat Robertson, owner of the Christian Broadcasting Network, who exploits "the anguish of the wounded and lost sinners of America." The new evangelicals offered "illusions of community" through televised group prayers and "tokens of mass produced affection . . . bumper sticker smiles [and] personalized form letters."

Unfortunately, Flake's review of the attack on secular culture by conservative evangelicals is not matched by her shallow analysis of their political impact. Indeed, most of the book is devoted to a discussion of "Christ and Culture": she spends only a few final chapters on "Christ and Politics," concluding, reassuringly, that the evangelical movement is now centering itself, moving away from the right. She takes heart from Billy Graham's new crusade against the arms race and from the campaigns for peace and social justice of radical and moderate evangelical groups, like the Sojourners. As evidence that even Jerry Falwell is moving toward the center, she notes that he permitted Edward Kennedy to speak at his Liberty Baptist College, after inadvertently sending him a Moral Majority membership card, which only confuses Falwell's canny public relations with his politics. She also cites the failure of the New Right, so far, to push its social issue agenda through Congress and suggests that earlier reports of an impending right-wing religious coup were exaggerated by a semihysterical liberal press. But her own review of the cultural changes wrought by evangelicals undermines her political optimism. What of the symbiosis of America's newly Christianized culture and its nonsectarian politics?

Flake ignores the substantial political inroads already made by conservative evangelicals via the culture, if not yet Congress itself. The rise of the religious right cannot be separated from resurgent public opinion favoring school prayer, capital punishment, cutbacks of civil rights and the rights of criminal defendants, and the suppression of pornography—opinion that translates into votes and then to law. It has already exerted considerable influence on the Supreme Court, whose dismal 1984 record on civil rights and criminal procedures is only a taste of what's to come if Reagan is reelected, with the help of a still active conservative evangelical community.

Christianity has already intruded on our supposedly nonsectarian political sphere to a dangerous degree. Allowing a local government to put a plastic baby Jesus in the town square may seem a small step in establishing religion, but it represents a marriage of faith and politics that, in the words of Justice Hugo Black, "tends to destroy government and to degrade religion." So do the Bible-thumping campaign speeches of Ronald Reagan and the general tendency of candidates to parade their religiousity. That the presidential race has been reduced to a debate about which party is closer to Christ is one measure of the evangelicals' political success—it's as if we were anointing a spiritual leader instead of electing a president.

"Our government needs religion," according to Reagan, to illuminate the official path of righteousness. (Apparently there is only one.) Those who insist on maintaining a wall between church and state, he says, are advocating not only freedom of but freedom from religion—and for once he gets it right. My freedom from his religion is precisely what the First Amendment guarantees. The battle over school prayer, abortion, and "traditional" moral values is not between God and the devil, whoever they may be, but rather between what Justice Brennan called "religious chauvinism" on one side and the constitutional legacy of "our remarkable and precious religious diversity as a nation" on the other.

SWEET SIN

(November 1988)

A Letter Home

On Tenth Avenue the hookers work fast and cheap, turning tricks for commuters from New Jersey. I used to watch them sliding in and stumbling out of cars that sometimes honked at me. "Hey, pretty mama," guys on foot would say, licking their lips. "I want some-a-that."

But except for the hookers and me and an occasional runner, there wasn't much pedestrian traffic on Tenth Avenue, midtown. I used to walk an eight-block stretch of it every morning, from the self-service gas station on the corner of Thirty-fourth Street to Manhattan Plaza, "the miracle on Forty-second Street." It's an ugly walk, gray and gritty. It's a fast walk, past parking lots and a slice of the Lincoln Tunnel. Tenth Avenue is for commuters—cars, cabs, vans, buses, and a limo or two and sometimes a horse and buggy en route to Central Park. Only the hookers linger. So while I walked, I watched them in their skin-tight pants, lace bras, and fake-fur jackets, and wondered whether any of them were worried about AIDS. Maybe getting through each day was tough enough to distract them from a disease that would or wouldn't strike tomorrow. Maybe they turned tricks the way some people smoked, believing in their immortality. Maybe they just didn't care. A few were still sassy enough to swing their hips and look down their noses at me, but most looked half-dead, not just stoned but resigned, with even the desperation drummed out of them.

On TV, the hookers are beautiful—sexy and streetwise in tiny black skirts, fishnets, and stiletto heels that could kill. They banter provocatively with TV cops: Kojak and Sonny Crockett are their friends. They're women of the 1980s—sensuous, assertive, entrepreneurial, *Cosmopolitan* girls on the wild side. No wonder Jimmy Swaggart likes to hear them talking dirty.

My friend Loretta met Jimmy Swaggart once. "He stared at me till I felt naked," she said. "He's so intense." I understand. I bought my first copy of *People* when they put Jimmy Swaggart on the cover. I was tempted and I fell, and I fear it's becoming a habit. I bought my second copy when Leona and Harry Helmsley graced the cover. (She's on his lap.) "Greedy, Greedy, Greedy," the headline proclaimed. The Helmsleys, who apparently share a grand passion for cash and a vision of heaven in Greenwich, Connecticut, are now in court, under indictment for tax fraud.* Jimmy Swaggart is back at the pulpit, defrocked but still intense, "serving notice on demons and devils and hell," and asking for money.

I suspect Jimmy Swaggart is about as close to God as TV hookers are to the street. I prefer subway sermonizers and the guys on Forty-second Street who preach for free. There's usually at least one slightly mad man with a megaphone on either the Seventh Avenue or Eighth Avenue corner, just around the block from the *New York Times*. Maybe the street preachers are only defrocked editorial writers, but I admire their fire. They seem to care so much about saving my soul. "It's not too late," they've assured me, although someday it will be.

Once I stopped worrying about pornography, I liked Forty-

* Leona Helmsley was subsequently convicted and imprisoned.

second Street. Sex (or some simulated version of it) is cheap and religion is free and everybody has an opinion. And there used to be an Indian restaurant called Nirvana at the top of One Times Square, overlooking everything. I went there once on my first date with Mark. I remember lots of drapery and women in saris and waiters in white jackets standing around with no one to serve but us. "I've never eaten off a gold plate before," I said. "And you're not going to now," he reminded me.

But I liked brass plates pretending to be gold and flashing lights and huge billboards selling running shoes, cameras, and jeans. I liked the shoeshine man at the corner of Eighth Avenue and Forty-second Street who called me sweetheart, nicely, and told me not to worry. I liked the guy who sat at the foot of the Seventh Avenue subway steps, chanting. I liked darting in and out of commuters trying only to get from the Port Authority to Sixth Avenue quickly. I liked watching pasty guys in polyester slipping into peep shows past the ever-hopeful preachers.

Now that I'm living in Cambridge, Massachusetts, I miss the daily cycle of sin and redemption. I miss the dramas on the Ninth Avenue bus. "You don't like it here, go back to South Africa," an elderly white lady in gloves and a hat yells at a black man cursing the MTA and Ronald Reagan too. "God Bless Rosa Parks," he yells back, one fist in the air, as he gets off the bus. I miss the $3 umbrellas you buy on the street, along with two-for-$5 all-cotton T-shirts, counterfeit Rolexes and Cartiers, and 100 percent acrylic "cashmere" scarves. I miss the night: Cambridge closes early. You can't get a cup of cappuccino past midnight, on weekends even, or a glass of wine past 1 A.M., much less a head of lettuce. I miss the twenty-four-hour greengrocers.

What I don't miss is the guy who used to stand near the corner of Sixth Avenue on Twelfth Street, in front of the New School, hawking his poetry, because he's now in Harvard Square. Maybe he followed me here (I used to live on Twelfth Street), and maybe he didn't. All I know is when I hear him say "Do you like poetry? Do you like poetry?" to people passing by, I feel at home.

I felt at home again when antipornography protesters picketed Alan Dershowitz's new deli in Harvard Square, where the price of a corned beef sandwich is truly obscene. But if the demonstration was silly enough to be entertaining, it was also a little sad. The picketers looked so glum, as if they really believed that not eating at Maven's Kosher Court would somehow be good for women. Besides, most people stay away from Maven's apolitically: "Let's go to the new deli," I hear them say in the square. "Nah," someone always replies, "I'm not in the mood for Indian."

THE BORROWING KIND

(January 1994)

Maybe too many books about the Kennedys were finally sufficient. Joe McGinniss's famously unoriginal biography of Ted Kennedy, *The Last Brother,* was famously unsuccessful in the marketplace. Or maybe there is such a thing as bad publicity. As practically everyone now knows, McGinniss was accused of borrowing his book from William Manchester and other historians the way I used to borrow my fourth-grade reports from the *World Book.*

Why does any of this matter? McGinniss's publisher responded by claiming that such unattributed use of source material is acceptable literary practice, and that Manchester borrowed part of his own Kennedy memoir from author Hugh Sidey. (Both Manchester and Sidey deny this.) Like a congressman caught trading votes for contributions, McGinniss's side offered a version of the "everybody does it" defense.

Well, maybe not everybody. But many writers do borrow liberally from unacknowledged or insufficiently acknowledged sources, although usually more skillfully than McGinniss, and often only the sources seem to mind. Neither readers nor publishers deserted Gail Sheehy when it was reported that she borrowed ideas for her 1976 best-seller, *Passages,* from Yale psychologist Daniel J. Levinson. She "relied heavily" on his work in writing *Passages,* according to the *Washington Post,* or, as the

New York Times said, she "drew upon" work by Levinson and other "seminal thinkers." One of her sources, UCLA psychiatrist Roger Gould, filed a copyright-infringement suit against Sheehy and obtained an out-of-court settlement of $10,000 and 10 percent of her *Passages* royalties. Sheehy characterized Gould's action as a nuisance suit. She denied taking undue credit for Levinson's work and did, in fact, make note of a "primary professional debt" to him in her acknowledgments and cited him occasionally throughout the book.

Levinson says that Sheehy borrowed considerably more than she acknowledged, but on balance he seems forgiving. He says he understands the importance of popularizing scholarly ideas and sees Sheehy's behavior in the context of the inherently conflicted relationship between the scholars who generate ideas and the journalists who make them accessible to lay readers. These readers, who keep buying her books, have not seemed at all concerned with questions about the originality or integrity of Sheehy's work. Her latest book, on menopause, *The Silent Passage,* reached the best-seller list and was heralded by her publisher as groundbreaking. But I suspect that Gail Sheehy would be the last person to write the first book about anything.

Sheehy's case was unusual mainly because it was so well publicized. There are occasional, high-profile cases of plagiarism— Alex Haley was accused in connection with *Roots*—but many instances of plagiarism go unreported. It is quite difficult to prove and not always illegal. Much of what a writer or scholar might consider plagiarism—stealing ideas or arguments or original research—is not technically a copyright violation. The questions about Sheehy's use of Levinson's work, for example, did not amount to a plagiarism charge: you can't copyright a fact and you can't copyright an idea, just your way of expressing it.

Fame, not law, provides writers with their most reliable, practical protection against plagiarism. It's difficult for one writer to take credit for ideas that are publicly associated with another. This means that the more obscure you are, the more likely it is that your work will be plagiarized. Scholars are particularly vulnerable to popular journalists, who recognize the commercial potential of the work and know how to package it.

What's the harm? Shouldn't scholars welcome the circulation of their ideas in the mainstream? Isn't it mere egotism that leads them to demand footnotes and other, more visible acknowledgments, not to mention shares of royalties? Perhaps, but the alternative to protesting plagiarism is self-effacement.

My own work has been appropriated by other writers four times that I've noticed, and each time I've felt outraged. When someone appropriates my work, she appropriates part of my identity, however clumsily. I relate to my writing the way I imagine models relate to their images, the way Bette Midler relates to her singing: she successfully sued the Ford Motor Company for using a Midler soundalike in a commercial. In this postliterate world, we understand that celebrities inhabit their images or styles, but we seem to be losing the sense that writers inhabit their words. We're disassociating language from identity, which is one reason some journalists routinely, unknowingly misquote people.

My own experiences as interviewee rather than interviewer have led me to assume that I'll be misquoted at least 50 percent of the time. Of course, even scrupulous journalists get a word or two wrong on occasion; the best of us make mistakes. But many misquotes are not mistakes—they're misapprehensions of what constitutes quotation.

This is what journalists often do: instead of recording your statement, they interpret it, put it in their own words, frame their paraphrase in quotation marks and attribute it to you. To people who are tone-deaf, insensitive to the nuances of self-expression, a paraphrase is the same as a quote.

In a copycat culture you not only don't possess a distinct identity, you may never even consider developing one. Someone who appropriates my work doesn't just appropriate part of my identity, she abdicates part of her own. Students who plagiarize to write their papers don't learn to think for themselves and don't seem to care. Instead, they appear to relish living in a consumer culture in which people actually aspire to looking and sounding alike. Madison Avenue has always depended on this longing to copy and conform. There is probably a subtle connection between a tendency to plagiarize and susceptibility to advertising.

The connection between plagiarism and commercialism is not subtle at all. As every designer knows, you're not a success until you're copied. Fashion is the art of eroticizing the familiar and making it profitable. Originality seems equally at risk in the worlds of music and visual art, where appropriation is less a crime than a style, like impressionism. Contemporary artists routinely use cultural objects and the works of other artists in collages and constructions, just as rap groups "sample" other people's songs.

For writers as well, the most familiar books—romance novels, self-help books, celebrity bios, and others that fall into recognized genres—are the most marketable. Publishers are wary of unrecognizable books that aren't easily categorized, which means that they value appropriative writers more than original ones.

Popular books are often ghost stories. We've divorced authorship from writing: Ivana Trump is the only named author of her novels, but her publisher doesn't even pretend she writes them (her ghost is Camille Marchetta). Martina Navratilova was recently signed to produce a mystery series with a coauthor. Think of this as a licensing agreement: Navratilova is lending her name to a series of books as she might lend her name to a line of tennis shoes.

Readers don't seem to care whether or not authors actually write their books, any more than voters care whether politicians actually write their speeches. Widespread knowledge that Ronald Reagan was mouthing the words of Peggy Noonan didn't seem to undermine public belief in his authenticity. During the 1988 presidential campaign, Senator Joseph Biden was greatly embarrassed by charges of plagiarism when the press revealed that he was parroting a stump speech by British Labour leader Neil Kinnock. But Biden would not have been the least bit embarrassed, would not have had to drop out of the campaign, if he had simply parroted a speechwriter on his payroll.

■ ■ ■

Perhaps politicians get away with buying other people's words partly because some political journalists do too. Carl Rowan, Evans and Novak, Jack Anderson, and John McLaughlin have relied heavily on staffers in producing their columns. They're not writers so much as shop foremen; like Renaissance painters, they preside over little factories of unheralded craftspersons who churn out the work.

Plagiarism is so easy and so insidious: the previous paragraph was lifted from a 1988 *New Republic* article, "The Culture of Plagiarism," by Ari Posner. I gleaned the information about Rowan, Evans and Novak, Anderson, and McLaughlin from Posner and stole his analogy to Renaissance painters; I paraphrased this sentence: "Some journalists are beginning to resemble the great painter-entrepreneurs of the 16th century, relying on a studio of unknown draftspersons to create their masterworks." Unattributed, my paraphrase would violate journalistic ethics, if not copyright law. But I doubt Posner would make a federal case out of my stealing one sentence; and if he did, how could anyone know that his analogy did not just occur independently to me?

In fact, different writers do sometimes formulate similar ideas simultaneously. Sometimes, ideas are like little revolutions erupting spontaneously in different places, which is why they should not be copyrighted, and why plagiarism must be a matter of ethics, not law. We have to govern ourselves, and the rules are simple: although we're not obliged to credit other writers for ideas we develop ourselves or information we possess independently, we are obliged to credit others for what we learn from their work or for the ideas they inspire. The only really hard cases are the rare ones involving moments of unconscious plagiarism. Sometimes a well-written sentence stays with you, like a song.

The less you think, the more you borrow or absorb unthinkingly. Popular culture feeds on thoughtlessness. It's the song, or rather the jingle, that gets stuck in your head—the styles, ideas, or modes of expression that resonate thanks to merciless repetition. How do you sort your own thoughts out of the messages that bombard you everyday? Turn on Oprah Winfrey and you hear different people saying the same thing, using the same jargon. Turn on MTV and you see only a different kind of sameness.

Attend a lecture on postmodern literary theory, and you may hear the underlying philosophy of groupthink, as Michiko Kakutani suggested last July in the *New York Times*. Current academic fashion denies even the possibility of the romantic, individual imagination, as Kakutani notes; ideas are said to be generated by the collective culture. (This may seem at odds with the equally fashionable insistence that we have only individual, subjective realities; only perceptions, not facts. But then, postmodernism thrives on paradox.) Still, if academia supplies the theory that ultimately justifies plagiarism (if there is no individual imagination, there can be no individual author), I suspect that the theory reflects more than inspires popular appropriative styles. Denigrating individual thinking may be useful to the minority of academics who have few ideas of their own, but it's essential to popular culture, as conformity is essential to consumerism. Originality would be the death of commerce.

---------------------- ■ ■ ■ ----------------------

THE BERLIN WALL OF
FOLEY SQUARE

(May 1985)

Tilted Arc, the massive steel wall created by Richard Serra, is
either a "hideous hulk of rusty scrap metal" or a "brilliant and
beautiful sculpture." This by now notorious arc of weathered
steel—112 feet high, 12 feet long, and weighing 72 tons—bisects
the plaza fronting the federal office buildings at Foley Square, to
the dismay of those who work there and the delight of artists,
critics, and curators who don't. William Rubin, director of the
department of painting and sculpture at the Museum of Modern
Art, considers *Tilted Arc* "a powerful work of great artistic
merit." Jessie McNab, an associate curator at the Met, says that it
cleaves across the courtyard with great beauty, "like a ship coming toward you in the water." But to people employed at Federal
Plaza, *Tilted Arc* is simply a metal barrier that has ended public
use of the plaza for concerts, rallies, lunchtime sunbathing, and
socializing. It has destroyed what was once an oasis of open
space, and it depresses them: they work in cubicles, surrounded
by walls all day; the last thing they need is another one.

Commissioned by the federal government in 1979 under the
Art and Architecture Program of the General Services Administration (GSA), at a cost of $175,000, *Tilted Arc* is a work of
public art that the segment of the public most affected by it

doesn't like. Federal employees—office workers and judges—
joined by some local residents, have been lobbying for the removal of *Tilted Arc* since it was installed in 1981. They want their
plaza back, and they may get it. The government has had at least
one offer for the work (from Storm King Art Center), and on
March 6, GSA Regional Administrator William Diamond con-
vened a three-day public hearing at Federal Plaza to determine
whether *Tilted Arc* ought to be relocated. The five-man hearing
panel (consisting of Diamond, two other GSA officials, Michael
Findlay, of Christie's, and Thomas Lewin, Senior Partner of
Simpson, Thatcher & Bartlett) have forwarded their recommen-
dation on relocation to the GSA administrator in Washington,
who is expected to issue a final decision on the matter by the end
of May.*

The government will not be making any "aesthetic judgments"
about *Tilted Arc,* Diamond claimed at the hearings; it will simply
decide on "the most effective use of the plaza." But the hearing
turned quickly into an impassioned forum on art and politics.
Members of the public, the art world, and a few politicians came
before a government panel to bury *Tilted Arc* or to praise it—and
to define the scope of artistic freedom when it's sustained at the
public's expense.

Serra was present throughout the proceedings, fit and feisty,
and vigorously protesting the proposed removal of his work. "I
don't make portable objects," he reminded the panel: *Tilted Arc*
is a site-specific work; to remove it would be to destroy it, along
with the integrity of the Art and Architecture Program. The
government has a legal as well as a moral obligation to keep the
piece on site, he stressed, and *Tilted Arc*'s ultimate fate may be
decided in court as a relatively mundane matter of contract law.
Serra may seek an injunction against any efforts to remove it,

* The sculpture was removed from Federal Plaza.

claiming that the contractual intent of both parties—artist and government—was to maintain *Tilted Arc* permanently at Federal Plaza. An impressive roster of artists, gallery owners, and official keepers of culture agreed. Frank Stella, George Segal, Kitty Carlisle Hart, and Leo Castelli, among others, testified in support of Serra in the name of government commitment to the arts, artistic freedom, and the sanctity of an artist's work. But, on the other side, a group of beleaguered civil servants voiced equally lofty concerns: *Tilted Arc* had been foisted on them by a few art experts and high-level government officials. Now, by speaking out against it, they, "the people," were defending the sanctity of the democratic process.

With so much at stake, much of the testimony was high toned and hyperbolic. Joan Mondale was on hand to extol the contributions of art (and the Art and Architecture Program) to American culture, to urge that history be allowed to judge *Tilted Arc,* and to quote Proust. Robert Frost was quoted by the other side: "Something there is that doesn't love a wall." And a few of those requesting the removal of *Tilted Arc* wrote their own poems about it: ". . . for those at the plaza I'd like to say / Please do us a favor—and take it away." Richard Serra was lauded as "one of the two or three greatest sculptors alive in the world today" and classed with Picasso and Michelangelo. *Tilted Arc* was often compared to the Eiffel Tower (greeted by the Parisian public initially with hostility) and Stonehenge, which, according to one museum curator, is the only equivalent experience in the history of art.

There was also much flag waving by both sides. Either it will be un-American to remove *Tilted Arc,* thereby censoring the work and silencing the artist, or it was un-American to install it in the first place without regard for public opinion.

Serra and his supporters branded the hearing an inquisition, a witch hunt, stressing the fact that Diamond is a Reagan appointee and suggesting that the campaign against *Tilted Arc* reflected the antilibertarianism of the current conservative administration: "The smell of burning books is in the air," declared Clara Weyergraf-Serra, the artist's wife. Marion Javits, reading a statement by her husband, Jacob, the former U.S. senator, in support of Serra, likened the proposal to remove *Tilted Arc* to the "enslavement of Soviet art."

Others contended that *Tilted Arc* itself is a symbol of Soviet enslavement. It was dubbed the "Berlin Wall of Foley Square," the "Iron Curtain," and was said to be a security risk. *Tilted Arc* not only encouraged loiterers, shielding the "bad guys" from police, but it was a potential "proterrorist device," Security Officer Vicky O'Dougherty warned: "It could vent an explosion inward and in an angle toward the buildings." So *Tilted Arc* may not represent a communist plot, but it is a threat to the national security and a totalitarian intrusion on the people's plaza. Many of those in favor of removing it prefaced their testimony by thanking Diamond for the opportunity to be heard. Holding a public hearing on *Tilted Arc* was the American way.

All the rhetoric, however, did little to resolve the conundrum at the heart of this case. The act of creation is not a democratic process, but determining how to use a public plaza or park is supposed to be just that. What should we value more in commissioning a work of public art—artistic freedom or the public's right to participate in shaping its own environment? On one side of the scale is the simple truth that art should never be subject to a popularity poll; on the other, the contention that public art is supposed to confer a public benefit.

What are the benefits of a work of art? Provocation may be one: art stirs up, challenges, and sometimes makes people angry, Serra's supporters stressed. The controversy over *Tilted Arc* was frequently cited as a measure of its worth. But those objecting to *Tilted Arc* and causing all the controversy were also condemned as "quacks and vigilantes," or dismissed, at best, as know-nothing petty bureaucrats. Only "art professionals," it was said, "know enough about the business of art to decide whether [*Tilted Arc*] is a good work of art." Moreover, it takes time for a great work of art to be accepted; people "will get used to *Tilted Arc.*" Some may even learn to like it. If not, the benefits of *Tilted Arc* will be evident to a more enlightened future generation.

Meanwhile, people using the plaza today want their benefits now, and they don't want to be patronized by experts. They've lived with *Tilted Arc* for three years and they know what they don't like: "We're not stupid and we're not philistines and we don't need some art critic to tell us in time we'll like it." Many see *Tilted Arc* as an "arrogant, nose-thumbing gesture" by a rich artist toward the "uncouth" working-class nine-to-fivers. Serra was paid $175,000 for his work. One federal employee complained, "Most of us don't make that much in ten years!" Daniel Katz, a law clerk at Federal Plaza, stressed that, before *Tilted Arc,* the plaza was a "small refuge" for people who commute in "steel tubes" and work in "steel cubicles." It was a gathering place, it relaxed people, and "there are some human values that are more important than the location of a work of art." Besides, art is supposed to celebrate the human spirit, not "assault a pathetic human activity."

But if the case against *Tilted Arc* is strong, it should have been made before, not after, its installation. Today, local community groups and officials are directly involved in selecting works for the Art and Architecture Program; *Tilted Arc,* however, was selected by NEA-appointed experts and GSA officials in Washington without consulting the community. Still, Serra's plans for *Tilted Arc* were painstakingly reviewed, and questions about its suitability for the site were asked and answered by government officials supposedly representing the public. It seems too late to veto *Tilted Arc*. A government arts program ought to keep faith with artists.

There may also be ways to mitigate the actual effect of *Tilted Arc* on the plaza. Some suggest removing the federal office buildings (which are indeed eyesores); others suggested a less drastic renovation of the plaza itself, to accommodate both the arc and the demand for usable public space. Unfortunately, the psychological effect of *Tilted Arc*, which generates the deepest opposition to it, was probably exacerbated at the hearing by the contempt expressed by Serra's side for the "barbarians" who don't want his work.

An artist who creates public art ought to respect the public. People like Tommy Farrell, a security guard at Federal Plaza, spend a lot of time staring at *Tilted Arc*. No one has ever asked Farrell his opinion of it (he doesn't like it) and no one has ever tried to explain it to him. Perhaps, says Farrell, if he understood "what the artist was trying to do," he'd "feel a little better about it." Farrell is a jazz musician, so he realizes, he adds, that art is not always accessible to everyone. "When a musician is improvising he's telling you how he feels about what he's doing." Perhaps Serra is telling something too, Farrell suggests. He doesn't like *Tilted Arc*, but he's curious about it: "If the artist could find a way to explain it to me, that would help. That's what I'm yearning for."

THE SHRUNKEN REALITY OF LIVES
IN THERAPY

(June 1993)

Two of our favorite lawsuits concluded this month, for the moment, with gratifying defeats for moral ambiguity. Dispensing with psychobabble, Justice Elliott Wilk, in rejecting Woody Allen's suit for custody of his three children, said that it was wrong for Allen to sleep with his surrogate daughter. Unimpressed by the mysteries of the literary process, a San Francisco jury found that it was wrong for New Yorker writer Janet Malcolm to fictionalize portions of her conversations with psychiatrist Jeffrey Masson. That so much time and money and so many experts were required to assert such common sense is surely a tribute to the absurdities of litigation. But it is also a parable of untempered subjectivism, which has been engendered by our therapeutic culture.*

Both Allen and Malcolm seemed sincerely befuddled by the charges and the judgments against them. "The heart wants what the heart wants," Woody Allen explained, assuming the indisputable rightness of desire. A famously devoted analysand and

---

* Masson subsequently lost a second action against Malcolm, who subsequently claimed to find written notes that belied Masson's charge that she made up quotes.

professional solipsist, Allen seemed puzzled by the notion that he had a duty to distinguish between what he wanted and what he ought to do. Janet Malcolm, a leading chronicler and student of analysis, suggested that the small lies she may have told in doctoring, if not reinventing, quotes and a *mise en scene* in a journalistic profile were justified, indeed required, by her commitment to a larger truth. Why, after all, should her vision have to be so carefully, objectively corroborated?

In defending the allegedly invented excerpts from her essay against the charge of libel, Malcolm implied that what she offered her readers was not fact so much as sensibility. Sensibility, however, is what we look for in novelists, artists, and shrinks, more than journalists. Sensibility was what his fans sought in Woody Allen, and it was finally the crudeness of his sensibility, his apparent cruelty, that disappointed them. Of course, no journalist is a purely objective transcriber, or a simply inartful one, as Malcolm has pointed out, overstating the obvious: as a journalist you "put a great deal of yourself" into your subjects. In a famous passage in "The Journalist and the Murderer" (reflections on convicted murderer Jeffrey MacDonald's libel suit against writer Joe McGinniss), she writes: "The characters of nonfiction, no less than those of fiction, derive from the writer's most idiosyncratic desires and deepest anxieties."

Not quite. Different journalists will, no doubt, describe the same "characters" and events differently, reflecting their different temperaments and experiences and the singular relationship they each have with their subjects. Still, they're supposed to strive for relative objectivity. As Malcolm acknowledges, nonfiction writers do not enjoy the same license to invent that fiction writers do. Their craft is based on the assumption that they can somehow manage not to do what Malcolm says they do instinctively—overidentify with their subjects, making them "what the writer wishes he was and worries that he is."

Beware the person who turns you into a character in the drama of his life or, Zelig-like, turns himself into a character in yours. In one case you're appropriated; in the other, you're betrayed. Someday, Soon-Yi Previn may believe she was appropriated, just as Mia Farrow believes she was betrayed. Jeffrey Masson, too, may rightfully feel the moral outrage of someone who has been not just ridiculed but deceived.

Malcolm's offense against Masson does, however, seem academic. The five quotations she was found to have fabricated, including the two found libelous, constituted only a moment in a 48,500-word book-length profile, the general accuracy of which was unassailed. Any harm to Masson's reputation appears to have been largely self-inflicted: the many remarks he did not challenge may have been as harmful as the few he did, which is perhaps why the jury deadlocked on the question of monetary damages. In the end, Malcolm's allegedly libelous behavior may have cost her more than it could ever cost him. But if Woody Allen's "crime" was much clearer and more grievous than Malcolm's "misdemeanor," it was also much less interesting.

Woody Allen doesn't seem to have broken the rules unwittingly: he just seems surprised that they apply to him. He is his own moral exemplar. (We thought he was a schlemiel; he knew he was an ubermensch). Janet Malcolm doesn't seem to have been knowingly untruthful. Grounded in the psychiatric tradition, she may have unthinkingly confused psychiatry and journalism: psychiatrists and pop psychologists alike routinely fictionalize patient profiles; the "case studies" presented as true in popular-psychology books are usually composites, at best. Like a shrink who publishes stories about her patients, Malcolm, according to her testimony at trial, tried to capture the "totality of [her] experience" with Masson—not such supposedly irrelevant details as exactly what he said and where.

Indeed, the line between journalism and therapy is not always clear, as Malcolm herself has eloquently observed. (The art of interviewing is, in part, the art of asking open-ended "How did you feel about that?" questions and tolerating long silences.) And sometimes, describing her methods, Malcolm sounded just like an ordinary journalist. She "selected the things that seemed most characteristic, most expressive" of Masson. This is precisely what journalists often do: they caricature. They approach every subject with a preconceived angle, seizing on whatever remarks support it, and ignoring, or even distorting, whatever contradicts it.

The *New Yorker,* however, is not supposed to be an ordinary journal, and Malcolm is not supposed to be the ordinary journalist who commits ordinary ethical lapses (she surely doesn't write like one). So she doesn't quite say "I wrote what I saw in Masson and chose to portray, at the expense of complete attention to detail." She asserts that what she wrote was true, not understanding that a literary "compression" of several months' worth of conversation into one dramatic afternoon encounter might, in fact, be subtly untrue. Accuse Malcolm of taking your remarks out of context and she wouldn't know what you mean. In her view, it seems, there is an essential self that emerges unchanged in different contexts, just waiting to be discovered by some perceptive journalist or shrink.

"I learned the same truth about [journalistic] subjects that the analyst learns about patients," she writes in "The Journalist and the Murderer." People "will tell their story to anyone who will listen to it, and the story will not be affected by the behavior or personality of the listener." Malcolm celebrates the subjective authority of the journalist, analogizing the journalist and her subjects to the novelist and her characters. (Citing Flaubert, she writes, "Masson, *c'est moi.*") But, contradicting herself, she also claims the objective authority of the all-knowing shrink: Masson is simply and unalterably Masson. Her perception of him is not simply her perception; it is an objective reflection of what's true.

Malcolm's greatest, or, at least, most unfashionable, sin was her apparent reliance on the traditional model of the omniscient shrink. Woody Allen may have been guilty of relativism in his attitude toward right and wrong; but Malcolm was not relativistic enough: she was too sure of her ability to perceive the truth. The emerging therapeutic orthodoxy about victimization, child abuse, and repressed-memory syndrome elevates the patient's notion of reality above the perceptions (or diagnosis) of the therapist. Supposedly progressive therapists are today as loath to question a patient's allegations of abuse as some progressive feminists are to question a woman's allegations of harassment or date rape. Underlying this cult of victimhood is a pervasive celebration of subjectivity. According to some proponents of campus hate-speech codes, for example, there are, in essence, no reliable, subjective standards for determining when speech is offensive; there are only the feelings of the person who has been offended, provided he or she is homosexual, a male person of color, or a woman.

Jeffrey Masson is part of this new therapeutic political culture. His work in the Freud Archives, which prompted Malcolm's profile, condemned Freud's refusal to credit his female patients' claims about their childhood sexual abuse (something Allen was accused of committing). His victory over Malcolm must have been sweet, for the jury chose to credit the subject's rather than the reporter's account of events, just as, in Masson's view, the progressive therapist credits the patient's version, or, in the view of some feminists, enlightened authorities believe the alleged victim.

In the end, however, Masson's victory was only symbolic. One lesson of this case lies in the jury's inability to agree on monetary damages. They were unable to do so partly because the subjectivism that dominates popular therapies, feminism, and other social movements hasn't yet taken over the law. Masson couldn't base his claim for damages simply on hurt feelings, on the wounding of his self-esteem. He was required to prove something more tangible—some measurable harm to his reputation.

Imagine, instead, a libel trial based on the proposition that people have a legally protected right to feel good about themselves, and that damages reflect an entirely subjective harm to the plaintiff's psyche. Imagine a sexual harassment trial in which the plaintiff is required only to show she felt offended or intimidated, however unreasonable her sensitivities. Imagine a society composed of competing interests and sensibilities without the benefit of generally accepted, more or less objective rules of conflict resolution. Imagine faith in the possibility of a fair enough legal process giving way to faith in identity politics and hearts that want what they want. That's the vision lurking in Masson versus Malcolm, the perils of which were demonstrated in Woody Allen's lawsuit. As Woody Allen might say, *"Le'etat c'est moi."*

DO YOU WANT TO TALK

ABOUT IT?

(*September 1992*)

If our enduring preoccupation with therapy is a reflection of our values, they comprise an enduring preoccupation with the family. Whether it emerges in Bill Clinton's testimony about his alcoholic stepfather or George Bush's reliance on the domestic virtues of his unsalaried wife, family life is a necessary subtext for both Democratic and Republican candidates. Traditional familial structures may be under siege, but Americans are not likely to devalue the family's role in character development or the pursuit of happiness anytime soon. James Hillman and Michael Ventura, coauthors of *We've Had a Hundred Years of Psychotherapy—and the World's Getting Worse,* question the power we accord both therapy and family. Stanley Siegel, coauthor of *The Patient Who Cured His Therapist,* celebrates it.

Siegel is a family therapist, formerly associated with New York's Ackerman Institute for Family Therapy, and a proponent of family systems theory, from which popular recovery experts draw many of their ideas. Family systems therapists view the individual in the context of family life. What appear to be individual problems—troublesome, aberrant behaviors—are often strategies for protecting and stabilizing the family, Siegel explains: a child falls ill or fails at school in order to divert his

304

parents from a marital conflict. Readers of mass-market recovery books will recognize in this example the hallmark symptom of "codependency"—the compulsion to sacrifice yourself on the altar of family life.

Siegel offers a less melodramatic, more nuanced view of this phenomenon, one that reflects considerably more respect for his craziest patients as actors, with the capacity for self-determination. Instead of presenting what is popularly labeled codependent behavior as a pathology, he regards it as a logical, creative, even noble individual response to a collective problem. He suggests throughout that people choose their behaviors. A chronic psychiatric inpatient who speaks only gibberish, for example, lets him know that she is capable of speaking clear English sentences; her gibberish is freely chosen.

The Patient Who Cured His Therapist is a collection of stories about the adaptive uses of deviancy and apparent neurosis. A man who resembles his wife cross-dresses to help her resolve her relationship with her twin. A couple who fulfill each other's complementary needs to parent and be parented refrain from having sex in order to preserve the filial purity of their relationship. A daughter of Holocaust survivors makes herself ill and overly dependent on her parents to spare her mother the pain of separation.

But if these behaviors are all functional solutions to underlying family crises, they can create crises of their own, which drive people into therapy. The cross-dressing husband worries about being in the grip of a compulsion. The celibate couple is turned down by an adoption agency. Siegel honors his patients' problems as coping strategies, but he is, after all, in the business of tempering or even "curing" them. He is an active, interventionist therapist and, by his own account, a very effective one: He sizes up people quickly; his epiphanies about their behavior can instantly transform their lives. "Therapy can be as sudden and powerful as a thunderbolt," he writes, and you hope he doesn't imagine himself to be Jehovah.

Arrogance, or at least the appearance of it, however, is an occupational hazard for therapists, especially ones who write books. Therapy stories are by nature a little self-serving: they're stories either of success or of therapists humbly, nobly learning from their failures. Siegel generally comes across as a likable, respectful healer, but it's difficult to know how much of this image is true. Although his book is written in the first person, it was coauthored by Ed Lowe, a columnist for *Newsday.* We're not hearing Siegel's voice directly; we're hearing Lowe's imitation of it.

Siegel's tales of therapy also raise questions about artifice. Therapy stories are often fictionalized; at their most accurate, they may only be composites. They're like television docudramas; conversations between Siegel and his patients, for example, are reconstructed and dramatically rendered in the present tense. Siegel's stories are said to be true, but they're not entirely believable. They're too pat, they illustrate their points too neatly. They're bedtime fables for posttherapy adults.

James Hillman, a Jungian psychologist, and Michael Ventura, columnist for the *L.A. Weekly,* offer a much more iconoclastic approach to writing about therapy, family, and selfhood, in keeping with their iconoclastic views. *We've Had a Hundred Years of Psychotherapy* is a collection of recorded dialogues and correspondence between Hillman and Ventura, a book of talking heads. Its narrative flow is the flow of thought and conversation. Hillman and Ventura don't generally tell stories, except about ideas.

To their credit, it's difficult to do justice to their ideas in a review. (The books that are easy to summarize are probably books that need not have been written.) Hillman and Ventura range energetically over such subjects as psychotherapy, politics and aesthetics, method acting and postwar ideas of the self, child abuse and inner child theory, romantic love, and America's tradition of anti-intellectualism.

They challenge what many of us accept as gospel: that personality development is reactive and we can understand ourselves by looking back and understanding what was done or not done to us as children. Hillman, in particular, is an essentialist: he suggests that we each carry within us from the beginning an essential, core self that is not shaped by the world but, rather, shapes the place we take in it. He quotes Picasso approvingly: "I don't develop; I am." According to Hillman, "rather than developmental psychology, we should study essential psychology," and, in an odd way, he may find himself aligned with religious conservatives, like Fulton Sheen, who railed against psychotherapy because it conceived of the newborn child as a tabula rasa, when it was inscribed with original sin; instead of sin, Hillman suggests we are marked by our self.

■ ■ ■

Therapy pathologizes the self. Hillman and Ventura focus their attack on the therapeutic tradition, including today's recovery movement, on its tendency to reduce all political problems to personal pathologies. (Shopping too much is blamed on codependency, not capitalism.) In their view, what are isolated and treated as individual neuroses are logical, even noble responses to a sick world. This sounds familiar partly because it is family systems therapy on the grand scale: an individual's private symptoms are expressions of a collective, public illness, which means that the patient is not just the family; the patient is the world.

Recovery gurus, such as John Bradshaw, seem to offer a similar message when they say that society itself is dysfunctional, but their focus is always on diagnosing and curing the individual, within the context of the family. "You have to work on yourself before you can work on the world" is a recovery movement refrain. The traditional therapeutic analog to this is the mandate not to externalize your troubles or, at least, not to externalize them beyond the limits of your family. As a consequence we have a therapeutic, personal-development tradition that effectively creates psychic problems, by offering them as explanations for political ones, a tradition, Hillman suggests, that teaches us to adapt to an unhealthy, oppressive environment, instead of encouraging us to rebel against it. Hillman and Ventura don't romanticize craziness, but they do suggest that therapy misconceives its causes and misdirects its energy.

That many people feel helped by therapy does not necessarily disprove this contention. What is individually helpful in the short term may have harmful, long-term social consequences. Or it may not. Hillman and Ventura are only speculating; they're thinking out loud, and that's the pleasure of this book.

Recording your conversations, reprinting your correspondence, seems at first a lazy way to write a book, one that demands more of its readers than its writers. But *A Hundred Years of Psychotherapy* is seductive precisely because it offers two live voices, actively engaged. So many books today are merely products, ghostwritten according to formula. You don't always get to hear a writer think.

---------------- ■ ■ ■ ----------------

I'M O.K., YOU'RE DEAD

(*October 1992*)

Inquiring minds will want to know about Robert Lindsey's new book, *Irresistible Impulse.* It's a true story about sex, romance, money, addiction, dysfunctional families, low self-esteem, and a particularly grisly murder. It even mentions weight loss; all that's missing are movie stars and unidentified flying objects. Lindsey, a former reporter for the *New York Times* who is also the author of other true-crime books, including *The Falcon and the Snowman* and *A Gathering of Saints,* tells a sordid story of uninteresting people, combining tabloid journalism with pop psychology, in the style of *Geraldo.*

The tale begins in 1980, in San Francisco. Monika Zumsteg, "a strikingly pretty young woman" with "long auburn hair highlighted by flashes of red," meets Michael Telling, a mysterious Englishman with "dark good looks . . . as handsome as a movie star," who claims to be a spy.

They were introduced by her parents. Monika's father, Leo Zumsteg, a motorcycle aficionado, spotted Michael on a Harley-Davidson and invited him home. Believing him to be "a British intelligence agent on an American holiday," the Zumstegs fix Michael up with their eldest daughter. Michael falls in love "within 24 hours." Monika takes a little longer—a couple of days. After a three-week courtship filled with flowers, jewelry, and fine wine, Michael asks Monika's father for her hand in marriage. They set a date. Trouble starts.

Monika inadvertently finds out that Michael is not a spy but the "non-employed" member of one of Britain's wealthiest families. She also discovers he has a wife, whom he is in the process of divorcing, and a two-year-old child, as well as a compulsion to lie and a penchant for guns. She marries him anyway, with her parents' blessing; they move to England, and the marriage quickly deteriorates. He hits her and threatens her with a gun, hangs out with skinheads, smashes windows and furniture in a "glassy-eyed frenzy," sets fire to Monika's possessions, and is arrested for illegal possession of firearms. She learns that Michael has a history of serious mental problems and spent part of his childhood in a psychiatric hospital, having tried to burn down his boarding school and kill his mother with a carving knife. She stays with him.

Monika starts drinking; she stops drinking, enters Alcoholics Anonymous, and decides that Michael suffers from low self-esteem and an addiction to lying (he still tells people he's a spy) caused by his dysfunctional family, notably his mother, who abandoned him emotionally. Her father, also a recovering alcoholic in A.A., agrees with Monika's diagnosis and urges her not to criticize Michael but to build up his self-esteem.

■   ■   ■

Soon he has enough confidence to shoot her at close range with a hunting rifle and hack off her head. In 1984, he was acquitted of murder but convicted of manslaughter "by reason of diminished responsibility," having convinced the jury that he lacked the will to resist the impulse to kill her. He was sentenced to life in prison and is expected to be released sometime this decade.

What are we to make of this awful tale? It is surely a comment on the perils of believing that life is a romance novel, that people fall in love in an instant, that there is a dark, handsome, absurdly wealthy, noble, trustworthy stranger out there, waiting to be smitten by you. Little girls should probably read about Monika instead of Cinderella.

But the more interesting moral to this story, which Mr. Lindsey does not draw, is that the little knowledge offered by self-help experts can be a very dangerous thing. You shake your head with wonder when Monika and her father excuse Michael's appalling behavior by attributing it to his history of emotional abuse and worrying about his self-esteem, but, as Lindsey reports, they are merely applying the lessons they have taken from A.A. and the recovery culture. Michael could have been a case study in a codependency book, just like any one of us.

According to some experts, virtually everything wrong with everybody is codependency—an inclusive disease with symptoms ranging from biting your nails to beating your wife. Monika's avoidable death demonstrates the dangers of the wholesale therapy practiced by mass-market self-help experts with their one-size-fits-all diagnosis.

What is striking about Monika and her father is that for all their familiarity with psychobabble, when it came to the subject of human behavior they were terminally stupid. At the risk of being bashed for blaming the victim, we ought to acknowledge that although Monika's death was unprovoked, unjustifiable, and undeserved, it was partly determined by her incredibly bad judgment and by the unfortunate advice of her father. That Michael was seriously unstable, violent, self-aggrandizing, manipulative, and compulsively dishonest was evident from the beginning, before the marriage. As Lindsey reports, he showed his dark side early on, throwing tantrums, buying guns, and lying about nearly everything; he was hardly a Jekyll and Hyde. From the day they met Michael, the gullibility of Monika's parents is almost inexplicable. You don't have to be a rocket scientist to be wary of a stranger on a Harley who tells you he's a spy.

■   ■   ■

Robert Lindsey, however, is not at all critical of the Zumstegs. He wrote *Irresistible Impulse* with the cooperation of Monika's parents and friends; his sympathy for her is palpable and entirely appropriate. Monika was vilified at Michael's trial as a shrew. That she could have been more discriminating in her choice of a husband does not make him less guilty of homicide.

But Lindsey's unqualified support for Monika and his suggestions that her choices were dictated by her own history as the child of a dysfunctional family make for a confused, even obtuse book. The author is justifiably outraged by Michael's acquittal on the murder charge and his irresistible-impulse defense. He believes that Monika's killing was premeditated, that Michael acted willfully and logically, not in the grip of some compulsion. Yet his analysis of this story is shaped by the same deterministic notions of dysfunction that Michael exploited. Both Michael and Monika were "programmed by the past to live as they did." She lacked the will not to marry him. "Like a moth to a flame, she was drawn irresistibly," Lindsey writes, and in the end he endorses Michael's defense, explaining that he was "emotionally insecure, deprived of parental love and hobbled by low self-esteem."

Oh. To say the least, Robert Lindsey lacks a sense of irony. He peddles the same personal-development pablum that Monika consumed to a dreadful end. She was not doomed by her dysfunctional family. She was doomed by popular psychology, when a little common sense would have saved her.

TOLSTOY, GANDHI, AND
SHIRLEY MACLAINE
(August 1992)

Once, on the *Donahue* show, Shirley MacLaine revealed to America the rules of reincarnation. "Is it possible to come back as a bird?" a woman in the audience asked. No, Shirley explained, we do not regress; we are not reborn as animals. Putting aside the question of how Shirley MacLaine became a nationally recognized authority on the mysteries of the universe, putting aside questions like "What makes her so sure?" I wondered about her theory of past and future lives. It seemed arrogantly anthropomorphic, not cosmically correct. Many New Agers would hesitate to call a nonhuman animal a lower life form or rebirth as a bird regression. Along with some zealous animal-rights activists, New Age movements include people generally inclined to condemn the "hierarchical" thinking that would characterize reincarnation, like evolution, as an ascent up the ladder of life forms. Still, there are many paths to many truths in the New Age; ideological inconsistency is part of its appeal.

Martin Green is sensitive to the inconsistencies of New Age, but he manages to delineate an ideological framework for it—or, at least, a temperamental orientation. (With its strong streak of antirationalism, New Age is less a state of mind than a state of temperament.) In *Prophets of a New Age,* Green, professor of

English at Tufts University, identifies the New Age temperament as a hopeful naïveté, an eagerness to believe that ideals can be realized, uncompromised, at no great cost. The weakness of New Age is its "lack of critical rigor" and tendency toward "self-indulgence," Green acknowledges, but he devotes himself to what he sees as its great strength—a belief in the possibility of spiritual and worldly progress that may be self-fulfilling. In the end, having selectively chronicled New Age movements in the eighteenth, nineteenth, and twentieth centuries, Green, in his own burst of naïveté, suggests that we need New Agers to save the world.

First, we have to take them seriously, and Green is generally successful in imbuing New Age with a measure of respectability. He begins by dismissing Shirley MacLaine, along with crystals and tarot cards, as New Age "caricatures." (Later, out of his own inconsistency or ambivalence, he resurrects her; comparing her to Doris Lessing's heroine, Martha Quest, he tries to make Mac-Laine respectable too.) But the New Age heroes around whom Green organizes his narrative have considerable intellectual credibility; Green challenges popular notions of New Age by choosing as its icons respectable, prominent, arguably saintly men—Tolstoy, Gandhi, Tom Paine, and Gary Snyder. Snyder, a Beat poet, seems less than conventionally respectable and somewhat marginal, but so, in his day, was Tom Paine.

A New Age movement is most likely to appear at a century's end, and Green focuses on three periods—1775 to 1805 and 1880 to 1919 in Western Europe (particularly England, including the empire) and 1960 to 1990 in America. The eighteenth century gives him a period of revolution to compare to the 1960s; the late nineteenth and early twentieth centuries give him a period of vegetarianism, occultism, feminism, and bohemianism, among other isms that have been part of our own New Age as well (not that feminism and other liberation movements haven't flourished outside New Age periods).

Green successfully conveys the eclecticism of New Age, but, in a sense, he's also defeated by it. A movement that stands for revolution and nonviolence, eroticism and asceticism, politics and aestheticism, women's liberation and the masculinism of Robert Bly or Gary Snyder, not to mention Tolstoy, is hardly a movement at all. Green is right to characterize New Age mostly by a particular temperament—aggressive ingenuousness—but temperament may be a better subject for a novelist than a historian.

An artist like D. H. Lawrence or George Bernard Shaw (both of whom Green mentions) can capture the spirit of New Age in a character, but it is difficult for an ordinary writer to describe with precision such a loose confederation of attitudes. Writing about New Age, you often end up sounding like a New Ager, discussing visions and paradigms, spiritual realities and transformative consciousness shifts.

Green usually avoids this trap (he only tumbles into it in the end), by focusing our attention more on the people involved in New Age than on its airy sensibilities. He has compiled a catalog of New Agers from each of the last three centuries that will give readers an understanding of how broadly New Age ranges. The trouble is that instead of an analytic history of ideas, we get a laundry list of names and places. Reading this book, you may feel as if you're cramming for a New Age segment on *Jeopardy. Prophets of a New Age* may be a good resource, a sort of New Age Who's Who, but it's not a terribly good read.

■   ■   ■

If Green's method of tracing New Age by citing its cast of characters is perfunctory, so is his writing. In the academic style, he's always taking us by the hand to tell us what he is going to tell us. He repeats himself, explaining at several points his theory that there are three basic types of human temperament: authoritarian (associated with soldiers and politicians); systematic (associated with academics and lawyers); and naïve (New Age).

He also relies heavily on a series of comparisons between modern and historic New Age figures, in chapters comparing the eighteenth and nineteenth centuries, respectively, to the modern American scene. He compares William Godwin to Paul Goodman; William Blake to Norman Mailer, as well as Allen Ginsberg; the fictional world of Doris Lessing to eighteenth-century London; and Mary Wollstonecraft to Betty Friedan and Germaine Greer. Feminist scholars may find the latter comparison particularly bizarre, and many of Green's comparisons seem arbitrary and unimportant. We might just as well compare Wollstonecraft to Elizabeth Cady Stanton or the fictional world of Balzac to New York in the 1980s. We can find analogous people, places, and books in virtually any two historical periods. That's not scholarship; it's a parlor game.

Emphasizing details at the expense of themes, Green barely touches on one of the more interesting thematic conflicts in New Age: the authoritarianism embodied in a succession of gurus (from Tolstoy to Werner Erhard) in what are supposed to be antiauthoritarian, even anarchic, movements. Green mentions several charismatic New Age authority figures without exploring what their presence signifies or questioning the search for prophets of any age. Green suggests that New Age prophets will lead us to the light—to a "shared sense of the holy of spiritual value"—and maybe he's right. But people whom prophets can lead to the light can be led to the darkness as well.

--- **. . .** ---

JUST GOOD FRIENDS

(*October 1985*)

One of these days, some graduate student, probably in southern California, will write a thesis on "self-help books as agents of social change in postfeminist America." He or she (as most of these books so carefully say) will examine the way new gender-based behavioral ideals are introduced to the mainstream by commercial publishers. How else did it become fashionable for men to cry and "share" their feelings and for women to question their "neediness"? Thanks to pop psychologists, millions of Americans, for whom feminism is still too radical, know that boys and girls are raised differently—if only for the sake of developing different syndromes, complexes, and dilemmas.

The problem this year is friendship—a relationship ripe for discovery. Demographic changes, like the rising divorce rate, have imbued friendship with emotional primacy. Feminism has legitimized relationships between women and, by extension, between men as well. Each of these three books rests on the premise that friendship can be as necessary, fulfilling, and painful as kinship. Each explores, through interviews and anecdotes, the role of friendship, primarily among middle-class heterosexuals (two focus solely on women). Each seeks to help readers make friends so they can lead happier lives.

Just Friends is the only one written for reasonably intelligent adults. Lillian Rubin, a psychotherapist and author of *Intimate*

Strangers, Women of a Certain Age, and *Worlds of Pain,* has a talent for talking about relationships and psychoanalytic theories without resorting to psychobabble. In *Just Friends,* she uses her skills to illuminate the developmental role of friendship—for children, adolescents, and adults; the place accorded friendships in the hierarchy of sexual and familial relations; and, of course, the difference between male and female bonds.

Because it presents friendship as a complex issue, this is not a typical self-help book; it may interest readers who don't need advice. Rubin raises provocative questions about the cultural devaluation of friendship, suggesting that myths about romantic love and nuclear families have shaped the traditional view of friendships as ancillary, temporary, and dispensable relationships. (Friends are the people you give up when you marry, the people you don't see on holidays or turn to in times of trouble.) She also points out the importance of ritual and social structure: friendships are considered secondary because, unlike families, they haven't been institutionalized. Neither, she argues, have they been given their due by developmental theories that focus on the first few years within the family. She believes, in the best self-help tradition, that people continue to grow and change throughout their lives and sees friends as important players in the process.

Whether discussing issues or telling stories about herself and the people she's interviewed, Rubin is earnest and likable, and some may find her analysis "helpful." Others may become impatient with her characterizations of men and women and the ways they relate: men, conditioned to be competitive and self-enclosed, drink beer and play ball together; women, trained to nurture and attend to feelings, talk. Rubin makes it clear that she prefers the female style, portraying men as emotional retards, capable only of silent bonding over a basketball. (Arguing that bonding is not necessarily intimacy, she dismisses one man's angry assertion that women simply don't appreciate the "vulnerability and intimacy" of the playing field.) Although its subject is men and women, *Just Friends* is aimed at women who talk about relationships and probably agree that most men are dolts who need women to help them along.

This may or may not be feminism; thirty years ago middle-class housewives must have said the same things about their husbands. Today, however, talking about women's superior capacity for intimacy, communication, and getting in touch with feelings sells books. Or so the authors of *Women and Friendship* apparently hope. Joel Block is a psychologist and author of several helpful-sounding books like *Lasting Love: How to Give It, How to Get It, How to Keep It;* his collaborator, Diane Greenberg, is a freelance writer. Together they have produced a well-intentioned, insipid, and painstakingly popular feminist tribute to intimate female bondings.

They begin with an endearing attack on stereotypes of women as jealous and catty, pointing hopefully to *Cagney and Lacey* and *Kate and Allie* as signs of our changing times. They remain vigilant against sexism and even make a few confused stabs at feminist historical analysis: on one page they note that sex roles in preindustrial America were relatively flexible and on another announce that sex roles were "strongly defined" and dichotomized by frontier life. Perhaps we should be grateful—this is how feminism trickles down.

With all the wisdom of a ten-year-old magazine article, *Women and Friendship* discusses marriage, childbearing, and divorce, single women and widows, friendship at home and in the office ("from backyard to boardroom"), in country, suburb, and town, friendship between men and women. It tells you how to "tend, mend, and end friendships" and offers "rules for effective communication" and "suggestions for moving closer." "Commitments" and "Caring" are said to be essential, and "Trust is a sensitive issue." There are also hot tips on making friends: "get to know your neighbors by inviting them over for drinks or dinner." Or get a pet: "One study done in London's Hyde Park found that people who walked their dogs talked to more people for a longer time than people who walked . . . alone." The authors illustrate most of their points with "case studies" presented as moral tales, written in the style of women's magazine fiction.

If none of this tells you anything new about friendship, it does clarify the self-help approach to life and publishing. Readers are treated like children and friendship is a product that can change their lives. Friendships "provide the psychological nutrients so important for optimal enjoyment of life." They're like Wheaties. Friendship is also a substitute for Midol: "the support and sharing provided by female friends who are going through the same season . . . can alleviate stress." Bad friendships, however, can be "potentially toxic," like tampons.

The Best of Friends, the Worst of Enemies exemplifies the other basic self-help technique: it presents friendship as a problem, which obedient readers will learn how to solve. Eva Margolies, psychotherapist and author of *Sensual Pleasure: A Woman's Guide,* believes women are deeply ambivalent about friendship because they all have ambivalent relationships with their mothers. She admits to borrowing her thesis from Jane Flax, whose ideas she summarizes.

It is especially difficult for girls to separate from their mothers because they're encouraged not to, unlike boys who are expected to be independent; girls are conditioned to believe they must choose between independence and mother love, which makes for lifelong difficulties in their relationships with other women. (Those who read both Margolies and Rubin in search of the Answer will have to choose sides. Rubin argues that separation from Mother is more problematic for boys, which makes men more homophobic than women and less adept at making friends.

This will seem a trifle convoluted to those who prefer Margolies's theory—which is, as she delightedly exclaims, "stunning in its simplicity.")

Margolies discusses the usual subjects—friendship for single, married, and divorced women, housewives, and corporate women seeking mentors. But her perspective is distorted by the effort to explain everything in terms of the "mother-daughter dyad": a woman who wants "nothing more" than to marry has probably enjoyed a "friendly, positive relationship with a traditional mother," which discouraged her independence. (Now women can blame Mom for their dependency needs.)

There is much harmless nonsense here, along with regressive stereotypes of women: the "ultimate purpose" of every single woman, we're told, "is to find a suitable mate." Women friends are, then, always second to male lovers, and her own experience has taught Margolies that "while it is fine to show another woman strength, it is not okay to show a woman need." Women learn to be cruel to each other early on: unspecified studies show that little boys "aren't nearly as vicious to one another as girls." Moreover, "the closer the mother-daughter bond, the more vicious a girl is likely to be."

Margolies says she has a troubled relationship with her own mother, and I believe her. Although she celebrates women as "the best of friends," this is a bitter book. It suggests women's friendships are shaped by an unhappy power struggle with their mothers that began in childhood, when the mother had more power than the daughter. "The bottom line in almost every mother-daughter relationship . . . is power."

Imagine. I always thought it was shopping.

--- ■ ■ ■ ---

IT'S A WONDERFUL LIFE

(*August 1985*)

Share this with me: Americans are confused about sex, gender, science, and religion; unsure of who we are and where we came from; afraid of where we're going. Battles over social issues, from reproductive rights to creationism, reflect a national identity crisis. Confronted with nuclear arms, terrorism, the decline of heavy industry, computers, the sexual revolution, and the women's movement, Americans feel out of control. Some seek refuge in nationalist bravado or religious fundamentalism; some beat their wives; some watch *Dynasty*. It's morning after in America.

Now don't get crazy. Buy this book and Phil Donahue will explain it all for you—gently, patiently, in short, simple sentences—just like he does on TV. *The Human Animal,* illustrated companion to an upcoming five-part television series, expounds on the vagaries of human behavior that got us into this mess, in order to help us out of it. After much consultation with experts, Donahue modestly explores the nature of good and evil, violence, aggression, male and female sexuality, and the human brain, reviewing the works of Darwin, Freud, and Einstein. All in two hundred pages.

■ ■ ■

This isn't a bad book, only a very simplistic one. *The Human Animal* is like a *Reader's Digest* version of Tuesday's *Science*

Times, condensing what science knows about such diverse matters as falling in love and atomic fusion. "All" that's required to understand the fusion process, Phil reassures us, is a "brief, rudimentary physics lesson," which he delivers in four or five paragraphs. "All" Freud did "was transform the speculations of old wives and poetic fancy of artists into something like a science," as if he simply had more common sense than the colleagues who thought he was crazy. After all, "what parent doesn't know it's true: as the twig is bent, so grows the tree."

The effort to explain or at least discuss absolutely everything about humankind releases a barrage of facile generalizations: "Throughout most of our history," we're told, religion has been our only source of transcendence, "the only thing that made [people] feel dignified, special, proud of being human." So much for art. Art appreciation, however, is not one of Donahue's strong points. He's been too long in a world that doesn't distinguish between talent and genius; to him, Michael Jackson is a "truly great artist," presumably along with Shakespeare and Matisse. Sometimes *The Human Animal* is like a children's book: "Humans are mammals," Phil informs us, "as are monkeys and dogs and cows and cats and almost any other animal you're likely to be friendly with."

Donahue is such an easy target. It could be very embarrassing to learn anything from his book. He doesn't sound sophisticated, even when he's telling you what you don't already know. But he's not writing for a sophisticated audience. There are people out there who don't want to believe they're descended from apes and probably some who don't know they're mammals. Others who do may not be familiar with or feel capable of understanding current theories about early child development, the chemistry of aggression, or the dynamics of sociosexual conditioning. Not everyone reads *Science Times.* Some who don't read much at all may pick up *The Human Animal* because it's by a brand-name author, goes with a TV show, and has lots of pictures.

How do you judge a book that's written for people who lack the time or inclination to read? Its weaknesses may be its greatest strengths. *The Human Animal* is valuable because it oversimplifies and generalizes, because it's accessible to anyone moderately literate and mildly curious or concerned about themselves and the world around them. I'd rather they listen to Phil Donahue than Jerry Falwell, not just because I prefer Donahue's politics, but because, despite his occasional inanities, he doesn't tell people what to think so much as endeavor to show them how. Instead of exploiting fear and confusion, he tries, oh so earnestly, to alleviate them.

You have to give Donahue credit for encouraging openmindedness. His basic message, delivered five mornings a week, packaged in language a twelve-year-old can understand, is "This is still America," where we respect each other's differences. He invites people to confront their prejudices: "So you don't like homosexuals," he'll say amiably to a woman who thinks they're not "normal." "What do you think we should do with them?" That we should all be free to be, regardless of race, sex, class, creed, or ethnicity, is a constant refrain, but he doesn't talk about discrimination in the abstract. Sexism is bad, he'll say, "because it puts the women you love at risk." Every political and social issue is personalized, every public problem becomes your problem too.

Donahue may not be Bill Moyers but neither is he Monty Hall. What other daytime television personality regularly compels his audience to "face the fact" that America is a racist country, that sexual stereotyping may be related to sexual violence, or that born-again Christianity is essentially anti-Semitic? How many pop sociology books discuss the exploitation of industrial workers and inequitable distribution of wealth? How many self-help books don't pretend to have the Answer?

The Human Animal is not intended to be precise or complete. It's the kind of book that teachers use to "stimulate discussion." Donahue is more concerned with attitudes than facts, with instilling in his readers a willingness to ask, to wonder and find out about themselves, because "only when we can control ourselves can we truly control our destinies." Like a careful politician, Donahue is cautiously optimistic, stressing that we have the capacity to change for the better. The moral could have been borrowed from a Frank Capra movie. It reflects the classic American ideal of men and women shaping their own destinies; not bound by the past, we can forge our own futures. If this is still America, "let every individual make his or her own history."

Donahue gets away with sometimes blaming America first by always reaffirming that it's still a great country, despite its problems, and by never appearing self-righteous. "I'm also here to learn," he'll say, and people believe him. He's smart enough not to act smarter than his audience. "Only recently," he concedes, "have I come to understand that nature and nurture . . . interact with each other in an astoundingly complex way." (Just in case you thought it was simple.) He never makes people feel stupid for asking stupid questions. Instead, he acknowledges their "contributions," prancing off into the "cheap seats" to "mine the gold."

Watching Donahue work a room is half the fun. Watching the room is the other half. (What's missing in his book is the audience.) I love it when the women hoot and whistle at male strippers. "What does your girlfriend think about your work?" they demand. "What about your mother? What are you doing after the show?" I love it when someone stands up to tell Phil what she doesn't like about her body. "My boobs sag," one lady confides to millions of people. Donahue is unabashed. He is, after all, the only man in America who can talk about menstruation with a straight face. That's why he's so effective. With Donahue, the political gets very personal indeed.